Microeconomic Studies

Edited by W. Güth, J. McMillan and H.-W. Sinn

T0402107

Microeconomic Studies

Klaus F. Zimmermann (Ed.)

Economic Theory of Optimal Population

With Contributions by
Z. Eckstein, K. Jaeger, M. C. Kemp, H. Kondo, D. Leonard
M. Nerlove, M. Neumann, P. Pestieau, J. D. Pitchford
A. Razin, E. Sadka, G. Schmitt-Rink, G. Schwödiauer
S. Stern, A. Wenig, K. I. Wolpin, K. F. Zimmermann

With 19 Figures

Springer-Verlag
Berlin Heidelberg GmbH

PD Dr. Klaus F. Zimmermann
Department of Economics
University of Mannheim
A 5, 6
6800 Mannheim 1, FRG

Printed with financial support of the Fritz Thyssen Foundation.

ISBN 978-3-642-50045-9   ISBN 978-3-642-50043-5 (eBook)
DOI 10.1007/978-3-642-50043-5

Typesetting: Kiliandruck, Grünstadt

2142/7130-543210

Preface

We are used to calling most developing countries overpopulated and considering some industrialized countries (like West Germany) "threatened by underpopulation". Analogous population policies with different objectives are discussed. However, none of the measures suggested can be justified or evaluated without an implicit concept of optimum population, a notion which has attracted attention ever since economics was made a science.

The relevance of the subject and the recent rise in interest by population economists has motivated the organization of a conference on "Optimal Population" in Bielefeld, where most of this book originates. Financial support for the conference and the publication of this book by the Thyssen Foundation and the editorial help provided by John De New and

Contents

IV. International Economics

List of Contributors

Zvi Eckstein, *Tel Aviv University,* Tel Aviv, Israel, and *Boston University,* Boston, USA

Murray C. Kemp, *University of New South Wales,* Kensington, Australia

Hitoshi Kondo, *Nanzan University,* Showa-ku Nagoya, Japan

Daniel Léonard, *University of New South Wales,* Kensington, Australia

Marc Nerlove, *University of Pennsylvania,* Philadelphia, USA

Manfred Neumann, *University of Erlangen-Nürnberg,* Nürnberg, Federal Republic of Germany

Pierre Pestieau, *University of Liège,* Liège, Belgium

John Pitchford, *Australian National University,* Canberra, Australia

Assaf Razin, *Tel Aviv University,* Tel Aviv, Israel

Efraim Sadka, *Tel Aviv University,* Tel Aviv, Israel

Gerhard Schmitt-Rink, *University of Bochum,* Bochum, Federal Republic of Germany

Gerhard Schwödiauer, *University of Bielefeld,* Bielefeld, Federal Republic of Germany

Steven Stern, *University of Virginia,* Charlottesville, USA

Alois Wenig, *University of Hagen,* Hagen, Federal Republic of Germany

Kenneth I. Wolpin, *University of Minnesota,* Minneapolis, USA

Klaus F. Zimmermann, *University of Mannheim,* Mannheim, Federal Republic of Germany

Optimum Population: An Introduction[1]

Klaus F. Zimmermann

> "A greater number of people cannot, in any given state of civilization, be collectively so well provided for as a smaller. The niggardliness of nature, not the injustice of society, is the cause of the penalty attached to overpopulation. An unjust distribution of wealth does not even aggravate the evil, but, at most, causes it to be somewhat earlier felt. It is in vain to say, that all mouths which the increase of mankind calls into existence, bring with them hands. The new mouths require as much food as the old ones, and the hands do not produce as much...
>
> If the population continued to increase at the same rate, a time would soon arrive when no one would have more than mere necessaries, and, soon after, a time when no one would have a sufficiency of those, and the further increase of population would be arrested by death.
>
> Whether, at the present or any other time, the produce of industry, proportionally to the labor employed, is increasing or diminishing, and the average condition of the people improving or deteriorating, depends upon whether population is advancing faster than improvement, or improvement than population. After a degree of density has been attained, sufficient to allow the principal benefits of combination of labor, all further increase tends in itself to mischief, so far as regards the avarage condition of the people."
>
> John Stuart Mill (1848, pp. 191-192)

1. The Threat of Population Growth

The Malthusian threat of overpoulation has inspired many writers ever since Thomas Robert Malthus' *"Essay on the Principle of Population"* appeared in 1798 (and 1830). Because the Malthusian framework is basically economic, the population question has always attracted many economists. Malthus hypothesised that families procreate to the point where they are living at the level of subsistence. "Before that a large and increasing population was generally favored; since that date it has never creased to be looked upon by some doubt and with fear. ... Before Malthus the criterion was the prosperity of the sovereign and of the ruling classes; thereafter it became the welfare of the increasing masses." (Fetter, 1913, p. 4)

For nearly a century, the Malthusian framework was a cornerstone of classical economics. However, the axiomatic authority of the population principle was considerably weakened by the demographic transition in many European countries. The

[1] The work on this paper was begun when I was a Research Fellow at the Center of Operations Research and Econometrics (CORE), Louvain-la-Neuve in 1986 and completed during my time as a Visiting Associate Professor at the University of Pennsylvania, Philadelphia, in 1987. I wish to thank Pierre Pestieau for a helpful discusssion and John De New for many useful comments.

Microeconomic Studies
K. F. Zimmermann (Ed.)
Economic Theory of Optimal Population
© Springer-Verlag Berlin Heidelberg 1989

substantial decline in fertility around 1900 and the concurrent increase in economic prosperity were induced by a spread of *rationality* in family decision making and *technical progress*—factors which Thomas Robert Malthus clearly had overlooked.

It was at that time when European and American authors such as Julius Wolf, Knut Wicksell, Edwin Cannan, Lujo Brentano, Frank Fetter, Simon Nelson Patten and Edwin R. A. Seligman where developing alternative ideas. One group of authors was concerned with the normative issue of the desired, ideal or *optimal* population size from the standpoint of society. This development of classical ideas lead to welfare economics. The other group rejected and revised the behavioral framework of Malthusian thinking, working in the context of positive economics. Whereas the former group assumed population to be exogenous, the latter reconsidered the endogeneity of familiy decision making.

A revival of Malthusian thinking was marked by the famous debate between John Maynard Keynes and William H. Beveridge in the 1920's, although the threat of population growth was also being expressed by other writers in many countries. The position taken by Keynes, that Britain was overpopulated at that time, can only be understood in the context of an optimum population framework. It is remarkable that only a few years later (in the 1930's), Keynes became a leading exponent of the group of population theorists attributing economic stagnation to population decline.

The concept of optimum population has always played a decisive role in models of economic growth since this strand of economics was developed. Influential contributions which treat population changes as exogenous are: Meade (1955), Dasgupta (1969), Pitchford (1974) and Lane (1977). Meade (1955), Dasgupta (1969) and especially Dasgupta (1984) also discuss ethical aspects of population policy. In recent years, more emphasis has been given to microeconomic models of endogenous family size following the seminal contribution by Becker (1960). This framework has been artfully applied to the problem of socially optimum population size by Nerlove, Razin and Sadka (1987).

This introduction is organized as follows: First, there is a summary of the doctrine of optimum population and a discussion of the issues of overpopulation and underpopulation. An evaluation of approaches to endogenous fertility follows. The introduction ends with a summary of the contributions in this volume.

2. The Doctrine of Optimum Population

Various definitions of optimum population can be found in the literature. "The word 'optimum' is a very innocent superlative; a synonym of 'best'. When one speaks of 'optimum population' one is seeking for (sic.) the best possible number of men. ... An optimum population is the one that achieves a given aim in the most satisfactory way. ... For the time being the optimum population will be no more than a convenient idea. The demographer may use it as an intermediate tool, as the mathematician uses imaginary numbers." (Sauvy, 1969, pp. 36-37) Spengler (1944) states that "a population factor — density, size, rate of growth — is at the optimum where some index which is conditioned by the population factor is at a maximum..." One could add age structure as a further population factor.

However, these definitions are rather vague. Therefore, most authors have related economic welfare to population size. Different population sizes are optimal depending on what is being maximized: income or consumption per capita, total income or consumption, life expectancy and military potential, among other criteria. In most cases, the problem is simplified by assuming that per capita income or output is maximized. Then, the particular population size that maximizes real output per worker is called the optimum population for a given nation.

There is no 'true father' of the doctrine of optimum population. The idea can be traced back to works of Plato and Aristotle. Generally, Knut Wicksell (1910, 1913) and Edwin Cannan (1888, 1928, see also 1964, pp. 80-87) are each credited with independently originating the economic concept, although the actual progression of ideas is not apparent "Naturally, when population grows, two opposing forces become operative. On one hand, the productivity of labor diminishes when everyone has a smaller share of land or natural resources in general, to work with. On the other hand, the united human efforts, the division of labor, the cooperation, the organization of industry, etc., are always important and under certain circumstances of considerable importance in the subjugation of the forces of nature. At the point where these tendencies cancel each other out is indeed the true optimum population. However, this stage is not fixed. The profusion of new discoveries and the growth of technical knowledge will most often, if not always, displace it. However, to argue that this stage has not yet been reached, because new inventions are still to come, shows a very unclear way of thinking. It can have been entirely exceeded at that particular time. " (Wicksell, 1910; cited from the English translation by Overbeek, 1977, p. 66)

"The truth is that the productiveness of industry is sometimes promoted by an increase of population and sometimes by a decrease of population... At any given time the amount of labour which can be exerted on a given extent of land, consistently with the attainment of the greatest productiveness of industry possible at that time, is definite... An increase of population is often one of the most essential requisites for increasing the productiveness of industry." (Cannan, 1888; cited from the unchanged third edition, 1903, pp. 22-23) Much later, Cannan (1928, p. 61) introduced the dynamic element of the theory: "We have to treat the ideal or optimum in regard to population as being the right movement (i. e. increase or decrease) of population rather than define it in reference to one particular point of time. The right movement is that which will give the largest returns to industry in the long run, the interests of the people of all the generations being taken into the account."

However, many distinguished economists had discussed the concept before or at the time Wicksell and Cannan introduced the doctrine. Among them there were Jean Charles Léonard Simonde de Sismondi, Henry Sidgwick, John Stuart Mill and Julius Wolf. Most notable are Mill (1848) and Wolf (1901, 1908), but also important are Wagner (1893, pp. 638-665) and Schmoller (1900, pp. 184-190). The concept of optimum population plays also an important role in the *Bevölkerungslehre* of Mombert (1929, pp. 240-271), the first economic analysis which extensively used the optimum population concept (see also Gottlieb, 1949, p. 157), though he traces the basic ideas back to Wicksell (1910) and surprisingly not to Julius Wolf (1901, 1908).

The contribution of Mill is well-known. Cannan's claim that Mill had overlooked that optimum population is changing over time is wrong. However, Mill had no clear view that a larger population size spurs technical progress. (See also Cohn, 1934, p. 13.)

The work of Wolf (1901, 1908) has been largely neglected, although he used the term *optimum population* in his 1908 book (p. 189) well ahead of Wicksell (1910) and Cannan (1928). Already in a review of Franz Oppenheimer's (1901) critical book on Malthus, Wolf (1901) had presented an outline of the theory. Oppenheimer (1901) suggested that population growth is beneficial, because the larger population density induces technical progress, allowing for division of labor and hence increasing labor productivity. Wolf (1901, pp. 288-289) cautioned that the impact on technical progress is not conclusive and that increasing returns in production would be soon followed by decreasing returns in either agriculture or industry. The crucial point of change was considered to be time -variant, depending on technical and economic conditions. Wolf (1901) also refuted the Malthusian law of population. Empirical evidence suggested that higher developed countries (presumably as a consequence of an increase in rationality and culture) were better balancing population growth and economic development. Population declined as a consequence of economic determinants (Wolf, 1901, pp. 280-287). In his 1908 book, which containes a paragraph on family economics (pp. 168-169), he explicitly presented his law of population using the notion of optimum population (pp. 188-192).

However, judging from the German literature at that time and earlier, the term must have been in common use before. Bortkiewicz (1908, pp. 24-33) has summarized these efforts and clearly used the term "optimal population size" (p. 27). Schmoller (1900, pp. 184-190), Wagner (1893, pp. 638-665), Marlo (1856, pp. 338-354) and von Mangoldt (1857, pp. 123-127) had a clear view on optimal, normal or ideal population size. Similar ideas can be found in the work of Wolff (1721, see Stangeland, 1967, pp. 209-211), who took a clear viewpoint of optimum population and economic welfare.

Overpopulation and underpopulation follow straightforwardly from a concept of optimum population. A revival of fears of overpopulation was induced by Keynes (1920, p. 213) after World War I who suggested the supposedly unfavorable trend in the terms of trade as evidence of overpopulation; but Beveridge (1923) showed that Keynes had ministerpreted the data. (See also Petersen, 1955, for further references and evaluations of the debate.) In the 1930's, economists were more concerned with the economic consequences of stagnating population. Again, it was Keynes (1937) who became a leading proponent of the group of population theorists attributing economic stagnation to population decline.

The notion of optimum population has been an influential concept in this century, though only a few authors have dared to calculate concrete numbers: Wicksell, for instance, found 3 million for Sweden in 1924 an Sauvy 50-75 million for France in 1956. After World War II, optimum population became an essential part of growth theory. However, for much too long, population was considered to be exogenous to the economic system in these models. This emphasis on exogeneity has only recently changed. Therefore, the next section concerns tracing the roots of endogenous fertility.

3. From Exogenous to Endogenous Fertility

A crucial step in the development of population theory has been the endogenization of fertility. Although such classic economists such as Adam Smith, Thomas Robert Malthus und David Ricardo (see also Pestieau, 1989; Eckstein, Stern, Wolpin, 1989) were treating population as endogenous, this tradition was ignored when the theory of optimum population emerged as an attractive instrument to economic demographers in the first half of the twentieth century. This has only recently changed.

The achievements in this field were inspired by seminal contributions of Leibenstein (1957) and Becker (1960) who studied fertility behavior within the framework of consumer theory. Hence the dominating model of fertility analysis today is based on a theory of rational individuals maximizing utility under given constraints.[2] However, the traditional framework of household choices was enriched in many ways. Parents decide about the quantity and quality of their children: they care about their well-being. A household production framework allows one to encorporate various restrictions in modelling individual choice. Specifically, the time-cost of childrearing is noted and children are considered to be more time-intensive then other home production activities. As a positive economic theory, home production must be assumed female time-intensive. The model therefore provides an explanation of female time allocation between work in the home and market work, as well as a rationale for the observed negative correlation between female labor supply and fertility. Both variables are seen as jointly endogenous to family decision making (Mincer, 1963).

A central puzzle of the analysis of population change is the observed negative correlation between fertility and economic development or income. The neoclassical theory of fertility suggests two major reasons for fertility decline: First, the *cost of time hypothesis* implies that the (relative) increase of female wages in the process of economic development is a particular relevant cause. Second, the *quantity-quality approach* to fertility choice predicts that, with rising income, there is a likely substitution effect from quantity to quality of children. An increase of quality per child implies an (endogenous) increase of expenditures per child and this endogenous (and negative) price effect may more than compensate the positive income effect. Hence, fertility may decline even if children are not inferior 'goods'. A precondition for this is, however, that the budget constraint is non-linear. Also, the assumption that children are time-intensive is occasionally criticized on empirical grounds (Robinson, 1987).

An alternative explanation for the negative correlation between fertility and income within the neoclassical framework was recently developed by Zimmermann (1987, 1989). It is argued that an increase in the *variety of goods* available to the consumers contribute to the *long-run factors* explaining fertility decline. This extends an idea presented by the German economist Lujo Brentano (1909, 1910). It is also

---

[2] This approach is sometimes called the Chicago school model. A rival framework is the Pennsylvania school model which gives more emphasis to preference formation, supply factors and behavior under imperfect information. See Easterlin, Pollak and Wachter, 1980. In this paper, I stay within the neoclassical framework.

worthy to note that Brentano (1909, 1910) had already fully outlined all central elements of modern family economics. Though this contribution was never completely forgotten in German demography (see Zimmermann 1988, 1989) it seems to be time to remember this old German tradition.

Although Leibenstein (1957) and Becker (1960) clearly used a cost-benefit approach to analyze fertility decisions, economics of the family had some way to go until the basic elements outlined in the last section were developed. This stage was reached with the publication of the Chicago conference volume edited by Schultz (1974). Becker (1960) applied the standard theory to the family treating children as consumer 'durables'. At a time when fertility was again rising in the United States, he supported the Malthusian view of a positive relationship between income and fertility. "Malthus' famous discussion was built upon a strongly economic framework; mine can be viewed as a generalization and development of his." (Becker, 1960, p. 209) He introduced the new element 'quality' of children, but concluded (p. 217) that theory suggests "that a rise in income would increase both the quality and quantity of children desired". This result was based on the assumption that children are not inferior goods. Different empirical correlations were explained by "general evidence that contraceptive knowledge has been positively related to income. ... Such evidence does little more than suggest that differential knowledge of contraceptive techniques might explain the negative relationship between fertility and income." (Becker, 1960, p. 218)

The persistence of a negative income effect in later empirical studies and an ongoing discussion about this problem inspired the ingenious paper by Becker and Lewis (1974). It demonstrates that given a certain non-linear interaction of costs for quantity and quality of children, an endogenous price effect may drive the observed income elasticities to be negative, though the linear (or 'true') income effect is positive. The basic idea can be traced to Becker (1960); especially to footnote 10 on page 215; however, this was not yet sufficiently developed. Also, the other central element of modern family economics, the time cost of rearing children, was later introduced by Mincer (1963). A general theory of home production was provided by Becker (1965), Lancaster (1966) and Muth (1966), and this theory is related to earlier contributions by Mitchell (1912) and Reid (1934). However, the basic elements of home production which are crucial for fertility decisions are implicitly contained in the Mincer (1963) study.

Brentano (1909)[3] contains already all key elements of the modern economic theory of the family: rational choice of utility maximizing individuals, time costs of rearing children, substitution of quantity by quality of children. Instead of 'quality', Brentano used the term 'refinement in the love of children', and he defines it in exactly the same way as Becker his concept of quality. The theory was already outlined in a series of newspaper articles in a public debate of Brentano with the German economist Adolph Wagner in 1901 (see Zimmermann, 1988, for a detailed discussion of this issue), in which Brentano took the position that an increase in income causes a fertility decline. Actually, the debate was life-long, originating in 1871 when Brentano completed his Habilitation with Wagner in Berlin. His critical

---

[3] Brentano (1910) is a poor summary of the brilliantly written German book.

evaluation of the wage fund theory of Malthus was closely related to the population issue (see Brentano, 1872, pp. 170-186; Brentano, 1924, pp. 206-207). The crucial point of his critique was that increasing prosperity would be linked with declining fertility. It is useful noting that fertility decline in Germany was only modest until 1900, but became drastic between 1901 and the first world war. Mombert (1907), a former student of Brentano, published a rich empirical study confirming Brentano's position and Brentano (1909) contains additional statistical material. In 1909, Brentano's aim was to defeat the whole Malthusian theory. In that, his motive was quite different from Becker's in 1960.

Brentano (1910, p. 372) criticizes the Malthusian "supposition that the cause of the increase of the human race is the desire for propagation, and that this remains constant in all circumstances. But there is no such thing as the desire for propagation. The causes responsible for the increase of population are the desire for sexual intercourse and the love of children. But sexual desire is under the influence of mental activity. ... And the love of children manifests itself in more ways than the mere bringing of them into the world." ... "The principle cause ... of the decline of fertility is the diminution of the desire for reproduction. As prosperity increases, so do the pleasures which compete with marriage, while the feeling towards children takes on a new character of refinement, and both these facts tend to diminish the desire to beget and bear children. The competition of other pleasures makes itself felt in the case of the woman as well as in that of the man, though in a different manner. In the woman it produces a distaste for the spending of her entire existence in pregnancy and child-bed; this distaste becomes more pronounced in proportion to the increased variety and tempting character of the pleasures which must be foregone." (pp. 385-386)

"She does not want to be cut off from all the joys of youth and the pleasures which wealth can offer by a series of pregnancies following on each other in uninterrupted succession. In the case of other modern women the decline in the desire to have children, or at any rate, many children, is attributed to the movement for emancipation. Women who follow intellectual pursuits or who wish to live their lives to the full, desire to be hindered as little as possible by the duties which the nursery imposes; others who follow a profession feel themselves hampered by motherhood in the earning of money which would make other pleasures possible. And of the factory worker ... the protective measures which prohibit her from returning to work for a definite number of weeks after child-birth, deprive her of the means of subsistence, and she naturally seeks to avoid the recurrence of such an enforced stopping of supplies.

With this we enter on the domain of economic causes, which are especially responsible for the decline in the desire for reproduction in the case of the man. ... The most potent check ... in his case is the consideration how far, if he were to call a great number of children into existence, the increased demand thus made on his resources would cut him off from other satisfactions. ... The advance in the technical arts, in trade and industry, in science and art, has made countless new pleasures accessible to everyone—pleasures, however, in which they can participate only if they can command the requisite means. ...

The greater delicacy of the feeling towards children works in the same direction. With increasing prosperity, mankind generally rises above the state of blindly giving way to its animal instincts, and so parents become more and more conscious of their responsibility both for the character and number of the human beings whom they bring into the world. This leads many weakly people to refrain from giving life to children to whom they might transmit their diseases. In other cases parents will rather strive to ensure to the children whom they have already brought into the world a good education and a larger patrimony, so as to equip them better for the modern struggle for life. Both these facts tend to restrict the number of births." (pp. 386-387)

Finally, Brentano (1910, p. 389) summarizes: "Thus the different behaviour of different classes of the same people and of the same people at different stages shows that sexual passion is no constant and regular motive as Malthus assumed. ... With increasing wealth and culture the variety of man's wants increases, and Gossen's law as to the limit up to which different kinds of pleasure are gratified, in order to realise the maximum of satisfaction on the whole, becomes applicable. Man limits his family when the increase of his family tends do diminish the sum total of satisfaction."

Beyond the modern analysis of fertility, Brentano emphasizes the concept of *variety of goods*. There are two aspects: (a) With an increasing variety of goods, the utility maximation principle becomes more relevant for individual decisions. (b) An increase of the variety of goods induces a pressure to substitute consumption goods for children. The validity of the second hypothesis was confirmed in a neoclassical framework by Zimmermann (1987, 1989).

There are comparable views to that of Brentano's in the American literature: "The increase of wealth will in itself set in motion those economic and sociological forces which tend to reduce the rate of increase of population." (Seligman, 1905, p. 64) "Productive power is really the connecting link, the equalizing force, between population and the food supply; it checks the former and increases the latter. As civilization is the principle antagonistic to the law of deminishing returns, so productive power is the principle antagonistic to the law of increasing population. With the growth of those qualities in men which lead to an increase in productive power, there is a diminution of the force of those passions which tend to increase population, thus gradually bringing about a harmony between population and food supply. In the primitive man, the cruder appetites and passions are the strongest motives to action. With the development of a higher type of man other pleasures become stronger and the natural impulses, which come from the primitive appetites and passions, are gradually subdued. A new society thus becomes possible, in which individuals act in a way that tends to secure a closer connection between population and productive power." (Patten, 1924, p. 199. The chapter from which this citation is taken was reprinted from an article in *The Political Science Quarterly*, Vol. 10, pp. 44-61, 1895.) And: "Increases in the standard of living, or the quantity of goods and services which people prefer to children, will slacken the rate of population growth." (Douglas, 1934, p. 344) The influencial book by Douglas (1934, pp. 349-351) also contains a summary of Brentano's and Mombert's work: "Brentano and Mombert have perhaps made the most thorough advocacy of the theory that an increase in real wages will cause a decline in the birth rate" (p. 349). Also Peterson (1955, p. 228) refered to Brentano's work.

The long and rich tradition of research on optimum population in self-evident, with recent work in this area emphasizing the crucial role of endogenous population, a line of research which itself has an impressive record. The articles found in this volume are built upon these solid foundations. The next section outlines the main findings of eleven papers covering a wide range of problems connected with optimum population.

4. An Overview of the Book

The volume consists of four parts: (I) Optimal Size and Growth Rate of Population, (II) Technical Progress and Social Security, (III) Limited Resources, and (IV) International Economics. In Section I, *Optimal Size and Growth Rate of Population*, three papers are concerned with positive and normative issues of optimum population: *"Socially Optimal Population Size and Individual Choice"* by Marc Nerlove, Assaf Razin and Efraim Sadka, "Endogenous Population with Discrete Family Size and a Capital Market" by Daniel Léonard and *"Is There an Optimal Growth Rate of Population?"* by Gerhard Schmitt-Rink.

In their paper *"Socially Optimal Population Size and Individual Choice"*, Marc Nerlove, Assaf Razin and Efraim Sadka examine the general equilibrium implications of endogenous fertility for a number of social issues of population policy. In studying the normative implications of endogenous fertility, they adopt the simplest possible formulation: In addition to their own consumption, the number of children and the utility of each child is assumed to enter the utility function of the parents. Thus, subject to whatever economic opportunities and contraints they face, parents are assumed to maximize their own utility functions in making choices with respect to numbers of children and investments in them. Non-coersive tax and subsidy policies may be devised to affect these decisions; in the absence of such policies, a laissez-faire solution will generally exist. They ask first whether the laissez-faire solution will be efficient from the standpoint of the present generation, i. e., whether individual choice in the absence of social intervention will lead to a Pareto-optimal solution. They then introduce the notion of an intergenerational social welfare function and ask whether laissez-faire leads to a social optimum under various criteria and, if not, what non-coersive social policies may be introduced to achieve one.

Nerlove, Razin and Sadka demonstrate that the implications of endogenous fertility for the questions of optimum population size are far-reaching. They show that endogenous fertility may, under certain circumstances, lead to the failure of laissez-faire to attain an efficient or Pareto-optimal solution from the standpoint of members of the present generation. To go beyond the issue of efficient allocations from the standpoint of only the present generation, the authors introduce a social welfare function which aggregates utilities of the present and future generations: the sum of individual utilities and the average of individual utilities. It is shown that the former always leads to a larger optimum population than the latter. When fertility is endogenous, a laissez-faire solution is well-defined, but exhibits no specific relationship with both social criteria.

In the literature, possible pitfalls of the basic structure of such models with endogenous fertility and bequest are examined, such as the lack of a utility maximizing choice, the non-existence of a non-trivial steady state, the unavoidability of extinction, and the restriction of family size to integer values. Whereas a unique stable non-trivial steady state would exist if the integer constraint were not imposed, the integer constraint if imposed interferes with the choice of bequests, resulting in discontinuities in the phase line. These may destroy the stability, uniqueness and even the existence of a steady state solution. In his contribution *"Endogenous Population with Discrete Family Size and a Capital Market"*, Daniel Léonard extends his previous work in this area. He adds another distinctive feature in an attempt to test the robustness of the previous analysis of the integer constrained model: a competitive market for the capital good. It is studied whether the existence of a capital market can smooth these discontinuities and re-establish the simplicity of real-valued analysis. Although the existence of capital markets affects both the population profile and the distribution of wealth, it is shown that the consequences of discrete family size cannot be ignored. The analysis of the real-valued case provides no clues to the actual dynamic behavior of the integer constrained system. Léonard shows that the integer restriction entails no loss of welfare and family consumption remains continous, but the level of bequests is discontinous.

In his paper, *"Is There an Optimal Growth Rate for Population"*, Gerhard Schmitt-Rink discusses the existence of properties of population growth rates which are optimal in the sense that (a) the demographic dependency rate, measured as the number of children and retirees which the average active person has to support, is minimized, (b) the economic dependency rate, measured as the relative share of per capita income which the average active person has to spend on children and retirees, is minimized, and (c) net per capita consumption is maximized. Minimization of the demographic dependency rate is only useful if one assumes that children and retirees have an average weight of one in the analysis. If the dependency burden is linked to gross or net consumption per active person, all maxima are located on golden-rule paths where the equilibrium growth rate equals marginal productivity of capital. Conversely, if the dependency burden is linked to the wage rate, the maximum of net per capita consumption is not located on golden-rule paths. Further results crucially depend on the relative size of the consumption weight of an average child and an average retiree: optimal population growth rates may be positive, zero or negative.

Section II, *Technical Progress and Social Security*, consists of two papers: one by Manfred Neumann on *"Technical Progress and Population Growth"* and one by Klaus Jaeger on *"The Serendipity Theorem Reconsidered: The Three-Generation Case Without Inheritance"*. The Malthusian and Ricardian tradition views economic development as a race between population and technical improvements. Technological change is modeled as an outward shift of the production possibility frontier allowing for a larger population size. Upon technical improvements, population size increases until the enlarged consumption possibilities are exhausted and consumption per head has come down to a stationary subsistence level. Hence, technical improvements elicit accelerated population growth.

In his contribution *"Technical Progress and Population Growth"*, Manfred Neumann contradicts this view. He shows that in a neoclassical growth model, technical progress lowers population growth under quite reasonable assumptions. Technological change is seen to be continuous and exogenously given. Instead of examining the optimum size of population which can be sustained by a given technology, the paper is concerned with a rate of growth of population sustainable at a given rate of technological change. The model of an eternal family is employed, which is concerned with the utility of a representative member of that family and all descendents. The family is assumed to control both capital accumulation and the rate of growth of the family, given production possibilities and their rate of increase due to technological change. The basic notion used is that rearing children can be considered as a kind of capital formation. Raising children affects the future size of the family and thus total utility, appropriately discounted. Similarly, accumulation of physical capital affects the sustainable level of consumption per head. Hence, both rearing children and expending part of the annual output for capital accumulation can be viewed as contributing to future utility of the family. The main results are that there is an inverse relationship between the rate of time preference that is used for discounting future utility on one hand and both capital formation and population growth on the other hand, and that the rate of population growth is adversely affected by technological improvements.

The Serendipity Theorem, in which private lifetime saving, at the optimal growth rate, will just support the most golden-rule lifetime state, as derived by Samuelson (1975), was criticized in the literature, as the implied optimal population growth rate is not optimal in the general case. For instance, in the special case in which both utility and production functions are Cobb-Douglas, Samuelson's solution, for those parameter values for which it exists, provides a global minimum of steady-state utility. Klaus Jaeger, in his contribution *"The Serendipity Theorem Reconsidered: The Three-Generation Case Without Inheritance"*, first evaluates this literature, concluding that depending on the exact specifications of both the utility and the production functions concerning their respective elasticities of substitution, an optimum population growth rate may or may not exist. Accordingly, the Serendipity Theorem holds or does not hold. However, two more crucial assumptions in the analysis are made: First, household utility does not depend on who consumes the family basket of goods; it is indifferent to the child-adult composition of the family. Second, children do not impose any costs, such as food and clothing, paid for by their parents.

Jaeger relaxes these restrictions. He assumes that each consumer lives and consumes for three periods, but provides labor in the second period only. Individuals in the working stage of their lives take care of their children's consumption by intergenerational transfers. The well-being of the representative person who works in the second period and retires in the third period of his life depends upon per capita real consumption of his children and upon his own consumption in the second and third periods of his life, but not on the number of his children. Population growth rate is exogenously given but changeable by an authority ensuring an utility maximizing optimal growth path. In this setting, it can be shown that the Serendipity Theorem does not hold even if an optimal population growth rate exists. The existence of such a growth rate is, in general, necessary but not sufficient for the validity of the Serendipity Theorem. However, a modified Serendipity Theorem is always applicable in a laissez-faire system, if an optimal growth rate exists. Moreover, introducing a suitable social security program in an otherwise laissez-faire organized old-age security system leads to the most golden-rule steady-state allocation of resources. Thus, if at all, then only a mixed system and not a strict privately organized capital-reverse system without inheritance can generate such an optimal allocation.

Section III of the volume, *Limited Resources*, contains three papers: *"Endogenous Population and Fixed Input in a Growth Model With Altruism"* by Pierre Pestieau, *"On the Malthusian Hypothesis and the Dynamics of Population and Income in an Equilibrium Growth Model With Endogenous Fertility"* by Zvi Eckstein, Steven Stern and Kenneth I. Wolpin, and *"Choice of Fertility and Population Pressure in Traditional Rural Societies"* by Gerhard Schwödiauer and Alois Wenig.

As already discussed above, modern growth theories are based on a constant proportional rate population growth as the essential driving force of economic growth with some aid from technological progress. The classical economists, especially Ricardo, however, rely on the idea that in the presence of fixed inputs per capita, consumption tends eventually to fall and to reach a floor at which population stops growing. Thus, there is not only the question of whether population is independent of economic considerations but also that of whether there is a natural resource constraint that cannot be removed by substitution with renewable inputs or by technological progress. The latter issue was neglected in recent literature, and it is the central point in the contribution *"Endogenous Population and Fixed Input in a Growth Model With Altruism"* by Pierre Pestieau.

Pestieau makes the point that the two basic Ricardian assumptions, endogenous population and fixed input, are usually discussed and objected to separately, whereas they are in fact inseparable: It is fixed supply of inputs which makes population dependent on per capita income. The argument is presented in an intergeneration model of consumption in which the utility of each generation depends on the level of its consumption, the size of the following generation and some index of altruism towards the future. Though the Ricardian stationary state cannot be avoided, it is shown, that the path of population growth and the stationary level of per capita income depend on the degree of altruism towards the future. It is also shown that if within each generation individuals are not alike, they might behave "demographically" as free riders and thus, lead to a growth of population which could be considered not socially optimal. Results can be summarized as follows: Either in the absence of altruism between generations or in case of unstable dynamics, population growth depends on and is eventually stopped by an exogenously given per capita consumption. If there is some altruism between generations, the rate of population growth and the stationary per capita income are normally a function of the degree of altruism. The absence of cooperation within each generation is likely to lead to a rate of population growth that is above the level that is optimal from each individual's viewpoint.

In their paper, *"On the Malthusian Hypothesis and the Dynamics of Population and Income in an Equilibrium Growth Model with Exogenous Fertility"*, Zvi Eckstein, Steve Stern and Kenneth I. Wolpin are concerned with the pessimistic Malthusian view that the existence of a fixed amount of land leads to the eventual decline in per capita consumption and capital. They choose an overlapping generations growth framework in which fertility is subject to individual choice. Starting with Malthus' postulates on decreasing marginal productivity, due to a fixed supply of land and exogenous exponential population growth, they demonstrate the Malthusian result that the competitive economy converges in finite time to zero consumption per capita. However, even if individuals care only about the number of their children and not about their children's welfare, there exists an equilibrium in which they would eventually choose to have only one child for each adult. Hence, by endogenizing their fertility decisions, the equilibrium with indefinite population growth is ruled out. Given a land market and fertility choice, the Malthusian result is no longer necessarily followed.

In the second part of the paper, an overlapping generations growth model is analyzed in which fertility is again subject to choice, but in which there is no essential fixed factor. It is shown that if offspring are assumed to consume time of adults before they reach adulthood, then the stylized fact of the demographic transition can be duplicated by the model. Further, it is shown that the economy may cycle or converge smoothly to the steady-state. This demonstrates that neoclassical growth theory with endogenous fertility is consistent with existing aggregate observations on population and income growth over long periods of time in many countries.

Gerhard Schwödiauer and Alois Wenig investigate the "*Choice of Fertility and Population Pressure in Traditional Rural Societies*". They first develop a general framework for the analysis of endogenous population in the context of overlapping generations long-run economic equilibrium models. They apply this approach to a traditional rural society characterized by a fixed supply of land, a productive role for children, and a fixed non-market institution for the distribution of social product and show that a stable generative tradition of such a society will, under empirically plausible assumptions, produce a continual pressure of population growth on the supply of food. Old-age social security may help to prevent progressive impoverishment of such a society. In reality, impoverishment may be checked by technological advances and/or institutional changes, or it will eventually be checked, at a low level of per capita consumption, however, by an increase in mortality. The model presented offers a theoretical concept to understand the nature of permanent population pressure in traditional rural societies, which is possibly superior to the mechanistic short-cut of viewing fertility as immediately causally related to per capita incomes. Fertility and per capita income are jointly determined by individual choices within a given institutional and technological environment. To reduce the population pressure in the Third World, the analysis suggests the usefulness of technological advances reducing the net productivity of child labor and of institutional changes like social security and/or competitive markets.

Section IV, *International Economics,* contains three articles by John Pitchford, "*Economic Interdependence and Optimum Population: An Examination of Meade's Objection to the Individual Utility Criterion",* Murray C. Kemp and Hitoshi Kondo, "*An Analysis of International Migration: The Unilateral Case",* and Hitoshi Kondo, "*Population, International Trade and Indebtedness: A More General Analysis".*

John Pitchford's contribution "*Economic Interdependence and Optimum Population: An Examination of Meade's Objection to the Individual Utility Criterion*" re-examines Meade's abandonment of individual welfare as a criterion for optimum population in favor of total utility. The analysis results only in an incomplete rehabilitation of the individualistic criterion, but it elucidates the nature of an individualistic utility based optimum population by showing how economic interdependencies such as trade and public goods determine how far population would be spread across regions of differing productivity. When all opportunities for beneficial trade and the sharing of the costs of public goods are exhausted it will not be optimal to extend population into further regions. All of this follows if there is one government and if that government insists on the equalization of consumption per capita in the populated world. Without one or both of these conditions, it is in the interests of the more productive regions that those less productive should be populated, as long as they can trade. Further, if tastes differ across but not within regions the individualistic criterion would have a place in the determination of each region's optimum population. Finally, the total utility criterion is unlikely to be one which each individual in the society will endorse.

Any fully satisfactory analysis of population change, whether of the descriptive variety or of the welfare-theoretical variety, must contain within it a sufficiently thorough analysis of the international migration of labor. Unfortunately, the analysis of migration lacks a firm basis in the decision-making of individual households. Murray C. Kemp and Hitoshi Kondo, therefore, present *"An Analysis of International Migration: The Unilateral Case"* to close this gap.

If a family is considering the possibility of migration to another country, it must decide whether to migrate at all and, if the desirability of migration is accepted, it must decide whether the entire family or only some portion of it is to move and whether the move is to be permanent or temporary. To capture all dimensions of the family's problem one must employ an overlapping-generations model in which individuals live for three periods: childhood, adulthood and retirement. The authors develop a general-equilibrium theory of migration based on an international disparity of preferences, where most of these preferences are determined in the country of birth. Furthermore, migration is assumed to be unilateral and permanent. Under these conditions it is shown that if an individual's preferences depend only on his country of birth, then all steady-state migration is from the country with the relatively high rate of time preference to the country with the relative low rate of time preference, but that if preferences can change after migration, then steady-state migration might be in the opposite direction.

In his paper *"Population, International Trade and Indebtedness: A More General Analysis"*, Hitoshi Kondo develops an open-economy, overlapping-generations model in which population, international trade and international indebtedness all appear as endogenous variables and in which intergenerational caring and bequests play a role. In particular, he examines the effects of international trade and investment on the steady-state values of capital ownership per worker, the capital-labor ratio, the level of income per family and the rate of population growth. If the rate of population growth is given exogenously then a modified Golden Rule implies the undesirable result that international trade between two countries leads to a constant flow of capital into the country with the higher autarkic rate of interest so that, in the steady-state, one country will have all the wealth. However, by allowing for endogenous population growth, it is possible to rule out this undesirable case. Furthermore, the modified Golden Rule implies that only an international disparity in the rate of discount or in marginal productivity causes an international difference in the rate of population growth under trade. In other words, if preferences or technology differ between countries in any respects other than those just mentioned then, as a result of international trade, those differences are absorbed by the disparities in family consumption and per-worker capital ownership, and the rate of population growth is the same in each country.

References

Becker, G. S. (1960) An Economic Analysis of Fertility. In: Demographic and Economic Change in Developed Countries. NBER. Princeton: 209-231

Becker, G. S. (1965) A Theory of the Allocation of Time. Economic Journal 75:493-517

Becker, G. S. and H. G. Lewis (1974) Interaction Between Quantity and Quality of Children. In: Schultz, T. W. (Ed.) Economics of the Family. Chicago: 81-90

Beveridge, W. H. (1923) Population and Unemployment. Economic Journal 33: 447-475

Von Bortkiewicz, L. (1908) Die Bevölkerungstheorie. In: Die Entwicklung der deutschen Volkswirtschaftslehre im neunzehnten Jahrhundert. Gustav Schmoller zur siebzigsten Wiederkehr seines Geburtstages. Vol. 1. Leipzig: Duncker & Humblot: XIII 1-57

Brentano, L. (1872) Die Arbeitergilden der Gegenwart. Zweiter Band. Zur Kritik der englischen Gewerkvereine. Leipzig: Duncker & Humblot

Brentano, L. (1909) Die Malthus'sche Lehre und die Bevölkerungsbewegung der letzten Dezennien. In: Abhandlungen der historischen Klasse der Königlich-Bayerischen Akademie der Wissenschaften 24. München

Brentano, L. (1910) The Doctrine of Malthus and the Increase of Population During the Last Decades, Economic Journal 20: 371-393

Brentano, L. (1924) Konkrete Grundbedingungen der Volkswirtschaft. Leipzig: Felix Meiner.

Cannan, E. (1903) Elementary Political Economy. London: P. S. King & Staples Limited. (Originally published in 1888.)

Cannan, E. (1928) Wealth. London: P. S. King & Staples Limited

Cannan, E. (1964) A Review of Economic Theory. London: Frank Cass. (Originally published in 1929)

Cohn, S. S. (1934) Die Theorie des Bevölkerungsoptimums. Ein Beitrag zur dogmengeschichtlichen und dogmenkritischen Behandlung des Bevölkerungsproblems. Berlin: Hanns Michel

Dasgupta, P. S. (1969) On the Concept of Optimal Population. Review of Economic Studies 36, 295-318

Dasgupta, P. S. (1984) The Ethical Foundations of Population Policies mimeo., Cambridge

Douglas, P. H. (1934) The Theory of Wages. Reprints of Economic Classics. 1964. New York: August M. Kelley

Easterlin, R. A., R. A. Pollak, and M.L. Wachter (1980) Toward a More General Economic Model of Fertility Determination: Endogenous Preferences and Natural Fertility. In: R. A. Easterlin (Ed.) Population and Economic Change in Developing Countries. Chicago: 81-149

Eckstein, Z., S. Stern, and K. I. Wolpin (1989) On the Malthusian Hypothesis and the Dynamics of Population and Income in and Equilibrium Growth Model With Endogenous Fertility. In this volume

Fetter, F. (1913) Population or Prosperity. American Economic Review 3 Supp., 5-19

Gottlieb, M., (1949) Optimum Population, Foreign Trade and World Economy. Population Studies 3: 151-169

Jaeger, K. (1989) The Serendipity Theorem Reconsidered: The Three-Generation Case Without Inheritance. In this volume

Kemp, M. C. and H. Kondo (1989) An Analysis of International Migration: The Unilateral Case. In this volume.

Keynes, J. M. (1919) The Economic Consequences of the Peace. London: MacMillan

Keynes, J. M. (1937) Some Economic Consequences of a Declining Population. Eugenics Review 29: 13-17

Kondo H. (1989) Population, International Trade and Indebtedness: A More General Analysis. In this volume

Lancaster, K. J. (1966) A New Approach to Consumer Theory. Journal of Political Economy 74: 132-157

Lane, J. S. (1977) On Optimal Population Paths. Berlin et al.: Springer

Leibenstein, H. (1957) Economic Backwardness and Economic Growth. New York: Wiley

Léonard, D. (1989) Endogenous Population With Discrete Family Size and a Capital Market. In this volume

Malthus, T. R. (1970) An Essay on the Principle of Population and a Summery View of the Principle of Population. Baltimore: Penguin. (Originally published in 1798 and 1830)

Von Mangoldt, B. (1857) Bevölkerung. In: J. E. Bluntschli and R. Brater (Eds.) Deutsches Staats-
    Wörterbuch 2. Stuttgart. Leibzig: 118-135
Marlo, K. (1856) Allgemeine Grundsätze der Volkswirthschaft. Second edition 1898. Tübingen:
    H. Laupp.
Meade, J. E. (1955) Trade and Welfare. Oxford: Oxford University Press
Mill, J. S (1965) Principles of Political Economy. Reprints of Economic Classics. New York:
    Augustus M. Kelley. (Originally published in 1848)
Mincer, J. (1963) Market Prices, Opportunity Costs and Income Effects. In: C. F. Christ (Ed.)
    Measurement in Economics. Stanford: 67-82
Mitchell, W. C. (1912) The Backward Art of Spending Money. In: American Economic Review 2:
    269-281
Mombert, P. (1907) Studien zur Bevölkerungsbewegung in Deutschland. Karlsruhe: G. Braun
Mombert, P. (1929) Bevölkerungslehre. Jena: Gustav Fischer
Muth, R. F. (1966) Household Production and Economic Demand Functions. Econometrica 34:
    699-708
Neumann, M. (1989) Technical Progress and Population Growth. In this volume
Nerlove, M., A. Razin, and E. Sadka (1987) Household and Economy: Welfare Economics of En-
    dogenous Fertility. New York: Academic Press
Nerlove, M., A. Razin, and E. Sadka (1989) Socially Optimal Population Size and Individual
    Choice. In this volume
Oppenheimer, F. (1901) Das Bevölkerungsgesetz des T. R. Malthus und der neueren Na-
    tionalökonomie. Darstellung und Kritik. Berlin. Bern: John Edelheim
Overbeek, J. (1977) The Evolution of Population Theory. Westport and London: Greenwood Press
Patten, S. N. (1924) Essays in Economic Theory. New York: Alfred A. Knopf
Pestieau, P. (1989) Endogenous Population and Fixed Input in a Growth Model With Altruism.
    In this volume
Petersen, W. (1955) John Maynard Keynes's Theories of Population and the Concept of 'Op-
    timum' Population Studies 8: 228-246
Pitchford, J. (1989) Economic Interdependence and Optimum Population: An Examinition of
    Meade's Objection to the Individual Utility Criterion. In this volume
Pitchford, J. D. (1974) Population in Economic Growth. Amsterdam et al.: North- Holland
Reid, M. G. (1934) Economics of Household Production. New York: Wiley
Robinson, W. C. (1987) The Time Cost of Children and Other Household Production, Population
    Studies 41: 313-323
Sauvy, A. (1969) General Theory of Population. London: Methuen
Schmitt-Rink, G. (1989) Is There an Optimal Growth Rate for Population. In this volume
Schmoller, G. (1919) Grundriß der Allgemeinen Volkswirtschaftslehre, 2 volumes. München:
    Duncker & Humblot. (The first volume was originally published in 1900, the second volume
    was originally published in 1904)
Schultz, T. W. (1974) Economics of the Family. Chicago: University of Chicago Press
Schwödiauer, G. and A. Wenig (1989) Choice of Fertility and Population Pressure in Traditional
    Rural Societies. In this volume
Seligman, E. (1905) Principles of Economics. London: Longmans, Green, and Co
Spengler, J. J. (1944) Pareto on Population, II. Quarterly Journal of Economics LXX: 107-133
Stangeland, C. E. (1967) Pre-Malthusian Doctrines of Population: A Study in the History of
    Economic Theory. New York: AMS Press
Wagner, A. (1893) Grundlegung der politischen Oekonomie II. Third edition. Leibzig: C. F. Winter
Wicksell, K, (1910) Das Optimum der Bevölkerung. Die Neue Generation, 383-391
Wicksell, K. (1913) Vorlesungen über Nationalökonomie auf Grundlage des Marginalprinzips.
    Jena: G. Fischer
Wolf, J. (1901) Ein neuer Gegner des Malthus. Zeitschrift für Socialwissenschaft 4, 256-289
Wolf, J. (1908) Nationalökonomie als exakte Wissenschaft. Ein Grundriss. Leibzig: A. Deichert
Zimmermann, K. F. (1987) The Variety of Goods and Fertility Decline. mimeo. Philadelphia
Zimmermann, K. F. (1988) Wurzeln der modernen ökonomischen Bevölkerungstheorie in der
    deutschen Forschung um 1900. Jahrbücher für Nationalökonomie und Statistik 205: 116-130.
Zimmermann, K. F. (1989) Die Konkurrenz der Genüsse: Ein Brentano-Modell des Geburtenrück-
    gangs. Forthcoming in: Zeitschriften für Wirtschafts- und Sozialwissenschaften

I. Optimal Size and Growth Rate of Population

Socially Optimal Population Size and Individual Choice[1]

Marc Nerlove, Assaf Razin, and Efraim Sadka

Since Becker's (1960) analysis, the implications of endogenous fertility in the sense of parental altrusim towards their own children, for consumption, labor supply and household unemployment decisions have been explored extensively in the literature. The purpose of this paper is to examine the general equilibrium implications of endogenous fertility for a number of social issues of population policy. We are thus concerned with the normative rather than the positive implications of endogenous fertility. In our analysis, we adopt the simplest possible formulation: In addition to their own consumption, the number of children and the utility of each child is assumed to enter the utility function of the parents. Thus, subject to whatever economic opportunities and constraints they face, parents are assumed to maximize their own utility functions (one per couple) in making choices with respect to numbers of children and investments in them. Noncoersive tax and subsidy policies may be devised to affect these decisions; in the absence of such policies, a *laissez-faire* solution will generally exist. We ask first whether the *laissez-faire* solution will be efficient from the standpoint of the present generation, that is, whether individual choice in the absence of social intervention will lead to a Pareto-optimal solution. We next introduce the notion of an intergenerational social welfare function and ask whether *laissez-faire* leads to a social optimum under various criteria and, if not, what non-coercive social policies may be introduced to achieve one.

1. Pareto Optimality

An allocation of economic resources is said to be Pareto efficient if it is impossible to reshuffle the resources across individual members of society so as to make somebody better off without making anybody worse off. The criterion of Pareto optimality, although it provides only a partial social ordering, is universally considered to be a minimal normative requirement which any individualistically oriented society should wish satisfied. An allocation is said to be feasible if, given everyone's initial endowments, it is technologically possible to produce a set of net outputs which, distributed across individuals, constitute the allocation. One feasible alloca-

[1] This paper draws from our book, *Household and Economy: Welfare Economics of Endogenous Fertility,* New York: Academic Press, 1987. We gratefully acknowledge the support of the U.S. National Institute on Aging, the U.S. — Israel Binational Science Foundation, the International Food Policy Research Institute, the Foerder Institute for Economic Research, and the University of Pennsylvania.

Microeconomic Studies
K. F. Zimmermann (Ed.)
Economic Theory of Optimal Population
© Springer-Verlag Berlin Heidelberg 1989

tion dominates another if everyone is at least as well off given the former as compared to the latter, and at least one individual is better off. A Pareto-efficient allocation is both feasible and dominated by no other feasible allocation. Since there are usually many feasible allocations given any initial distribution of endowments and, among these allocations, more than one that are Pareto-efficient, the criterion does not distinguish among them or rank them from a social point of view. To do so, we need some other criterion which permits comparisons among losses in welfare on the part of some individuals with gains achieved by others. However, in an efficient allocation, the gainers, in theory at least, would be in a position to compensate the losers, whereas in a non-efficient allocation, they might not be. This is why we should wish to achieve Pareto otimality; we can quibble later about how to redistribute the utility pie.

The problem with the Pareto criterion applied to many generations, all but one of which are as yet unborn, is that the set of individual utilities to be compared is not well defined in general. It is clearly not when fertility is endogenous, nor is it well defined when population size is a variable in the welfare calculation. What does is mean to compare allocations in which some individuals are never born with those in which they are? Thus the criterion of Pareto optimality is minimal only from the standpoint of the present generation and has no meaning in an intergenerational context when population is variable. When fertility is endogenous, however, allocations across individuals include variables reflecting the sizes of future generations and the resources available to them, so that allocations be Pareto-efficient from the standpoint of the present generation provides at least a partial ordering of states in which future generations and the welfare of individuals composing them are variable. In a sense, this is not so incompatible with an intergenerational welfare criterion taking into account the welfare of potential individuals as yet unborn since such a criterion must be applied now by the present generation.

Most of the literature of welfare economics is concerned with the kinds or methods of social organization that are compatible with the achievement of Pareto efficiency. In particular the fundamental propositions of welfare economics deal with the relationships between allocations resulting from equilibrium in perfectly competitive markets and Pareto efficiency. The basic result is, roughly speaking, that every competitive equilibrium is Pareto-efficient from the standpoint of the present participants in the resulting allocation, and that every Pareto-efficient allocation could be made, after a redistribution of income, the outcome of exchange in competitive markets. If all individual utility functions are strictly increasing and if there are no externalities (to be discussed in the next section), a competitive equilibrium, where it exists, is Pareto-efficient. Not every allocation can be sustained by a competitive equilibrium, but those that are, under some convexity conditions, can be achieved in the market place through competition, after some redistribution of initial incomes, which are determined by initial endowments.

When, given a particular initial allocation of endowments, a competitive process does not lead to a Pareto-efficient allocation, the allocation to which it does yield, is dominated by one or more allocations which are Pareto-optimal. We know then that there exists some redistribution of income via lump-sum taxes and transfers to redistribute initial endowments which will make one of these Pareto-efficient allocations the outcome of a competitive process. But it may not always be possible to effect such a reallocation in a non-distortionary way, which is equivalent to a rearrangement of initial endowments. (Income taxes or excise taxes are not, for example, non-distortionary.) If the appropriate set of non-distortionary taxes and transfers are not available, it will not be possible to achieve every Pareto-efficient allocation by a competitive process, but this does not mean that we cannot do better than achieving the competitive allocation when no lump-sum taxes and transfers are available. If a Pareto-optimal solution, denoted as first-best, is not attainable by a competitive process due to externalities or non-convexities, there may exist a set of taxes and subsidies which would lead to a situation in which no individual is worse off and at least one individual is better off. Such solutions are second-best; they may still be dominated by other allocations, also not attainable by competitive processes, but they dominate the competitive allocation for the given initial endowments.

2. Externalities and Public Goods

The conditions under which every Pareto-efficiency allocation can be sustained by a competitive equilibrium are of two kinds: (1) Conditions referring to the production technologies and individual preferences which characterize the economy, which require diminishing marginal rates of substitution in both production and consumption and rule out increasing returns to scale. (2) Conditions referring to the existence and organization of markets, which essentially require that there are competitive markets for every commodity. When there is an unpriced commodity, we say there is an externality. Such commodities are usually produced jointly with another commodity, for which there is no market and therefore no price. Such commodities are typically produced or consumed by one economic agent but affect one or more other agents. In principle (Coase, 1960), an appropriate system of enforcable contractual arrangements could be established that would give rise to the markets necessary to eliminate unpriced commodities, but the transactions needed to effectuate such markets may be prohibitively expensive and, therefore, such externalities continue to exist. The famous, if biologically inaccurate, example of the honey bees and the apple blossoms is an example of a positive externality or an external economy. If my use of abortion or other means to prevent *my* family from having additional children appals *you* and lowers your utility independently of your own choices, it is an example of an external diseconomy.

In this paper, we confine ourselves to market failures arising from externalities and assume that all convexity conditions are satisfied.

By its very definition, an externality is unpriced. Thus an agent who generates an externality by his action does not fully perceive the social consequences of that action since the prices he faces do not reflect the value (positive or negative) of the externality. Therefore, the competitive agent who acts in response to market prices does not act properly from the point view of efficiency of resource allocation i.e. he fails to internalize the externality.

Because transactions costs may prevent the creation of certain markets, Pigou (1947) suggested a system of corrective taxes and subsidies. Instead, in the apple-blossom/honey-bee example, of creating a separate market for apple blossoms, we subsidize the price of apples. If the subsidy is set at a level equal to the marginal value product of apple blossoms in honey production, then the cost of apples to the grower will reflect the full social value of apples. But the funds for such subsidies must be raised by nondistortionary lump-sum taxes. In the case of abortions, a tax would have to be levied reflecting the disutilities borne by the right-to-lifers, but the resulting distribution of income might cause suffering not only to those obligated to pay the tax. An external diseconomy caused by the fact that air pollution is a byproduct of electricity production is more easily corrected by a Pigouvian corrective tax. Pigouvian taxes and subsidies which are uniform across individuals are often only a second-best remedy (see Diamond, 1973).

Most goods, with which we deal, are ordinary private goods in the sense that they can be parcelled out among different individuals or, at least, among different families. But there are many examples, such as national defense, television or radio broadcasts, etc., which ". . . all enjoy in common in the sense that each individual's consumption of such a good leads to no subtraction from any other individual's consumption of that good" (Samuelson, 1954, p. 387). In order to achieve Pareto optimality, a price for individual use of the public good would have to exist equating the sum of individual benefits to the marginal cost of producing the good. But the relative cost of enforcing such a price and of excluding individuals who don't pay it from use of the good may be prohibitively high. So the existence of public goods may create conditions for externalities.

The question we now ask is whether endogenous fertility can create possibilities for market failure, that is, give rise to externalities which lead to competitive equilibria which are not optimal from the standpoint of the present generation.

3. Endogenous Fertility and Potential Market Failure: False Issues

In this section, we consider three potential sources of market failure. First, if there are *pure* public goods such as national defense, basic research, weather forecasts, etc., the per-capita costs of providing these goods fall as the population size is increased. Since all enjoy these goods at no additional cost, it is possible that there exists a market failure in relation to population size resulting in the inefficiency of *laissez faire*. Second, a fixed resource, such as land, which must be combined with labor to produce goods for consumption, could lead to Malthusian diminishing returns to a larger population size. This suggests a potential source of external diseconomies and market failure in relation to population size. Third, there is the problem associated with the infinity of generations in an over-lapping generation model. In his seminal paper, Samuelson (1958) showed that even without the standard sources of market failure (externalities and nonconvexities), the competitive equilibrium may fail to achieve Pareto-efficiency when there are an infinite number of generations.

It is a remarkable fact that none of these three potential sources lead to market failure when fertility is endogenous; competition leads to Pareto optimality from the standpoint ot the present generation.

Consider, for the sake of simplicity, a two period model with one parent in the first period. (Extension to the infinite horizon case is without difficulty.) We assume a fixed resource, land, and a fixed supply of labor per-capita (i.e. no labor-leisure decisions). Land is used in each period together with labor to produce a single good which can be used as private consumption (c^i) and public consumption (P^i) in period $i = 1,2$. Due to the Malthusian fixed factor (land), there is a diminishing marginal product of labor. Assuming that the labor endowment is one unit, output is $f(1)$ in the first period. The parent in the first period bears n children. Therefore, output is $f(n)$ in the second period. We assume that $f' > 0$ and $f'' < 0$.

The consumption possibilities of this economy can be described by the following two resource constraints:

$$c^1 + P^1 + b = f(1), \tag{1}$$
$$nc^2 + P^2 = b + f(n), \tag{2}$$

where b is the quantity of consumption transfered from the parent in the first period to her children in the second period. Constraint (2) implicitly assumes that consumption can be stored from the first to be second period without cost. These two constraints are combined to yield a single constraint:

$$c^1 + nc^2 + P^1 + p^2 = f(1) + f(n) \tag{3}$$

A competitive profit-maximization implies that:

$$w^1 = f'(1), \qquad\qquad w^2 = f'(n),$$
$$\tag{4}$$
$$\Pi^1 = f(1) - f'(1) \text{ and } \Pi^2 = f(n) - nf'(n),$$

where w^i is the market wage rate and Π^i is the land rent (profit) in period $i = 1,2$. The wage rate is simply the marginal productivity of labor and the land rent is the residual of output over the wage bill.

The government provides the public goods in each period and finances them by a lump-sum tax (T) which is imposed on the parent and all of her progeney, that is, the dynasty as a whole. Notice that in our model a head tax is not a lump-sum tax, since the number of children is endogenous. This is the reason for imposing a fixed tax T on the whole dynasty rather than a head tax on each of its members. The government budget constraint is written as:

$$p^1 + p^2 = T. \tag{5}$$

The government is thus restricted to a balance budget over the whole horizon rather than at each period.[2]

We consider here any *arbitrary* pair (P^1, P^2) of public good provisions; this vector includes the optimal pair under any desired objective. It can be shown that there is no market failure, despite a seemingly non-internalized benefit that a greater population size has a lower cost per-capita of providing the public good. Since we are considering *any* pair of public good provisions, our result holds therefore whether or not the government optimizes with respect to the provision of public goods.

---

[2]   In fact, it does not matter here whether the government is restricted to a balanced budget at each period or only over the whole horizon, because the parent cares for his children. As long as his bequest is strictly positive, he can always use his bequest to undo any intergenerational distribution of taxes by the government.

The parent in period 1 maximizes her utility function subject to her budget constraint.

$$u(c^1, c^2, n, P^1, P^2), \tag{6}$$

Obviously, P^1 and P^2 are not choice variables by the parent, so that the utility maximization is carried out with respect to c^1, c^2 and n, subject to the budget constraint:

$$c^1 + nc^2 = w^1 + nw^2 + \Pi^1 + \Pi^2 - T \tag{7}$$

The parent who cares about her children makes plans for their consumption, taking into account their earnings (nw^2) and the land rent (Π^2) accruing to them in the second period. She also takes into account the entire tax bill (T) of the dynasty. The fact that the children as a group receive both labor income and land rent is really the key to our conclusion.

Given the choice of P^1, P^2 and T by the government in *compliance* with the budget constraint (5), a competitive equilibrium is a 7-tuple $(\tilde{w}^1, \tilde{w}^2, \tilde{\Pi}^1, \tilde{\Pi}^2, \tilde{c}^2, \tilde{n})$ of wage rates, land rents, parent and child consumptions and number of children such that: (1) $(\tilde{c}^1, \tilde{c}^2, \tilde{n})$ maximizes (6), subject to (7), i.e., the parent maximizes her utility subject to her budget constraint; (ii) the wage rates and land rents are compatible with firm profit maximization, i.e., $\tilde{w}^1$, $\tilde{w}^2$, $\tilde{\Pi}^1$ and $\tilde{\Pi}^2$ are given by (4).

Our main result is summarized in the following proposition which we state without proof:

Proposition: An unfettered competitive equilibrium is efficient from the current generation point of view; that is, any other feasible allocation (i.e. an allocation which satisfies the resource constraint (3)) cannot yield a higher utility to any parent, who already takes into account the welfare of her offspring.

We can provide an intuitive explanation of this result that there is no market failure. A market failure arises whenever there is a divergence between *private* and *social* evaluation of *marginal* costs or benefits. We can see that such a divergence in the evaluation of marginal changes in the *endogenous* variables c^1, c^2 and n does not arise here. On the benefit side, both the private and the social objectives are represented by the parent's utility (6), since we are concerned only with the parent's welfare (who herself is concerned about her offspring).

Now, let us turn to the cost side. The parent's perception of the costs associated with c^1, c^2 and n is derived from her budget constraint (7) which we rewrite as

$$c^1 + n(c^2 - w^2) + T = W^1 + \Pi^1 + \Pi^2. \tag{7'}$$

The social costs are given by the resource constraint (3) which can be rewritten as

$$c^1 + nc^2 - f(n) + P^1 + p^2 = f(1). \tag{3'}$$

It is evident from (3′) and (7′) that there is no difference between the private and social marginal cost of c^1 and c^2. (They are 1 and n, respectively, both for the parent and for the society). The private marginal cost of n is seen from (7′) to be $c^2 - w^2$. The social marginal costs of n is seen from (3′) to be $c^2 - f'(n)$. Recalling that, at equilibrium, $w^2 = f'(n)$ (see (4)), it follows that there is no divergence between the private and social marginal costs of children.

It is more difficult to demonstrate that the Samuelsonian proposition that, under the conventional assumptions the fact that . . . each and every today is followed by a tomorrow . . .'' may lead competitive markets to fail in achieving Pareto optimality (Samuelson, 1958, p. 482). We will not attempt a proof here (the reader is referred to our book, 1987, for a demonstration), but it is nontheless true that endogenous fertility removes this source of failure. This is because there is a direct utility link between each generation and the one immediately following it (and thus an indirect utility link extending into the infinite future), so that the welfare of all generations as perceived by the current one is taken into account by the efficiency criterion in a natural way.

While the pathological behavior of competitive markets in the Samuelsonian model must indeed be attributed to the infinity of the economy's time horizon (in the sense that in finite-horizon economies the efficiency of competition is guaranteed even with Samuelson's assumption of exogenous population), the fact that in our model each representative individual has an infinite time horizon (even though she herself lives only a finite time) can be shown to be sufficient to restore the efficiency properties of competitive markets.

4. Endogenous Fertility and Potential Market Failures: Real Issues

Although the obvious cases of externalities when fertility is endogenous do not appear to occur, there are two real sources of market failure in a model in which parents care about their children arising from bequests, since in the absence of such care parents will never transfer (bequeath) anything to their children in a world of perfect foresight and lack of any uncertainty about the time of death.

Consideration of bequests and of marriage suggests a potential source of market failure as follows: First, if bequests benefit both partners in a marriage (as a public good *within* marriage), parents may fail to include benefits to other children's parents in deciding on the amount of bequests to make to each of their own children. Thus, bequests generate an external economy. Second, when children have different abilities, investments in their human capitals are not equally productive. If parents cannot enforce transfers among their siblings, then an egalitarian attitude toward children may lead to inefficient investment in human and non-human capital. For example, the parents may invest too much in the human capital of low-ability children, so that they will be equal (in utility sense) to their more able siblings.

Consider first the problem of marriage: Let there be two families in the current generation and only two generations (periods). The problem may be formulated as follows:

c_i = the consumption of the i_{th} family in the first period,
n_i = the number of children of the i_{th} family,
b_i = the per child bequest of the i_{th} family,
K_i = the resources available to the i_{th} family for consumption and bequest,
$\quad$ i = 1,2.

The total bequest of two children who marry one another will be the sum of the bequests to each child, i.e. $b_1 + b_2$. We assume that this sum is also the consumption of the second generation. If each family's utility function, u, is identical and if each family is endowed with the same amount of a resource, K, each will behave in an identical manner, so that the number of children available to marry each other will be identical.

The ith family chooses c_i, n_i and b_i so as to maximize

$$u(c_i, n_i, b_1 + b_2), \tag{8}$$

subject to the resource constraint

$$K = c_i + b_j n_i, \tag{9}$$

where b^j, $j \neq i$, is taken as a parameter by the ith family. (This is called a parametric externality.) A competitive (Nash) solution is the 6-component vector $(\bar{c}_i, \bar{n}_1, \bar{b}_1, \bar{c}_2, \bar{n}_2, \bar{b}_2)$ such that $(\bar{c}_i, \bar{n}_i, \bar{b}_i)$ solves the maximization problem (8)-(9) defined above, $i = 1,2$. Because of the assumed symmetry, we have:

$$\bar{c}_i = \bar{c}_2 \equiv \bar{c}, \quad \bar{b}_1 = \bar{b}_2 \equiv \bar{b}, \quad \text{and } \bar{n}_1 = \bar{n}_2 \equiv \bar{n}.$$

The competitive allocation is characterized by the following first-order conditions (assuming an interior solution):

$$\frac{u_2(\bar{c},\bar{n},2\bar{b})}{u_1(\bar{c},\bar{n},2\bar{b})} = \bar{b}, \tag{10}$$

and

$$\frac{u_3(\bar{c},\bar{n},2\bar{b})}{u_1(\bar{c},\bar{n},2\bar{b})} = \bar{n}. \tag{11}$$

These conditions state the familiar equalities between *private* marginal benefits and costs.

There are many possible Pareto-efficient allocations in this model. We restrict our attention to a symmetric Pareto-efficient allocation which treats the two families equally in order to be able to compare the allocation to the competitive allocation which is symmetric.

A symmetric Pareto-efficient allocation (c*, n*, b*) is obtained by a choice of (c, n, b,) so as to maximize

$$u(c, n, b + b) \tag{12}$$

subject to the *aggregate* resource constraint of the two families:

$$K + K = c + bn + c + bn. \tag{13}$$

Thus, this Pareto-efficient allocation yields the highest equal utility to the two families, given their *joint* resources.

The symmetric Pareto-efficient allocation is characterized by the following first-order conditions (again, assuming an interior solution):

$$\frac{u_2(c^*, n^*, 2b^*)}{u_1(c^*, n^*, 2b^*)} = b^*, \tag{14}$$

$$\frac{2u_3(c^*, n^*, 2b^*)}{u_1(c^*, n^*, 2b^*)} = n^*. \tag{15}$$

These conditions state the familiar equalities between the *social* marginal benefits and costs.

A comparison between conditions (10)-(11), which describe the competitive allocation, and conditions (14)-(15), which characterize the symmetric Pareto-efficient allocation, reveals that the two allocations differ from each other. Thus, the competitive allocation is not Pareto-efficient. We can also see the reason for the market failure from this comparison: the *social* marginal rate of substitution of c for b is twice the *private* marginal rate of substitution of c for b. (Compare the right-hand sides of (11) and (15).) This is because the parents' willingness to give up their own consumption (c) to secure an additional unit of consumption for their children (b) stems from their care for their own children only; they do not take into account the utility they generate for the parents in-law of their children.

Observe that if, in the competitive case, marriages are "arranged" in such a way as to be a symmetric solution to a cooperative bargaining game (non-Nash), there will be no difference between the competitive and symmetric Pareto-efficient solutions.

The preceding analysis can be used to show that too little is bequeathed to children in the competitive solution as compared to the symmetric optimum, i.e., $\bar{b} \leq b^*$. In general, however, one cannot draw any general conclusion about the numbers of children in the two cases. The bequest b is the "price" of children in the budget constraint (9) or (13). The implications are as follows: First, since b is smaller in the competitive solution, children are essentially "cheaper". Second, there is a smaller real income (welfare) in the competitive solution, due to the externality. Thus, if children are a normal good, the income effect tends to counteract the price effect. Third, since the level of bequests affects the marginal rate of substitution between children (n) and family consumption (c), the projection of the indifference map in the c-n plane must shift. Therefore, it is impossible to draw any general conclusion about the relationship between $\bar{n}$ and n^*.

If parents do not take into account the effect of their bequests on the welfare of families to whom they are potentially related by the marriage of their children, they will bequeath too little. In this case bequests should be subsidized on efficiency grounds rather than taxed. This is the standard Pigouvian remedy to an external economy.

In the standard economic models of externalities, this kind of a Pigouvian subsidy is all that is needed. Only the good that generates an external economy should be subsidized and only the good that generates an external diseconomy should be taxed. In our case, the bequest generates an external economy. But in this case, it is not sufficient simply to grant an appropriate subsidy to the bequest. This is because the bequest b is also the "price" of n. Thus, subsidizing b distorts i.e. reduces the price of n. This distortion must be removed by an appropriate simultaneous tax on children.

The second source of potential market failure which we have identified arises from the fact that parents cannot control the actions of their offspring after a certain point. In particular, they cannot enforce transfers among siblings. Parents who care about their children may wish to transfer resources to them. These transfers can take various forms: direct transfers of consumption (bequests), or indirect transfers by investing in the human capital of the children, which investments increase the future consumption-possibility sets of the children, etc. The most efficient method of transfer may depend on the specific charateristics of the child. Thus, the parent may wish to use different methods of transfer for different children. Furthermore, it may happen that it will be more efficient to make transfers only to some of the children and force them to transfer later on in life to the siblings who did not receive transfers from the parent. But this possibly most efficient mode of transfers to children depends on the parent's ability to enforce the required transfers among them. This poses a difficulty which cannot be eliminated, for instance, by appeal to Becker's "rotten-kid" theorem or by appeal to vaguely defined social norms (see Becker, 1974, 1976; and Hirschleifer, 1977). Becker and Tomes (1976) note the difficulty, but suggest in passing that ". . . social and family 'pressures' can induce . . . children to conform to the terms of implicit contracts with their parents." Such norms might be effective in some circumstances in some societies but they have certainly not generally been effective even in ancient societies (as the biblical episode of Cain and Abel attests), let alone in modern societies.

The most important case in which equal transfers to siblings are not efficient even for an equity-among-children conscious parent is when children differ in their abilities. In this case it might be most efficient to invest only in the human capital of the able children if parents could guarantee that these children would later on transfer part of the return to this investment to their less able siblings. However, if transfers among siblings cannot be enforced by the parents, then they may not be able to take advantage of high rates of return to investment in the human capital of their more able children. In this case, transfers in the form of investment in human capital from parents to children will be too low relative to bequests in the form of physical capital. Moreover, the investment in human capital will be inefficiently allocated among the children in the sense that the rates of return are not the same for all children.

When ability can be identified by the social planner, he can devise a system of taxes and transfers based on ability in order to achieve an efficient allocation of resources. However, when identification of more able and less able children is impossible or prohibitively costly except for the parents themselves, a first-best solution to the problem of optimal investment in human capital and bequests cannot be achieved.

It can be shown that a linear tax on earned income and a subsidy to inheritance are welfare improving and are therefore second-best corrective policies. Such policies make the parents better-off because they redistribute income from able to less able siblings and allow parents to allocate investments in human and physical capital which they make on their children's behalf more efficiently. Other policies, such as public investment in human capital or a tax/subsidy for education, can be shown to reduce welfare. Public investment in human capital (e.g., free education) is redundant as long as parents are investing positive amounts in children of all abilities, because parents can always undo the effects of each policies by reducing their investments in the human capital of their children dollar for dollar. Instead of direct government investment in human capital, we might consider a subsidy to education. Such a subsidy in the first period must be financed by a lump-sum tax in the same period, because the government cannot transfer resources from the future to the present. Moreover it creates a distortion by artificially lowering the cost of education to the parents. Indeed, since it can be shown that parents could have achieved the post-subsidy allocation under *laissez faire* it is apparent that the subsidy must be welfare reducing.[3]

5. Socially Optimal Population Size: Beyond the Pareto Principle

If one considers a number of different "states of the world" resulting from alternative social policies interacting with individual maximizing behavior and attempts to rank them, the principle of Pareto efficiency provides only a partial ordering. Given a particular allocation, Pareto-efficient or not, there exist many alternatives in general which cannot be compared with it according to the criterion. To achieve a complete ordering, it is necessary to assume an analogue to the individual utility functions which "aggregates" states of the world in the same manner as individual utility functions "aggregate" bundles of consumption. If aggregation is based on individual utilities we call this a *Paretian social welfare function*. Such a social welfare function is individualistic in the sense of respecting individual values but requires a certain comparability across individuals (see Sen, 1977).

Criteria for a social optimum usually concern choices in which the number and identity of the individuals are given; in this case, although many difficulties of comparability are involved, the criteria are otherwise unambiguous. The classical utilitarian criterion is to maximize the sum of individual utilities:

$$\sum_{h=1}^{n} u^h = W^B(u^1,...,u^n)$$

We call W^B a Benthamite social welfare function. Since scaling all utilities up or down by a constant multiplicative factor doesn't affect any essential property of W, if n is known, this criterion does not differ from the maximization of average or per capita utility:

$$\frac{1}{n} \sum_{h=1}^{n} u^h = W^M(u^1,...,u^n)$$

We call W^M a Millian criterion.

An alternative to utilitarianism, in either Benthamite or Millian form, has been proposed by Rawls (1971) who gives a nonrigorous argument to justify maximizing the welfare of the worst-off individual in society, the so-called maximin principle:

---

[3] This is a standard theorem in the theory of taxation. See, *inter alia,* Diamond and McFadden (1974).

$$\underset{h}{\text{Min}} \{ u^h, h = 1,...,n\} = W^R(u^1,...,u^n)$$

The argument of Harasanyi (1955) shows that if individuals maximize expected utility, the contract argument of Rawls, for example, leads to maximizing average utility if population sizes are different in different hypothetical societies, and total utility, if they are the same. An axiomatic justification of the maximin principle requires another type of argument, e.g., on the basis of extended sympathy. (Arrow, 1978). If all individuals have identical preferences, maximizing the Rawlsian social welfare function leads to an egalitarian solution, but not necessarily to the highest average or total.

Note that there is no difference between the two social welfare functions in situations concerning choices among alternatives which have the same effects on population levels. If population is constant, average utility differs from total utility only by a multiplicative constant. It is only in a situation in which different choices produce a different population level that the two criteria can lead to different conclusions. For example, suppose that the question concerns adding an additional person to the existing population. If the utility of the additional person called into existence is positive but less than the average of the population in the status quo ante, then adding the person will produce a greater total utility but a smaller average.

Our purpose here is not to decide the issue of which criteria, or if some other, should be used, but rather to compare the two with each other and with the *laissez faire* solution when fertility is endogenous. We show that the Benthamite social welfare function always leads to a larger population than the Millian criterion, but that the *laissez faire* solution may yield a population larger than the Benthamite or less than the Millian. We carry out the analysis for a two-generation case, but the result can be extended trivially to any finite number of generations and to an infinite number of generations, provided only that in the infinite-generation case we restrict ourselves to stable population growth paths (so that the relationship between two consecutive generations is always the same).

Consider an economy with two generations, each consisting of just one type of consumer. In the first period there is only one adult person. She consumes (together with her children) a single private good (c^1). She also raises identical children who will grow up in the second period. She dies at the end of the first period and bequeaths b to each one of her children. The number of children (n) that are born in the first period is a decision variable of the parent living then. The number of persons living in the second period is n. Each one consumes a single private good (c^2).

The parent's utility includes the children's utilities. In a reduced form we can write the parent's utility as

$$u^1(c^1,n,u^2(c^2)). \tag{16}$$

u^1 is concave in c^1 and u^2; u^2 is monotonically increasing and concave in c^2; both u^1 and u^2 are non-negative (people enjoy positive happiness). u^1 is also monotonically increasing in c^1 and u^2, but it is not necessarily monotonic in the number of children n. Assume that the parent lives only one period and that her budget constraint is

$$c^1 + nb = K; \qquad c^1,n \geq 0, \tag{17}$$

where K is her initial endowment which is nonrenewable and does not depreciate over time. This is like having an exhaustible resource capable of producing K units of consumption.

Although we do not restrict the bequest, b, to be nonnegative, it can be shown that it will never be negative. Thus, institutional arrangements which do not allow b to be negative — parents cannot obligate their children to pay their debts — are superfluous here.

The exact specification of the supply side is not very important for this problem, although for some issues it would be important to introduce production and capital accummulation.

Assume that the children are born with no endowments. Thus, the exhaustible resource has to suffice for the consumption of the current and all future generations. The children's per capita consumption is therefore equal to their per capita inheritance:

$$c^2 = b. \tag{18}$$

Constraints (17)-(18) can be consolidated into one budget constraint for the parent:

$$c^1 + nc^2 = K; \qquad c^1, c^2, n \geq 0. \tag{19}$$

A competitive or *laissez faire* allocation (LFA) is obtained when (16) is maximized with respect to c^1, c^2, and n, subject to (19). Denote this allocation by (c^{1L}, c^{2L}, n^L).

Observe that the feasible set determined by the constraint (19) is neither convex nor bounded. The nonboundedness may pose some difficulties. In particular one may let n go to zero and c^2 approach infinity or vice versa. That is, one may opt for as small a number of children as possible and let each one of them enjoy unbounded consumption and vice versa. This means that some restrictions have to be imposed on the utility function to ensure that this course of action does not yield an unbounded utility so that a *laissez faire* allocation exists. For example, one may have to restrict a term like $nu^2(c^2)$ to be bounded when $n \to 0$ (and $c^2 \to \infty$). Similar considerations of boundness arise with respect to the Benthamite and Millian allocations discussed below.

In our model the Benthamite social welfare function is defined by:

$$B(c^1, c^2, n) = u^1(c^1, n, u^2(c^2)) + nu^2(c^2). \tag{20}$$

As mentioned, it is assumed that there is diminishing marginal utility of c^1 and c^2, i.e., $u^1_{11}, u^2_{11} < 0$, where subscripts stand for partial derivatives. A Bentham optimal allocation (BOA) is obtained by maximizing (20) with respect to c^1, c^2 and n, subject to (19). Denote this allocation by (c^{1B}, c^{2B}, n^B).

The Millian social welfare function, namely the per-capita utility, is

$$M(c^1, c^2, n) = \frac{u^1(c^1, n, u^2(c^2)) + nu^2(c^2)}{1 + n} = B(c^1, c^2, n)/(1 + n) \tag{21}$$

The Millian optimal allocation (MOA) is obtained by maximizing (21) with respect to c^1, c^2, and n, subject to the resource constraint (19). Denote this allocation by (c^{1M}, c^{2M}, n^M).

It is important to emphasize that we assume that the parent's utility function represents her *interest* (e.g. happiness from being a parent, guilt relief in providing for the children, etc.) rather than her *moral* (social) preferences (e.g. believing that it would be wrong to have children and let them starve). This is why we add $nu^2(c^2)$ to $u^1(c^1, n, u^2(c^2))$ when we define our Benthamite and Millian social welfare criteria. Otherwise, were we to adopt the second interpretation that parents get no happiness at all from caring for their children, adding $nu^2(c^2)$ to $u^1(c^1, n, u^2(c^2))$ would be superfluous. However, in this case we would not have a theory of *endogenous* fertility.

Observe that both the BOA and the MOA satisfy the same resource constraint (19). Since the Millian allocation maximizes M and since $M = B/(1 + n)$, it follows that

$$\frac{B(c^{1M}, c^{2M}, n^M)}{1 + n^M} \geq \frac{B(c^{1B}, c^{2B}, n^B)}{1 + n^B}. \qquad (22)$$

Since (c^{1B}, c^{2B}, n^B) maximizes B, it follows that

$$B(c^{1B}, c^{2B}, n^B) \geq B(c^{1M}, c^{2M}, n^M). \qquad (23)$$

Therefore

$$\frac{1 + n^M}{1 + n^B} \leq \frac{B(c^{1M}, c^{2M}, n^M)}{B(c^{1B}, c^{2B}, n^B)} \leq 1,$$

from which it follows that $n^B \geq n^M$.

Since the Millian criterion calls for a maximization of the average utility, intuition suggests that *laissez faire* results in overpopulation. However, although this may be true under some circumstances, it does not hold in general.

Since the LFA satisfied the same resource constraint (19) as does the MOA, it follows from the definition of the MOA that

$$M(c^{1M}, c^{2M}, n^M) \geq M(c^{1L}, c^{2L}, n^L). \qquad (24)$$

Since $M = B/(1 + n)$, it is implied by (15) that

$$B(c^{1M}, c^{2M}, n^M) \geq \left(\frac{1 + n^M}{1 + n^L}\right) B(c^{1L}, c^{2L}, n^L). \qquad (25)$$

Since $u^2 \geq 0$, it also follows that

$$B(c^{1L}, c^{2L}, n^L) = u^1(c^{1L}, n^L, u^2(c^{2L})) + n^L u^2(c^{2L}) \qquad (26)$$

$$\geq u^1(c^{1L}, n^L u^2(c^{2L}))$$

$$\geq u^1(c^{1M}, n^M, u^2(c^{2M})),$$

because (c^{1L}, c^{2L}, n^L) maximizes u^1 subject to the overall resource constraint (19). Thus, we conclude from (25) and (26) that

$$B(c^{1M}, c^{2M}, n^M) \geq (\frac{1 + n^M}{1 + n^L}) \, u^1(c^{1M}, n^M, u^2(c^{2M})),$$

so that

$$\frac{1 + n^M}{1 + n^L} \leq \frac{B(c^{1M}, c^{2M}, n^M)}{u^1(c^{1M}, n^M, u^2(c^{2M}))}$$

$$= \frac{u^1(c^{1M}, n^M, u^2(c^{2M})) + n^M u^2(c^{2M})}{u^1(c^{1M}, n^M, u^2(c^{2M}))} = 1 + \frac{n^M u^2(c^{2M})}{u^1(c^{1M}, n^M, u^2(c^{2M}))}. \tag{27}$$

Since the extreme right-hand side of (27) is strictly greater than 1, it is impossible to say anything about the ratio on the extreme left-hand side, in particular we cannot conclude that $n^L \geq n^M$.

Since the Benthamite criterion calls for a maximization of total utility of parents and children, while the competitive allocation maximizes the parent's utility only, intuition suggests that *laissez faire* leads to a smaller than socially optimal population. However, this is not necessarily true: when $nu^2(c^2)$ is added to the parent's utility, as suggested by the Benthamite criterion, increasing the product $nu^2(c^2)$ is indeed desirable; but it does not follow that we have to increase both n and c^2.

To see this, observe that it follows from the definition of the LFA and the BOA that

$$u^1(c^{1L}, n^L, u^2(c^{2L})) \geq u^1(c^{1B}, n^B, u^2(c^{2B})),$$

and

$$u^1(c^{1B}, n^B, u^2(c^{2B})) + n^B u^2(c^{2B}) \geq u^1(c^{1L}, n^L, u^2(c^{2L})) + n^L u^2(c^{2L}).$$

Hence,

$$n^B u^2(c^{2B}) \geq n^L u^2(c^{2L}).$$

Thus, indeed the total utility from children (nu^2) must be larger at the BOA than at the LFA.

The assumption that fertility is endogenous enables us to consider noncoercive policies aimed at moving the economy from the LFA to either the BOA or the MOA by changing the incentives (prices) which parents face.

We consider all possible direct and indirect taxes and subsidies as candidates for the optimal policy. Notice that, in our case, children themselves are a commodity and may be subject to a tax or a subsidy. Such a tax, which is a head tax, is *not* a lump-sum nondistortionary tax as in the traditional economic literature with exogenous population. Here such a head tax affects fertility decisions on the margin.

Among the set of possible direct and indirect taxes and subsidies to achieve a social optimum, it is necessary to utilize interest rate subsidies (to encourage future consumption) and child allowances (positive or negative to encourage or discourage having children). It can be shown that an interest rate subsidy is warranted under both the Benthamite and the Millian criteria; a positive child allowance is necessary under the Benthamite criterion; but the child allowance needed under the Millian criterion may be positive, zero, or negative. It should be emphasized that these policies are *first-best* policies in that they actually achieve the BOA and the MOA.

Consider first the BOA. It is obtained by maximizing.

$$u^1(c^1, n, u^2(c^2)) + nu^2(c^2),$$

subject to the resource constraint:

$$k - c^1 - nc^2 = 0$$

(see (19) and (20) above).

Letting $\lambda \geq 0$ be the Lagrange multipler, the following first-order conditions for an interior solution may be derived:

$$u^1_1 = \lambda, \tag{28 a}$$

$$u^1_2 + u^2 = \lambda c^2, \tag{28 b}$$

$$u^1_3 u^2_1 + nu^2_1 = \lambda n. \tag{28 c}$$

Didiving (28 b) and (28 c) by (28 a) we obtain

$$\frac{u^1_2 + u^2_2}{u^1_1} = c^2, \tag{29 a}$$

$$\frac{u^1_3 u^2_1 + nu^2_1}{u^1_1} = n. \tag{29 b}$$

Equation (29 a) asserts that the *social* marginal rate of substitution of c^1 for n (the willingness of society to give up parent's consumption for an additional child, which is $(u^1_2 + u^2)/u^1_1$) must be equated to the *social* "cost" of an additional child, which is equal to its consumption c^2. Similarly, equation (29 b) asserts that the *social* marginal rate of substitution of c^1 for c^2 must equated to the *social* "cost" of a unit of the child's consumption, which is n, since every one of the n children consumes this unit.

In order to achieve the BOA allocation (via the market mechanism), it may be possible for the government to subsidize c^2 at the rate of α (for instance, by subsidizing the interest rate which is implicitly assumed here to be zero), to give child allowances (possibly negative) of β per child, and to balance its budget by a lump-sum tax (possibly negative) in the amount T. In this case the parent's budget constraint becomes

$$c^1 + nc^2(1 - \alpha) = K + \beta n - T. \tag{30}$$

Given this budget constraint, the parent maximizes

$$u^1(c^1, n, u^2(c^2))$$

by choosing c^1, n and c^2 (see (17) above). Letting $\Theta \geqslant 0$ be the Lagrange multipler for this problem, we obtain the following first-order conditions for an interior solution:

$$u^1_1 = \Theta, \tag{31 a}$$

$$u^1_2 = -\Theta\beta + \Theta c^2(1 - \alpha), \tag{31 b}$$

$$u^1_3 u^2_1 = \Theta n(1 - \alpha). \tag{31 c}$$

Dividing (31 b) and (31 c) by (31 a) we obtain:

$$\frac{u^1_2}{u^1_1} = c^2(1 - \alpha) - \beta , \tag{32 a}$$

$$\frac{u^1_3 u^2_1}{u^1_1} = n(1 - \alpha) . \tag{32 b}$$

Equation (32 a) states that the marginal rate of substitution of c^1 for n (i.e., parent's willingness to give up her own consumption for an additional child) must be equated to the "price" of a child as perceived by the parent from the budget constraint (30). The "price" consists of two components: (i) the cost of providing the child with c^2 units of consumption which is only $c^2(1 - \alpha)$ due to the subsidy α and (ii) the tax on children which is $-\beta$. Equation (32 b) states that the marginal rate of substitution of c^1 for c^2 must be equated to the "price" of c^2 which is the number of children times $1 - \alpha$.

If it is possible to achieve a BOA in this way, we can find the optimal level of α and β by comparing the first-order conditions for the BOA (namely, (29)) with those of the individual parent's optimization problem (32). First, compare (29 b) with (32 b) to conclude that

$$n(1 - \alpha) = n(1 - \frac{u^2_1}{u^1_1}) ,$$

so that the optimal subsidy to children's consumption under the Benthamite criterion is

$$\alpha^B = \frac{u^2_1(c^{1B}, n^B, u^2(c^{2B}))}{u^1_1(c^{1B}, n^B, u^2(c^{2B}))} . \tag{33}$$

Next, compare (29 a) with (32 c) to conclude that

$$c^2 = \frac{u^2}{u^1_1} = c^2(1 - \alpha) - \beta ,$$

so that the optimal child allowance under the Benthamite criterion is

$$\beta^B = \frac{u^2(c^{2B})}{u_1^1(c^{1B}, n^B, u^2(c^{2B}))} - \alpha^B c^{2B} . \tag{34}$$

Notice that α and β play the role of a Pigouvian tax/subsidy. Since the term $nu^2(c^2)$ of the Benthamite criterion (10) is ignored by the parent objective (15), we have a case where c^2 generates an external economy from a social point of view; hence, it ought to be subsidized in order to achieve the BOA. The optimal magnitude of this subsidy has to be determined according to what the parent ignores (at the margin). When the parent considers increasing c^2 she ignores the social benefit nu_1^2 at the margin. This benefit is measured in utility units. Its equivalent in terms of the numeraire consumption good is nu_1^2/u_1^1. From the parent's budget constraint (30), we can see that if we subsidize c^2 at the rate α, then each unit of c^2 receives a subsidy of $n\alpha$. Thus, the Pigouvian subsidy ought to be set at a level such that $n\alpha = nu_1^2/u_1^1$ which explains the magnitude of the optimal α in (33).

For the same reason, n ought to be subsidized by u^2/u_1^1, so that the price of n for the parent will be $c^2 - (u^2/u_1^1)$. Since, by the parent's budget constraint (6.36), the price of n is $c^2(1 - \alpha) - \beta$, we have to equate $c^2 - (u^2/u_1^1)$ to $c^2(1 - \alpha) - \beta$. Thus, it follows that $\beta^B = (u^2/u_1^1) - \alpha^B c^2$, as in (34).

Note that $\alpha^B > 0$ and can be implemented by a subsidy to the rate of interest, assumed zero in this model. To find the sign of β^B, observe that

$$\beta^B = \frac{u^2}{u_1^1} - \alpha^B c^2 = \frac{u^2 - c^2 u_1^2}{u_1^1} ,$$

by substituting (33) into (34). Since u^2 is concave, it follows that

$$u^2(c^2) - u^2(0) \geq u_1^2(c^2)(c^2 - 0).$$

Since u^2 is assumed nonnegative, it follows that

$$u^2(c^2) \geq c^2 u_1^2(c^2) ,$$

so that $\beta^B > 0$: The optimal child allowance under the Benthamite criterion must be positive.

Fixed α and β may not in fact lead to the BOA because the parent's optimization problem is not convex; therefore, the second-order conditions may not hold. In case the second-order conditions do not hold with fixed α and β, it is possible to achieve a BOA with nonlinear taxes, i.e., with instruments α and β which are *functions* of c^1, c^2 and n. In other words, we can always satisfy the second-order conditions by functions $\alpha(\cdot)$ and $\beta(\cdot)$ The *values* of $\alpha(\cdot)$ and $\beta(\cdot)$ *at the optimum* will be exactly α^B and β^B as given in (33) and (34), i.e.,

$$\alpha^B = \alpha(c^{1B}, n^B, c^{2B}) ,$$

and

$$\beta^B = \beta(c^{1B}, n^B, c^{2B}) .$$

Exactly the same kind of analysis may be carried through for the Millian social welfare function. In this case, one finds that the subsidy to children consumption, namely α^M, is positive as in the Benthamite case. However, the sign of the optimal child allowance (β^M) is ambiguous in this case. The reason for this ambiguity can be seen by comparing the Millian objective which is $(u^1 + nu^2)/(1 + n)$ with the parent's objective which is just u^1. On the one hand, the Millian objective adds nu^2 to the parent's objective and in this way n generates a positive externality; but, on the other hand, we also divide $u^1 + nu^2$ by $(1 + n)$ and in this way n generates a negative externality. Thus, one cannot determine *a priori* whether n should be taxed or subsidized.

6. Conclusion

The implications of endogenous fertility for the question of optimal population size are far-reaching. We show that endogenous fertility may, under certain circumstance, lead to the failure of laissez-faire to attain an efficient or Pareto-optimal solution from the standpoint of members of the present generation. To go beyond the issue of efficient allocations from the standpoint of only the present generation, it is necessary to introduce a social welfare function which aggregates utilities of the present and future generations. In this paper we consider two: the sum of individual utilities and the average of individual utilities and show that the former always leads to a larger optimal population than the latter. When fertility is endogenous a laissez-faire solution is well-defined, but it cannot be shown to lie between the results produced by the two social criteria or, indeed, to bear any particular relation to them.

References

Arrow, K. J. (1978) Extended Sympathy and the Possibility of Social Choice, Philosophia 7: 223-237

Becker, G. S. (1960) An Economic Analysis of Fertility. In: R. A. Easterlin (Ed.) Demographic and Economic Change. Princeton: Princeton University Press

Becker, G. S. (1974) A Theory of Social Interaction. Journal of Political Economy 82: 1063-1093

Becker, G. S. (1976) Altruism, Egoism and Genetic Fitness: Economics and Sociobiology. Journal of Economic Literature 14: 817-826

Becker, G. S. and Tomes, N. (1976) Child Endowments and the Quantity and Quality of Children. Journal of Political Economy 84: S142-63

Coase, R. H. (1960) The Problem of Social Cost. Journal of Law and Economics 3: 1-44

Diamond, P. A. (1973) Consumption Externalities and Imperfect Competitive Pricing. Bell Journal of Economics 4: 526-538

Diamond, P. A. and McFadden, D. L. (1974) Some Uses of the Expenditure Function in Public Finance. Journal of Public Economics 3: 3-21

Harasanyi, J. (1955) Cardinal Welfare, Individualistic Ethics and Interpersonal Comparisons of Utility. Journal of Political Economy 63: 309-321

Hirschleifer, J. (1977) Shakespeare vs. Becker on Altruism: The Importance of Having the Last Word. Journal of Economic Literature 15: 500-502

Nerlove, M., Razin, A., and Sadka, E. (1987) Household and Economy: Welfare Economics of Endogenous Fertility. New York: Academic Press.

Pigou, A. C. (1947) A Study in Public Finance (3rd Edition). London: Macmillan
Rawls, J. (1971) The Theory of Justice. Cambridge: Harvard University Press
Samuelson, P. A. (1954) The Pure Theory of Public Expenditure. The Review of Economics and
    Statistics 36: 387-389
Samuelson, P. A. (1958) An Exact Consumption Loan Model of Interest with or without the Social
    Contrivance of Money. Journal of Political Economy 66: 467-82
Sen, A. K. (1977) Social Choice Theory: A Re-Examination. Econometrica 45: 53-89

Endogenous Population With Discrete Family Size and a Capital Market

Daniel Leonard[1]

1. Introduction

The work of Becker (1960, 1981) on the economics of the family where the number and the "quality" of children are endogenous has in recent years given rise to studies in population policy such as Nerlove et al. (1984) and Kemp et al. (1983). In these analyses the number of children a family chooses to have and the size of the bequest left to them are the result of utility maximization by a typical family; hence the size and age structure of the population can be made endogenous and the effect on them of various policy parameters can be studied.

In Kemp et al. (1984) three possible pitfalls of such models are examined: the lack of a utility-maximizing choice, the non-existence of a non-trivial steady state, and the unadvoidability of extinction; some ways to prevent these are suggested.

In Leonard (1984) a new feature is added on to such models: the number of children of a typical family is restricted to integer values. This feature causes some of the problems pointed out in Kemp et al. (1984) to emerge. Whereas in the version of the model analyzed in Leonard (1984) a unique stable nontrivial steady state would exist if the integer constraint were not imposed, the integer constraint interferes with the choice of bequests, resulting in discontinuities in the phase line. These may destroy the stability, uniqueness and even the existence of a steady state.

In this paper we add another distinctive feature in an attempt to test the robustness of the previous analysis of the integer constrained model. Specifically it is assumed that there exists a competitive market for the capital good − the substance of bequests. The question we seek to answer is this: can the hypothesis of a capital market smooth away these discontinuities and restore the simplicity of the real-valued analysis?[2] Although the existence of capital markets affects both the population profile and the distribution of wealth, on the whole, the answer to the above question is negative: the consequences of a discrete family size cannot be ignored; indeed the analysis of the real-valued case provides no clues to the actual dynamic behaviour of the integer constrained system. The introduction of a capital market does reduce the amount of discontinuity in the sense that the integer restriction entails no loss of welfare and the family consumption level remains continuous throughout but the level of bequests is discontinuous.

[1]   I am grateful to an anonymous referee for many useful comments.
[2]   This was elicited by constructive criticism by Gary Becker.

Microeconomic Studies
K. F. Zimmermann (Ed.)
Economic Theory of Optimal Population
© Springer-Verlag Berlin Heidelberg 1989

In Section 2 we describe the model. In Section 3 we derive the behaviour of the typical family. In Section 4 we discuss the dynamic path.

2. The Model

There are many identical families in each generation. All individuals are born identical; they live for one generation during which they all marry, choose the family's consumption, the number of their children and the bequests left to these children.

There is only one good which can be used for current consumption or bequeathed as capital. A family's income is determined by the combined inheritance of both parents; they can use their own capital to produce output, or sell it and live off their revenue, or buy more capital for their own firm. The capital market is assumed to be competitive.

All decisions are made by the adults. The typical family's objective is to maximize a utility function which is additive across current and future periods. Specifically the first term has current family consumption as its sole argument and the second term depends on the total wealth of the families formed by the children. This second term reflects the interest shown by parents in the number and well-being of their offsprings. Because parents may not control the inheritance of their children's spouses, clearly an externality in the choice of bequests may exist even though all families are identical. For simplicity we assume here that the externality has been internalized (e.g. by arranging marriages). This does not substantially affect the analysis. See Kemp et al (1983) for a complete discussion. Thus we can express the utility of a family in period t as

$$V = u[c(t)] + v[n(t) \cdot \tilde{f}[b(t)]] \tag{1}$$

where $c(t)$ is family consumption, $n(t)$ is the number of children and $b(t)$ is the inheritance of each child (as well as of his or her spouse). u and v are utility functions and $\tilde{f}(b)$ is the income derived by a child and his spouse, as adults, when each inherits b. With the same notation the budget constraint is

$$\tilde{f}[b(t-1)] = c(t) + n(t) \cdot b(t) \tag{2}$$

We now turn to the production technology and the capital market. As demonstrated in Kemp et al (1984) the nonconvexity and unboundedness of the constraint set defined by (2) give rise to the possibility that an arbitrarily large level of utility may be reached with either n or b becoming arbitrarily large whilst their product remains bounded. It was shown in Leonard (1984) that a necessary and sufficient condition for ruling out such unbounded outcomes is that marginal product exceed average produce for small b and the reverse for large b. This and some regularity conditions yield a familiar S-shaped production function $f(b)$, as depicted in Figure 1. Here we simply postulate this shape. A family can use its own capital to produce output with this technology but the existence of a competitive capital market allows for other possibilities as we now show.

The point at which average product is maximized is b^* where $f'[b^*] = f[b^*]/b^*$. If each family receives $b < b^*$ we now show that it would be advantageous for some families to pool their resources to create firms with capital b^*. (It is presumed that

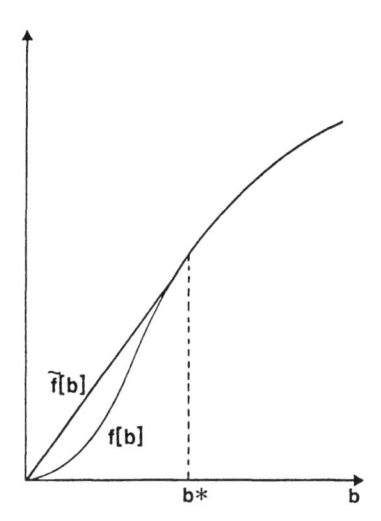

Fig. 1

there cannot be more firms than families, therefore $\bar{f}$ (b) and f(b) are identical for $b > b^*$.) Let us then derive the shape of $\bar{f}$ (b) for $b \leq b^*$ in the presence of a competitive capital market. Formally, suppose there are N families with capital $b \leq b^*$; if N is large enough it is always possible to form I firms each with capital (bN/I) $\simeq b^*$, with a suitable choice of an integer I. The income (after trading) of a typical family is

$$\bar{f}(b) = \max_{T}\{f(b + T) - RT \mid T + b \geq 0\}$$

where R is the competitive price of capital and T is the amount of capital borrowed by that family. The optimality conditions are

$$f'(b + T) - R \leq 0, \; T + b \geq 0, \; (T + b)\,(f'(b + T) - R) = 0.$$

There are two possibilites: if $T + b = 0$ we have $\bar{f}(b) = Rb$; if $T + b > 0$ we have $f'(b + T) = R$ and $\bar{f}(b) \equiv f(b + T) - f'(b + T)\,T$. This latter expression exceeds Rb if $b + T > b^*$, which induces families with $b + T = 0$ to shift to $b + T > 0$ and this in turn leads to an increase in the competitive price of capital R. The reverse applies if $b + T < b^*$ and the unique stable equilibrium is at $b + T = b^*$. We then have

either $\bar{f}(b) = Rb, \; T + b = 0$
or $\quad \bar{f}(b) = f(b^*) - f'(b^*) \cdot (b - b^*) = f'(b^*)b \equiv Rb, \; T + b = b^*$.

The first case must hold for N-I families and the second case for I families; for any one family it is a matter of indifference as to whether it is a buyer or a seller of capital. The new addition to the technology is represented in Figure 1 by a line segment from the origin to the point of coordinates (b*, f(b*)) and recall that $\bar{f}(b)$ and f(b) are identical for $b \geq b^*$. Thus $\bar{f}$ is the concave upper contour of f; this is the result of optimizing in the capital market by individual families. We are familiar with such outcomes from duality theory.

Remark

In the above analysis, no explicit mention was made of any variable input. We introduce this concept albeit in a very restrictive fashion in the appendix. Our aim is to show that optimization in regard to the choice of a variable "smoothes" the production function in the same way as did the hypothesis of a competitive capital market. The input is taken to be free; we show at the end of the appendix that a costly input would yield similar results.

3. Family Choice

In period t the typical family chooses its consumption $c(t)$, the number of its children, $n(t)$ (an integer) and the bequest to each of these, $b(t)$, so as to maximize its utility given by (1) subject to its budget constraint, (2).

Let us first ignore the integer restriction on n. Denoting income by $\bar{f}$ and skipping all time arguments, the first-order conditions are:

$$\bar{f} = c + nb \tag{3 a}$$

$$v'\,[n\,\tilde{f}(b)]\,\tilde{f}'(b) = u'\,[c] \tag{3 b}$$

$$v'\,[n\,\tilde{f}(b)]\,\tilde{f}(b) = b\,u'[c] \tag{3 c}$$

where (3b) and (3c) characterize the optimal choice of b and n, respectively. The last two conditions yield $\tilde{f}(b)/b = \tilde{f}'(b)$; this is equal to $f'(b^*)$ and we are free to choose any $b \leq b^*$. Thus there is an indeterminacy in the choice of b and n, with only their product bn being well defined by the family's choice.

However in this situation (n real) there is no reason why a capital market should develop since b^*, which is optimal, can always be chosen without it. Therefore we will assume that b^* is always chosen: parents always choose the smallest optimal number of children, guaranteeing the highest income to each of their children. Given this assumption, the first-order conditions (3) determine the optimal values of n and c and the optimal solution with n real, *given income* $\bar{f}$, is denoted by $(\bar{c}, \bar{n}, b^*)$.

We now introduce the integer restriction on n and consider the choice of (c, n, b) given the same initial income $\bar{f}$ as before. If we select n below $\bar{n}$, the value of b determined by (3b) will be above b^*, where the strict concavity of $\tilde{f}$ makes this a seond-best choice which cannot better $(\bar{c}, \bar{n}, b^*)$.

On the other hand if we select n larger than $\bar{n}$, the b value is below b^* where $\tilde{f}$ is linear: $\tilde{f}[b] = b \cdot f'[b^*]$. Substituting this into (3) we find that (3b) and (3c) are identical; thus selecting b, given n, amounts to the same thing as selecting both b and n optimally. Therefore choosing n as an integer larger than $\bar{n}$, and b and c according to (3) yields the same level of utility as the smooth optimum; thus we never select n below $\bar{n}$. Note also that the integer restriction causes no loss of welfare since we have $nb = \bar{n}b^*$ and consequently $c = \bar{c}$.

We have shown that a first-best optimum is still attainable under the integer restriction. However there still remains to resolve the indeterminacy about the choice of b and n since only the value of nb (and of c) are uniquely determined. Clearly, there are countably many suitable n values since n can be any integer larger than $\bar{n}$. There is however a clear incentive for a family to choose b as large as possible, as we now show.

Let us denote the optimal value of nb by nb $= \alpha b^*$ where α is real. For an arbitrary integer $n(n \geq \bar{n})$ each child receives b $= \alpha b^*/n$ and they form nM families (if there were 2M parent families). Hence the aggregate capital is $2M\alpha b^*$ and the number of firms should approximate $M\alpha$, which is not an integer and in practice each firm's capital differs slightly from b^*. Thus taking into account the probability that some of the children may be left out (because it benefits firms to get b^* exactly) there is an incentive to choose the largest possible b value so as reach the highest average product.

To sum up, the optimal procedure is as follows, given the initial income $\bar{f}$:

(i) Find the 'smooth' optimum value $(\bar{c}, \bar{n}, b^*)$ according to (3).
(ii) Select the smallest integer $n \geq \bar{n}$, b $= (\bar{f} - \bar{c})/n$ and c $= \bar{c}$.
(Note that nb $= \bar{n}b^*$.)

Formally

$$\bar{f} = c + nb \tag{4 a}$$

$$v'[nbf'[b^*]]\, f'[b^*] = u'[c] \tag{4 b}$$

n is the smallest integer with $n \geq \bar{n}$ and $\bar{n}$ is defined by

$$v'[\bar{n}b^*f'[b^*]]\, f'[b^*] = u'[\bar{f} - \bar{n}b^*]. \tag{4 c}$$

We now turn our attention to switch points where the chosen number of children suddenly increases by one. These will occur at income levels for which $\bar{n}$ is an integer. According to the above rule in equation (4), any increase in income from that point yields a slightly larger real value for $\bar{n}$, hence the integer n increases by one unit. Consider now what happens to the associated values of b and c as income passes that threshold. When all variables are real, strict concavity insures that $\bar{c}$ and $\bar{n}b^*$ rise continuously with $\bar{f}$. Recall however that the integer constraint on n results in nb $= \bar{n}b^*$ and c $= \bar{c}$. Therefore when n shifts by one unit the b value alone adapts to the change. Since b^* is the bequest value when $\bar{n}$ is optimally chosen as an integer, there is a decrease in bequest to $b^* \cdot \left\{ \dfrac{\bar{n}}{\bar{n} + 1} \right\}$ as soon as income increases slightly; $\bar{c}$ doesn't change. Note that the gaps between b^* and $b^* \bar{n}/(\bar{n} + 1)$ become narrower as $\bar{n}$ increases.

With regard to the switch between n $= 0$ and n $= 1$, note that in the smooth case we would always select n $b^* > 0$ if income was positive. In the discrete case (and when the optimal value of n is less than unity) we can duplicate the level of utility by choosing n $= 1$ and b accordingly but we cannot do it with n $= 0$. Therefore the latter is never chosen and if income is positive, families have at least one child.

We can summarize the above results in the following proposition.

Proposition 1

The imposition of the integer restriction with a competitive capital market leads to larger and poorer families, although childless families are ruled out. The size of bequests never exceeds b^*. Family consumption rises continuously with income but the size of bequests exhibits discontinuities when the number of children increases. More precisely, when a family switches from n to (n + 1) children as income rises, the size of bequest switches from b* to b*(n/(n + 1) but family consumption doesn't change. No loss of welfare is incurred by resricting n to integer values when a competitive capital market is present. Finally the exact shape of f is irrelevant except for the values of b* and f'(b*). □

We can understand the results summarised in Proposition 1 if we note that the introduction of a competitive capital market has created a linear technology valid below b* which is superior to the old technology still operating above b*. Hence bequests are always chosen below b* and the linearity of the technology allows the size of bequests to adjust to integer restrictions on the number of children thereby smoothing the consumption path and incurring no loss of utility.

The results of Proposition 1 are illustrated in Figure 2 where the arrows indicate the rise in income. To do this we need to summarize all the implications of the above analysis for the paths of c, b and n as income rises. Both c and nb rise monotonically with income, hence an income expansion path which gives c as a function of nb can be obtained by eliminating $\bar{f}$; this in no way implies functional dependence of c on nb but describes both their movement as income rises.

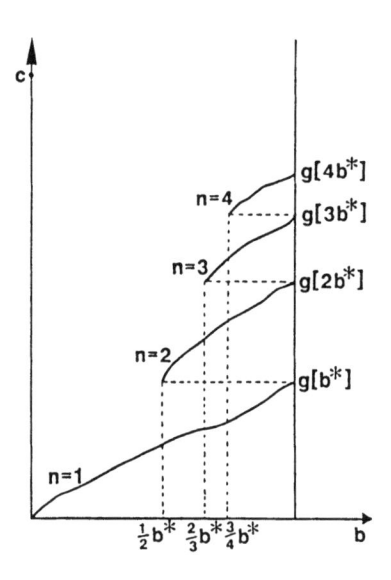

Fig. 2

In order to generate this income expansion path all we need to do is to equate the marginal utilities of (c) and (nb):

$$u'[c] = v'[f'[b*]nb] \, f' \, [b*]$$

This defines a function c = g [nb] where the form of g depends on u, v and f'[b*]. We can show that g is increasing.

$$\frac{dc}{d(nb)} = \frac{v''[f'[b*]nb]}{u''[c]} \, (f'[b*])^2 > 0 \tag{5}$$

but we cannot restrict g any further except to require it to be positively valued (zero) when nb is positive (zero) because we posess no save information on u'' and v'' for their sign. We now show how to construct Figure 2.

First we plot the graph of

$$c = g[b] \qquad \text{for} \qquad 0 \le b \le b^*.$$

Then we plot the graph of

$$c = g[2b] \qquad \text{for} \qquad \frac{b^*}{2} < b \le b^*.$$

In general we plot the graph of

$$c = g[nb] \qquad \text{for} \qquad \frac{n-1}{n} b^* < b \le b^*, n = 1, 2...$$

Note that when the switch from n to (n + 1) occurs the slope changes from $ng'[nb^*]$ to $(n + 1)g'[nb^*]$. However we cannot claim that the slopes of the higher segments are larger because we do not know the overall shape of g [b].

Plainly, in order to construct Figure 2 we only need to choose an increasing function g that goes through the origin and a value for b*; the exact income expansion path can be mapped from them.

4. Dynamics

Parents, by their choice of bequests, determine the income of their children's families and thus taking into account the analysis of family choice in the previous section, the value of bequests in one period determines the value of bequests in the next period. Formally we use the function $c(t) = g[n(t)b(t)]$ defined in Section 3 plus the budget constraint

$$f'[b^*] b(t - 1) = c(t) + n(t)b(t)$$

to obtain

$$b(t - 1) = \frac{1}{f'[b^*]} (g[n(t)b(t)] + n(t)b(t)). \tag{6}$$

From this equation we can construct a phase diagram in the $(b(t - 1), b(t))$ space. All we need to do is draw the graph of equation (6), for given values of n, on the various intervals

$$\frac{n}{n + 1} b^* < b(t) \le b^*, \qquad n = 0, 1, 2... \tag{7}$$

Equations (5) and (6) yield

$$\frac{db(t - 1)}{db(t)} = n(t) \left[\frac{1}{f'[b^*]} + f'[b^*] \frac{v''[f'[b^*] n(t)b(t)]}{u''[g[n(t)b(t)]]} \right] \tag{8}$$

Although this slope is clearly positive we have little to say about its size except that it must exceed $n(t)/f'[b*]$. We do however know that the relevant part of the phase space (the one which is reached after one period) is a square including the origin and of side length $b*$ since b is never chosen to exceed $b*$ and c and nb reach zero together.

Proposition 2

Whereas when family size is a real number, the value of the typical bequest is $b*$ for any positive initial condition, complications arise if the integer nature of the number of children is taken into account and we discover that:

(i)   After one period all bequests are less than or equal to $b*$ and families are larger than at the smooth optimum.
(ii)   There is a trivial steady state at the origin but there may exist no non-trivial steady state. All steady that do exist may be stable or unstable.
(iii) Possible outcomes include extinction, chaotic behaviour and cycling as well as convergence to a steady state. The exact outcome depends on the value of $f'[b*]$ and the slope of g.
(iv)   There can be no steady state at $n > f'[b*]$. $\square$

The first point follows from Proposition 1. Point (ii) is a consequence of the fact that $b \leq b*$ and both consumption and bequests are zero when income is zero but we do not know the slope $db(t)/db(t-t)$ and in particular whether it is larger or smaller than 1. The third point follows from the same reasoning: extinction may occur if the $n = 1$ line has a slope less than unity; many configurations may give rise to periodic cycles and even an a-periodic motion (chaos) as demonstrated below; the last point follows from equation (6).

The main conclusion from our analysis is that any inferences made from such a model with a real-valued family size are irrelevant when the actual integer-valued family size is taken into account.

We conclude with an illustration example which also serves to establish the possible occurrence of chaos.

Example: $u(c) = Ln(c)$, $v(n \cdot \tilde{f}(b)) = 0.1\, Ln(n \cdot \tilde{f}(b))$, $f'[b*] = 30$, $b* = 1$.
We must solve

Maximize $Ln[c(t)] + 0.1\, Ln[30n(t)b(t)]$
subject to $30b(t-1) = n(t)b(t) + c(t)$

Following the procedure outlined in section 3, this yields

$$b(t) = \frac{3b(t-1)}{1.1n}, \qquad \frac{(n-1)\,1.1}{3} < b(t-1) \leq \frac{n1.1}{3} \quad n = 1, 2, 3\ldots$$

and the only relevant segments are (all coefficients are rounded to the 4th digit)

$$\left.\begin{array}{lll}
b(t) = 2.727\ b(t-1) & 0.0000 < b(t-1) \leq 0.3667 & (n = 1) \\
b(t) = 1.363\ b(t-1) & 0.3667 < b(t-1) \leq 0.7333 & (n = 2) \\
b(t) = 0.9091\ b(t-1) & 0.7333 < b(t-1) \leq 1.1 & (n = 3)
\end{array}\right\} \quad (9)$$

This phase line is depicted in Figure 3. There are no nontrivial steady states. Because the slope of the first two lines is larger than unity, individuals born in families of one or two children always bequeath more to each child than they themselves inherited and have an equal or greater number of children. On the other hand because the slope of the third line is less than unity individuals born into families of three children bequeath less and have two or three children.

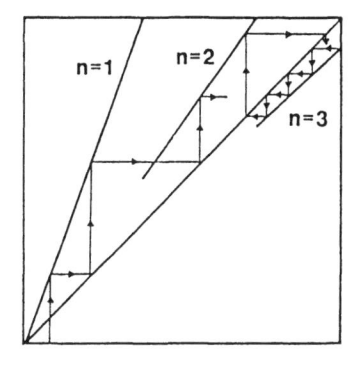

Fig. 3

Thus after a finite number of periods, the phase line will be confined to the top right corner of the diagram and families will have either 2 or 3 children. Furthermore we now show that the trajectory will not reach any stable cycle or indeed any cycle at all but will be chaotic. The reader is referred to Collet and Eckman (1980) or Lichtenberg and Lieberman (1983, ch. 7) for more details. Briefly we speak of a chaotic orbit when there is "no pattern to it", that is, it never repeats itself although it is bounded. The end result is that as time goes on the phase line densely fills some interval. Proving the existence of chaos usually involves proving that all cycles are unstable and entails some measure of the mean slope of the orbit such as the Liapunov exponent. However in our example we can prove our point much more simply.

Consider the interval $(0.9086, 1)$; it consists of two subintervals $(0.9086, 0.9761)$ and $(0.9761, 1)$. Let us follow some orbits, using equation (9). First let $b(0) = 0.9999$ be the starting point on the second subinterval, then $b(3) = 0.7513$ still is on the $n = 3$ line but $b(4) = 0.6830$ moves on to the $n = 2$ line, hence $b(5) = 0.9313$. This pattern is the same for all starting points in the second subinterval: they involve four points on the $n = 3$ line and one on the $n = 2$ line and result in a slightly smaller number after five periods. Secondly let $b(0) = 0.9500$ be the starting point on the first subinterval; the trajectory will move onto the $n = 2$ line at $b(3) = 0.7137$ but $b(4) = 0.9733$ is again on the $n = 3$ line and is above $b(0)$. This pattern is typical of points on that subinterval.

To sum up, depending on the starting point (on a subset of $(0.8873, 1)$) we will return to the $n = 3$ line in either 4 or 5 periods and consequently either above or below the starting point. These are the only two patterns and given an arbitrary starting point. These are the only two patterns and given an arbitrary starting point β, if we are to ever return to it there must be m 4-period runs and q 5-period runs such that:

$$\beta \left[\left(\frac{3}{3.3}\right)^3 \left(\frac{3}{2.2}\right)\right]^m \cdot \left[\left(\frac{3}{3.3}\right)^4 \left(\frac{3}{2.2}\right)\right]^q = \beta$$

$$\left(\frac{3}{3.3}\right)^{3m+4q} \left(\frac{3}{2.2}\right)^{m+q} = 1$$

$$\left(\frac{3}{3.3}\right)^{\frac{3m+4q}{m+q}} = \frac{2.2}{3}, \quad \text{m and q are integers.}$$

This requires the rational number $(3m+4q)/(m+q)$ to be irrational and thus cannot be. In conclusion although we can find an appropriate number of runs of both kinds to approximate our starting point, we can never reproduce it and we have an infinite-periodic orbit; furthermore since this is true for an arbitrary starting point, the orbit eventually fills the interval.

The ease with which this example was constructed makes it obvious that this behaviour is by no means rare. Other patterns can also emerge; for instance a low enough value of $f'[b*]$ would result in families ever having but one child and extinction.

Appendix

Let ℓ be the input level and with it is associated a productvity index per unit of capital $p(\ell)$, which rises from zero to a maximum at ℓ^* and then decreases. Given a capital stock b, the family must use an input level $\ell \geq b$. The linear form of this constraint is not restrictive since the scale of measurement of ℓ is arbitrary. The inequality reflects the need to man so many machines or tend to many heads of cattle for instance. The product which is to be maximized is thus $b \cdot p(\ell)$ and the production function is defined as:

$$\phi(b) = \max_{\ell} \{ b \cdot p(\ell) \mid \ell \geq b\}$$

The outcome is obvious: if $b \leq \ell^*$ we choose $\ell = \ell^*$, hence $\phi(b) = b \cdot p(\ell^*)$; if $b \geq l^*$ we choose $\ell = b$ and $\phi(b) = b \cdot p(b)$.

We now show that the restrictions imposed on $p(\cdot)$ are compatible with those imposed on $f(\cdot)$ so that $\phi(b)$ has the same shape as $\tilde{f}(b)$. Suppose that the functional forms p and f are such that $p(x) = f(x)/x$ so that p is some average product. Since p reaches a maximum we have:

$$p'(x) = \frac{f'(x) \cdot x - f(x)}{x^2} > 0$$

below the maximum and negative above it. This indicates that the marginal product of x exceeds its average product from the origin up to the maximum of p and the reverse is true afterwards. These restrictions, it will be recalled, are exactly those imposed on the function f as illustrated in Figure 1. The ϕ function then takes the following form (note that $\ell^* = b^*$):

$$\phi(b) = \begin{cases} b \cdot p(b^*) = b \cdot f(b^*)/b^* = b \cdot f'(b^*), & \text{if } b \leq b^* \\ b \cdot p(b) = f(b) & \text{if } b \geq b^*. \end{cases}$$

Therefore ϕ and $\tilde{f}$ are identical if we take $p(x) = f(x)/x$. Thus given a production function such as $f(\ell)/\ell$ which represents the output per unit of capital with l units of input we can define $\phi(b)$ by choosing the input that maximizes production of output, subject to a constraint, and we obtain a function which is the concave upper contour of f. (If the constraint is $\ell = b$, then $\phi(b) = f(b)$.)

We now briefly consider the case where the input is costly. Suppose that the unit cost of input in terms of the capital good is w.

$$\phi(b) = \max_{\ell} \left\{ b \left[\frac{f(\ell)}{\ell} - w \right] \mid \ell \geq b \right\}, \quad \text{and}$$

$$\phi(b) = \begin{cases} b [f'(b^*) - w], & \text{if } b \leq b^* \\ f(b) - wb, & \text{if } b \geq b^* \end{cases}$$

Therefore it is as if we were dealing with a net production function $f(b) - wb$ which exhibits a maximum, but we again obtain its concave upper contour. A similar occurrence would have followed the imposition of transaction costs in the capital market version.

References

Becker, G. S. (1960) An Economic Analysis of Fertility. In: R. A. Easterlin (Ed.) Demographic and Economic Change. Princeton: Princeton University Press

Becker, G. S. (1981) A Treatise on the Family. Harvard University Press, Cambridge MA

Collet, P. and Eckman, J-P. (1980) Iterated Maps of the Interval as Dynamical Systems. Birkhauser, Boston

Kemp, M. C., Leonard, D., and Long, N. V. (1989) A Contribution to the Theory of Economic Planning: A Family-based Model of Population growth. In S. Bhagwan Dahiya (Ed.) Theoretical Foundations of Development Planning. Inter-India Publiccations, New Delhi

Kemp, M. C., Leonard, D., and Long, N. V. (1984) Three Pitfalls in the Construction of Family-based Models of Population Growth. European Economic Review 25 : 345-354

Leonard, D. (1984) Solomn's Dilemma: the Consequences of Restricting Variables to Integer Values. Paper Presented at the 1984 Australasian Meetings of the Econometric Society. Sydney, Australia

Lichtenberg, A. J. and Lieberman M. A. (1983) Regular and Stochastic Motion. Applied Mathematical Sciences Series No. 38. Springer Verlag, New York

Nerlove, M., Razin, A., and Sadka, E. (1986) Bequests and the Size of Population When Population is Endogenous. Journal of Political Economy 92, No. 3: 527-531

Is There an Optimal Growth Rate for Population?

Gerhard Schmitt-Rink

1. Introdcution

This contribution discusses the existence and properties of population growth rates which are optimal in the sense of (1) the number of children and retirees which the average active person has to support, i.e. the overall demographic dependency rate is minimized, (2) the economic dependency rate, i.e. the relative share of per-capita income which the average active person has to spend in order to support children and retirees is minimized and (3) net per-capita consumption, i.e. per-capita income less dependency burden of the average active person is maximized. The corresponding optimal population growth rates are denoted by n*, n**, and n*** respectively.

Criterion (1), according to which the optimal population growth rate n* minimizes the demographic dependency rate, i.e. the number of young and old dependants which the average active person has to support, makes sense only if one assumes that children as well as elderly dependent have an average income or consumption weight of one. Otherwise this indicator, although frequently used in the context of population problems, would not make any sense at all. The following considerations concentrate therefore on criteria (2) and (3). As will be seen, (2) and (3) coincide with (1) in very special cases only.

2. The Golden Rule of Accumulation

According to the Golden Rule of Accumulation, per-capita consumption is maximized if marginal productivity of capital equals the equilibrium growth rate g = n + h, where g is the growth rate of total production, n the growth rate of population and, the participation rate being given, the growth rate of the labour force and h the rate of Harrod-neutral technical progress, i.e. the equilibrium growth rate of both labour productivity and capital intensity. On steady-state paths, total production and capital input grow at the constant rate g = n + h, labour input at the constant rate n, and labour productivity and capital intensity expand at the constant rate h, the growth rate of capital productivity being zero. Under the assumptions of the neo-classical standard growth model there is one and only one golden-rule path for any given equilibrium growth rate g = n + h, and the equilibrium magnitudes of labour productivity, capital intensity, capital productivity, per-capita consumption and per-capita savings and investment change with the equilibrium growth rate g = n + h, regardless of whether the change of the equilibrium growth rate is caused

Microeconomic Studies
K. F. Zimmermann (Ed.)
Economic Theory of Optimal Population

by a change of the population growth rate (n) or of the rate of neutral technical progress (h).

Is there then, the rate of neutral technical progress (h) being given, an optimal population growth rate (n) in the sense that it maximizes golden-rule per-capita consumption, a "goldenest golden rule" according to Samuelson (1975). And, if this optimum optimorum exists, does it also imply the minimization of the economic and/or demographic dependency burden per active person, or, in other words, does it also imply the maximization of net consumption in relation to gross consumption per active person? The answer is, as will be shown, that the optimum growth rate does exist which maximizes per-capita consumption, but that it neither minimizes the economic nor the demographic dependency rate necessarily. The population growth rate n***, which maximizes net per-capita consumption, differs from the population growth rate n**, which minimizes the economic dependency rate, the share of gross per-capita consumption, which is absorbed by young and old dependants of the active part of population, and population growth rate n** normally differs from population growth rate n*, which minimizes the demographic dependency rate, the number of young and old dependants which on average one active person has to support out of gross per-capita consumption.

The Golden Rule of Accumulation, as originally formulated by Phelps (1961) and others, refers to per-capita consumption (z) in the sense of $z = C/L$, where C is total consumption and L the active labour force. Per-capita consumption z in this sense equals per-capita production, i.e. labour productivity (y) minus per-capita investment (i). In equilibrium, growth per-capita investment is $i = nk + hk = (n + h)k$, where nk is capital widening, hk capital deepening per unit of labour. In other words, nk is that part of total per-capita investment which increases the number of jobs at rate n, if capital intensity is constant, whereas hk is that part of total per-capita investment which increases capital intensity at the given equilibrium rate h of technical progress. In equilibrium growth consumption per worker $z = y - (n+h)$ k is maximal, if

$$\frac{dz}{dk} = \frac{dy}{dk} - (n + h) = 0, \tag{1}$$

and

$$\frac{dy}{dk} = n + h.$$

The neo-classical production function in per-capita terms $y = y(k)$ with $y'(k) > 0$, $y''(k) < 0$ and $y(0) = 0$, $y'(0) = \infty$ determines the golden-rule magnitudes of labour productivity (y*), capital intensity (k*), per-capita investment (i*) and per-capita consumption (z*) for any given rate of population growth (n) and equilibrium rate of technical progress (h).

Diagrams 1a and 1b demonstrate that steady-state per-capita consumption $z(k) = y(k) - i(k)$ is maximal, if and only if $dy/dk = n + h$. Whether the economy expands on the golden-rule path or not, depends upon the magnitude of the average propensity to save (s). Equilibrium growth necessitates that per-capita savings sy(k) equal equilibrium per-capita investment $i(k) = (n + h)k$. Golden-rule growth

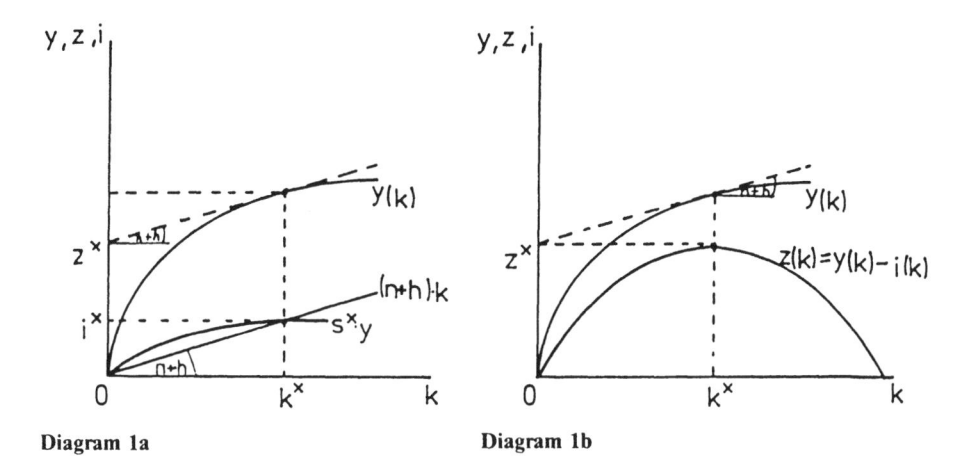

Diagram 1a   Diagram 1b

therefore implies an average propensity to save $s^* = (n + h)k^*/y^*$. If the average propensity to save is greater (smaller) than s^*, the equality of actual and required per-capita savings and investment $i(k) = (n + h)k$ implies that capital intensity and labour productivity are greater (smaller) than k^* and y^*, and in both cases per-capita consumption $z(k)$ is smaller than z^*.

The per-capita production function $y(k)$ exists only in the short run. In the long run technical progress continuously shifts the production function radially at the constant rate h of technical progress. On steady-state paths $y(k)$, $z(k)$ and therefore y^*, z^* and k^* all increase through time at the constant equilibrium rate h of technical progress.

3. Demographic Dependency Rates and Participation Rate

The active labour force (L) is smaller than that part of the total population which is potentially productive. If for instance the productive life-span reaches from the age of A (first year of productive age-span) to that of B (first year of post-productive age-span), the potentially active part of the total population comprises (1) the employees, (2) the self-employed, (3) profit and interest receivers who are working neither as employees nor as self-employed, and (4) the dependants of groups (1), (2) and (3), who are not actually but potentially active because they are in their productive life-span A-B. If m is the number of potentially active, but actually non-active persons per active worker, the participation rate of the potentially productive part of the total population is $1/(1+m)$. Besides the potentially active groups, i.e. people in the productive life-span A-B, total population comprises (1) the pre-productive persons, i.e. children and (2) the post-productive individuals, i.e. retirees. If the number of pre- and post-productive persons per potentially active person equals v, per-capita consumption in the sense of average consumption per unit of total population is

$$c = \frac{C}{N} = \frac{C}{L} \frac{1}{(1+m)(1+v)} = z \frac{1}{(1+m)(1+v)} = zq. \tag{2}$$

The ratio $q = 1/((1+m)(1+v))$ is the overall participation rate, i.e. the share of the active labour force in total population and therefore the ratio of net consumption (c) to gross consumption (z) per active person. The participation rate m may be assumed to be independent of the population growth rate. This is found not to be the case for the dependency rate v. The greater the population growth rate, the larger normally the number of pre-productive individuals v_1 and the smaller normally the number of post-productive individuals v_3 per active person. The overall dependency rate $v = v_1 + v_3$ changes with the population growth rate, and this poses the question whether (1) there exists a growth rate of population which minimizes the dependency rate (v) and whether (2) the growth rate of population which minimizes the dependency rate (v) maximizes per-capita consumption $c = C/N$, i.e. consumption per unit of total population.

4. Minimization of the Demographic Dependency Rate, Maximization of the Demographic Participation Rate

Any given series of age-specific birth rates b(x) and age-specific survival rates l(x) implies an asymptotically stable population, which is characterized by a constant growth rate of the population size on the one hand and a constant age-distribution on the other. The constant age-composition of the stable population implies constant dependency rates v_1 and v_3, i.e. constant numbers of young and elderly dependants which one potentially active person has to support.

$$v_1 = \frac{\sum\limits_{0}^{A} (1+n)^{-x} l_x}{\sum\limits_{A}^{B} (1+n)^{-x} l_x} = e_1 (1+n)^{-(\bar{x}_1 - \bar{x}_2)} \tag{3 a}$$

$$v_3 = \frac{\sum\limits_{B}^{M} (1+n)^{-x} l_x}{\sum\limits_{A}^{B} (1+n)^{-x} l_x} = e_3 (1+n)^{-(\bar{x}_3 - \bar{x}_2)} \tag{3 b}$$

The ℓ_x are the constant age-specific survival rates $\bar{x}_1$, $\bar{x}_2$ and $\bar{x}_3$ are the (approximate) mean ages of the pre-productive, productive and post-productive parts of the total population, and e_1, e_3 the ratios of the sums of the survival rates of the respective age-spans 0-A, A-B and B-M, where M is the maximal retirement age. Obviously, e_1 and e_2 equal the dependency rates v_1 and v_2 which would prevail in the case of a stationary population, i.e. if $n = 0$.

Dependency rate v_1 increases (decreases), dependency rate v_3 decreases (increases), if linear increases (decreases) of all age-specific birth rates increase (decrease) the stable population growth rate, the age-specific survival rates being constant:

$$\frac{dv_1}{dn} > 0 \qquad\qquad (4\,a)$$

$$\frac{dv_3}{dn} < 0 \qquad\qquad (4\,b)$$

Increases (decreases) of the stable population growth rate, which would be caused by linear increases (decreases) of all age-specific survival rates l_x would leave the age-composition of the stable population and consequently the dependency rates v_1 and v_3 constant. According to (4 a) and (4 b) there is one and only one stable population growth rate, which minimizes the overall dependency rate $v = v_1 + v_3$

$$\frac{dv}{dn} = \frac{dv_1}{dn} + \frac{dv_3}{dn} = 0, \qquad\qquad (5)$$

and

$$-\frac{dv_1}{dn} = \frac{dv_3}{dn}.$$

According to Bourgeois-Pichat (1950), Coale, Demeny (1966), Deistler, Feichtinger et al. (1978), Arthur, McNicoll (1977), Meyer-Thoms (1983), Wander (1971, 1975) and other authors the stable population growth rate n*, which minimizes the overall dependency rate, is slightly negative, if one bases the computations on the life-tables and productive life-spans of industrialized countries. Diagrams 2a and 2b demonstrate this fact:

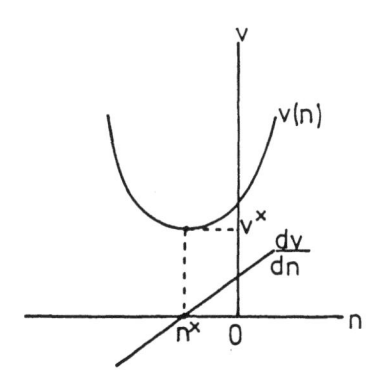

Diagram 2a

Diagram 2b

In diagram 2 a the optimum population growth rate n*, which minimizes the dependency rate v(n), is negative. The rate which minimizes the dependency rate v, maximizes the participation rate q $= 1/((1+m)(1+v))$, i.e. the share of the economically active people in the total population. This is shown in diagram 2b. It is assumed that rate m is exogenously fixed, i.e. that the participation rate of the potentially productive part of the total population is independent of the population growth rate. In reality, m and n may well be interlinked.

The population growth rate n*, which minimizes the dependency rate v or which, in other words, maximizes the participation rate q $= 1/((1+m)(1+v))$, does not maximize per-capita consumption c $= C/N = z/((1+m)(1+v)) = zq$. Maximization of c $=$ zq implies

$$\frac{dc}{dn} = \frac{dz}{dn}q + \frac{dq}{dn}z = 0 \tag{6}$$

$$-\frac{dz}{dn} = \frac{dq}{dn}\frac{z}{q} \, .$$

Since z(n) $=$ y(k(n)) $-$ (n+h)k(n), the first derivative of z with respect to n is

$$\frac{dz}{dn} = \frac{dk}{dn}\left(\frac{dy}{dk} - (n + h)\right) - k. \tag{7}$$

According to (1) maximization of per-capita consumption (z) at any given equilibrium growth rate g $=$ n+h implies dy/dk $=$ n+h. Maximization of per-capita consumption c $=$ zq therefore implies

$$k = \frac{dq}{dn}\frac{z}{q} \, . \tag{8}$$

Since golden-rule k* $= -$ dz/dn is always positive, maximization of per-capita consumption c $=$ C/N implies dq/dn $>$ 0. In other words, the population growth rate n***, which maximizes per-capita consumption (c), is smaller than the population growth rate n*, which maximizes the participation rate (q) and minimizes the dependency rate (v).

Under the assumptions of the neoclassical standard growth model per-capita consumption z $=$ C/L and participation rate q $=$ L/N are steady and twice differenciable functions of the population growth rate. Therefore the existence of an interior solution for n* and n*** is secured.

5. Minimization of the Economic Dependency Rate, Maximization of the Economic Participation Rate

Up to this point, the dependency rate (v) and the participation rate (q) have been taken as purely demographic variables. Thus per-capita consumption was defined as consumption per person, i.e. children, active people and retired persons were all given the same weight of one. Instead one could take into consideration that on average children and the elderly consume less per capita than those active in the labour force. If one attaches relative consumption weights u_1 and u_3 to the demographic dependency rates v_1 and v_3, the overall economic dependency rate, the number of children and retired people per active person in terms of consumer-equivalents is $p = u_1v_1 + u_3v_3$, and per-capita consumption in terms of consumption per consumer-equivalent is

$$c = \frac{C}{Z} = \frac{C}{L}\frac{L}{Z} = z\frac{1}{(1+m)(1+p)} = z\frac{1}{(1+m)(1+u_1v_1+u_3v_3)}, \qquad (9)$$

where $Z = uN$ is the number of consumer-equivalents, i.e. the fictitious size of total population which one gets if one attaches a relative consumption weight of u_1 to the pre-productive part and u_3 to the post-productive part of the total population. Minimization of the economic dependency rate $p = uv = u_1v_1 + u_3v_3$ implies

$$\frac{dp}{dn} = u_1\frac{dv_1}{dn} + u_3\frac{dv_3}{dn} = 0, \qquad (10)$$

and

$$-\frac{dv_1}{dn} = \frac{dv_3}{dn}\frac{u_3}{u_1}.$$

Obviously, (10) is reduced to (5) if $u_1 = u_3$. If, instead, (1) $u_3 > u_1$, if the average retiree consumes more than an average child, the optimum population growth rate n^{**}, which minimizes the economic dependency rate $p = p_1 + p_3$, is greater than the population growth rate n^*, which minimizes the demographic dependency rate $v = v_1 + v_3$, and if (2) $u_3 < u_1$, if the average retiree consumes less than an average child, the optimum population growth rate n^{**}, which minimizes the economic dependency rate p, is smaller than the population growth rate n^*, which minimizes the demographic dependency rate v. Rates n^{**} and n^* are equal, if the consumption weights for children and retirees are the same. Diagram 3a demonstrates case (1), diagram 3b case (2):

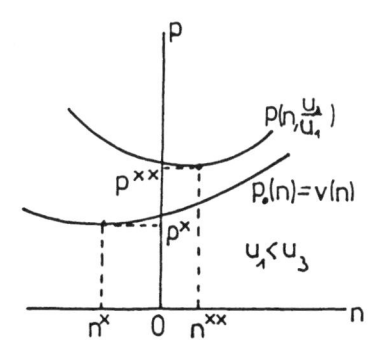

Diagram 3a

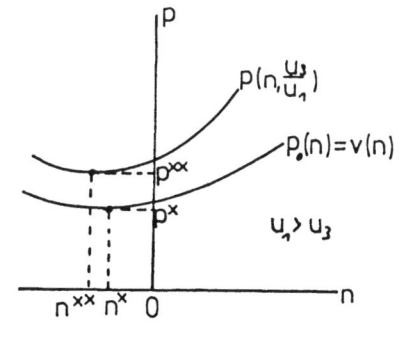

Diagram 3b

The curves $P_o(n) = v(n)$ show the economic dependency rate for the case $u_1 = u_3 = 1$. In relation to this case, where $p = v = v_1 + v_3$, because $u_3 = u_1 = 1$, the optimum population growth rate n^{**} is (1) greater than n^*, if $u_3 > u_1 = 1$ and (2) smaller than n^*, if $1 = u_3 < u_1$. If the lower consumption weight is taken as unity, the economic dependency rate $p(n)$ is always greater than the demographic dependency rate $v(n)$.

The population growth rate n^{**}, which minimizes the economic dependency rate $p(n)$, is not the population growth rate n^{***}, which maximizes per-capita consumption in the sense of consumption per consumer-equivalent $c = C/Z$. According to (8) per-capita consumption is maximal, if $k = (dq/dn)(z/q)$. Since k, z and q are all positive, a positive dq/dn is required, and this implies that the population growth rate n^{***}, which maximizes per-capita consumption $c = C/Z$, is smaller than the growth rate of population n^{**}, which minimizes the economic dependency rate $p(n)$.

6. Maximization of Net Per-Capita Consumption: Concept I

In the above analysis consumption has been determined as gross consumption (C) per unit of population: $z = C/L$, $c = C/N$ or $c = C/Z$, where L = active labour force, N = total population and Z = total population in terms of consumer-equivalents. Instead, per-capita consumption could be determined in terms of net consumption per active person, where net consumption is gross consumption less dependency burden. Whether the population growth rate, which maximizes net per-capita consumption, is the same as or different from the growth rate of population, which maximizes gross per-capita consumption, depends upon the way in which per-capita contributions for young and old dependants are determined.

If the participation rate of the potentially active part of the total population, i.e. of those in the productive age-span A-B is unity, if, in other words, m = 0, gross consumption per active person is $z = C/L$. If the dependency burden is linked to net consumption (c) per active person, i.e. if

$$c = z - cp = z \frac{1}{1 + p} = zq, \tag{11}$$

where $q = 1/(1+p)$ ist the overall participation rate, i.e. the share of the labour force in the total population (calculated in terms of persons or in terms of consumer-equivalents), maximization of the net per-capita consumption c implies, the growth rate and therefore the participation rate being given,

$$\frac{dc}{dk} = \frac{dz}{dk} q = 0. \tag{12}$$

Thus maximization of gross per-capita consumption (z) implies that of net per-capita consumption (c), i.e. net per-capita consumption is maximized in the golden-rule constellation. The same holds if the dependency contribution is linked to gross per-capita consumption (z) instead of net per-capita consumption (c). Now the net consumption of the average active person is

$$c = z - zp = z(1 - p) = zq \tag{13}$$

$$\frac{dc}{dk} = \frac{dz}{dk}(1 - p) = \frac{dz}{dk}q = 0. \tag{14}$$

The participation rate and therefore the relation of net consumption to gross consumption is now $q = 1 - p$ instead of $q = 1/(1+p)$. Conditions (12) and (14) are the same, i.e. maximization of gross consumption per active person (z) implies that of net consumption per active person (c), if the dependency burden is linked to gross instead of net per-capita consumption. In other words, net per-capita consumption (c) is maximized in the golden-rule constellation.

Regardless of whether the dependency contribution of the average active person is linked to gross or net consumption, to z or c, net consumption per active person is maximized in golden-rule constellations only, i.e. under the condition $n + h = dy/dk$. If the participation rate $1/(1+m)$ of those in the productive age-span A-B, is less than unity, net consumption is smaller than in (11) and (13)

$$c = z \frac{1}{(1+m)(1+p)} = zq_c \tag{15 a}$$

$$c = z \frac{1-p}{1+m} = zq_z. \tag{15 b}$$

(15 a) describes the case where the dependency contribution is linked to net consumption c, (15 b) the case, where it is linked to gross consumption z. Since, all other things being equal, the ratio q of net consumption c to gross consumption z differs in both cases, the population growth rate which maximizes net per-capita consumption, is different too in the two cases.

7. Maximization of Net Per-Capita Consumption: Concept II

The maximum of net per-capita consumption is not located on the golden-rule path, if the dependency burden is not linked to per-capita consumption z or c, but to the wage rate w or to per-capita income y. Diagram 4a demonstrates the case where the dependency burden is linked to the wage rate, diagram 4b the case, where it is linked to per-capita income.

In diagram 4a $w(k)p$ is the dependency burden per active person, and net per-capita consumption is $c(k) = z(k) - w(k)p$. Maximization of $c(k)$ implies

$$\frac{dc}{dk} = \frac{dz}{dk} - \frac{dw}{dk}p = 0, \tag{16 a}$$

and

$$\frac{dz}{dk} = \frac{dw}{dk}p \ .$$

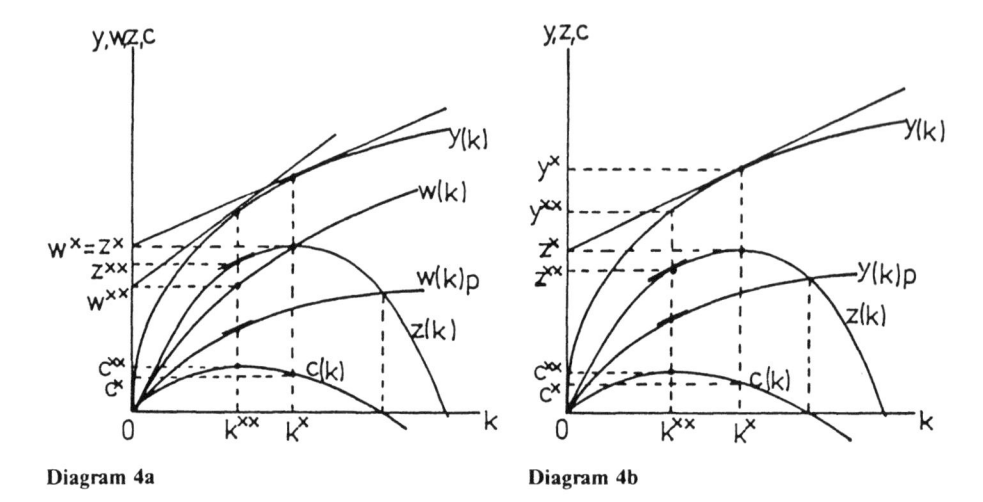

Diagram 4a   **Diagram 4b**

Since dw/dk is positive, the optimal magnitudes w^{**}, k^{**}, z^{**} and c^{**} are located to the left of the golden-rule constellation w^*, k^*, z^* and c^*, if $0 < p < 1$. The golden-rule solution would imply $p = 0$, which is no plausible case.

In diagram 4b $y(k)p$ is the dependency burden per active person, and net per-capita consumption is $c(k) = z(k) - y(k)p$. Maximization of $c(k)$ implies

$$\frac{dc}{dk} = \frac{dz}{dk} - \frac{dy}{dk} = 0, \tag{16 b}$$

and

$$\frac{dz}{dk} = \frac{dy}{dk}p.$$

Since dy/dk is positive, the optimum magnitudes y^{**}, k^{**}, z^{**} and c^{**} are located to the left of the golden-rule constellation y^*, k^*, z^* and c^*, if $0 < p < a$, where a is the wage share, i.e. $a = w/y$. In these cases maximization of net per-capita consumption does not imply golden-rule solutions. The golden-rule solution would imply $p = 0$. The optimum magnitudes y^{**}, k^{**}, z^{**} and c^{**} would be located to the right of the golden-rule constellation y^*, k^*, z^* and c^*, if the economic dependency rate (p) were greater than the share of wages in total income (a).

The population growth rate which maximizes net consumption $c = z - wp$ per active person, is determined by

$$\frac{dc}{dn} = \frac{dz}{dn} - \frac{dw}{dn}p - \frac{dp}{dn}w = 0, \tag{17 a}$$

and

$$\frac{dp}{dn} = \frac{dk}{dn}\left(\frac{dz}{dk} - \frac{dw}{dk}p\right)\frac{1}{w}.$$

According to (16 a) the expression in parentheses equals zero. Thus the maximization of net per-capita consumption $c = z - wp$ implies the minimization of the dependency rate p, i.e. the optimum growth rates n*** and n** coincide. The same holds in the case where net per-capita consumption is determined as $c = z - yp$. Maximization of net per-capita consumption $c = z - yp$ implies

$$\frac{dc}{dn} = \frac{dz}{dn} - \frac{dy}{dn}p - \frac{dp}{dn}y = 0, \tag{17 b}$$

and

$$\frac{dp}{dn} = \frac{dk}{dn}\left(\frac{dz}{dk} - \frac{dy}{dk}p\right)\frac{1}{y}.$$

According to (16 b) the expression in parentheses equals zero, i.e. the maximization of net per-capita income implies $dp/dn = 0$ and therefore $p(n) = min$. In other words: The optimum population growth rate n***, which maximizes net per-capita consumption, is equal to the population growth rate n**, which minimizes the economic dependency rate, if the dependency burden is linked to the wage rate or to per-capita income instead of to gross or net per-capita consumption.

8. Different Impact of Age-Specific Birth Rates and Age-Specific Survival Rates

Linear increases or decreases of the age-specific survival rates, different from linear changes of the age-specific birth rates, do not have any impact on the age-composition of the stable population. Consequently the demographic dependency rates v_1 and v_3 do not depend upon the level of the age-specific survival rates. But the optimal growth rates n*, n** and n*** increase or decrease along with the level of the age-specific survival rates, the age-specific birth rates being given. Linear increases (decreases) of the age-specific survival rates shift the p(n)- and the q(n)-curves and consequently the minima of these functions and the respective optima to the right(to the left). In other words, the relationship between dependency rate and stable population growth rate implies a constant set of age-specific survival rates.

9. Summary

To summarize the results of the above analysis: (1) If the dependency burden is linked to gross or net consumption per active person, all maxima of gross consumption (z) and net consumption (c) per-capita are located on golden-rule paths, where the growth rate $g = n + h$ equals marginal productivity of capital. (2) If the dependency burden is linked not to gross or net per-capita consumption, but to the wage rate (w) or to per-capita income (y), the maximum of net per-capita consumption is not located on golden-rule paths. (3) The population growth rate n***, which maximizes net per-capita consumption (c), is smaller than the population growth rate n**, which minimizes the economic dependency rate p(n), if the dependency rate (p) is linked to gross consumption (z) or net consumption (c) per active person. If the dependency rate (p) is linked to the wage rate (w) or to per-capita income (y), the population growth rate n^{***} which maximizes net per-capita consumption equals the population growth rate n^{**} which minimizes the economic dependency rate. (4) The population growth rate n^{**}, which minimizes the economic dependency rate, is smaller (greater) than the population growth rate n^*, which minimizes the demographic dependency rate $v = v_1 + v_3$, if the consumption weight u_1 of an average child is greater (smaller) than the consumption weight u_3 of an average retiree, if, in other words, on average, a child is more (less) "expensive" than a retiree; the population growth rates n^{**} and n^* are equal, if the relative consumption weights of children and retirees are the same. (5) The population growth rate n^*, which minimizes the demographic dependency rate $v = v_1 + v_3$ is slightly negative, if determined on the basis of typical life tables and productive age-spans of industrialized countries. (6) The magnitude of population growth rate n^{***}, which maximizes net per-capita consumption, depends upon whether the dependency burden is linked to gross per-capita consumption (z), to net per-capita consumption (c), to the wage rate (w) or to per-capita income (y). (7) Because of the lack of sufficient empirical data, which would allow one to decide whether u_1 is greater or smaller than u_3, it is not feasible to say whether the population growth rate n^{**}, which minimizes the economic dependency rate and/or the population growth rate n^{***}, which maximizes net per-capita consumption (c), are positive, zero or negative.

References

Arthur, W. B., G. McNicoll (1977) Optimal Time Paths With Age-Dependence: A Theory of Population Policy. The Review of Economic Studies: 111-123

Bourgeois-Pichat, J. (1950) Charges de la Population Active. In: Journal de la Societe de Statistique de Paris: 94-114

Coale, A. J. (1972) The Growth and Structure of Human Populations. A Mathematical Investigation, Princeton N.J.

Coale, A. J., P. Demeny (1966) Regional Model Life Tables and Stable Populations, Princeton N.J.

Dasgupta, P. S. (1969) On the Concept of Optimal Population. The Review of Economic Studies, 107: 295-318

Deistler, H., G. Feichtinger, M. Luptacik and A. Wörgötter (1978) Optimales Wachstum stabiler Bevölkerungen in einem neoklassischen Modell. Zeitschrift für Bevölkerungswissenschaft: 63-73

Diamond, P. (1965) National Debt in a Neoclassical Growth Model. The American Economic Review: 1126-1150

Dunsdorfs, E. (1953) The Optimum Theory of Population. Weltwirtschaftliches Archiv: 221-233

Felderer, B. (1976) Environment and Population Optimum. In: Beckmann, M., Künzi, H. P. (Eds.) Lecture Notes in Economic and Mathematical Systems, No. 127, Berlin-Heidelberg-New York

Meyer-Thoms, G. (1983) Demographische Grundlagen der sekundären Einkommensverteilung. In: Schmitt-Rink, G. (Ed.) Probleme der Bevölkerungsökonomie, Bochum: 3-59

Phelps, E. S. (1961) The Golden Rule of Accumulation. A Fable for Growthmen. In: The American Economic Review: 638-643

Phelps, E. S. (1966) Golden Rules of Economic Growth: Studies of Efficient and Optimal Investment, New York

Pitchford, J. D. (1972) Population and Optimal Growth. Econometrica: 109-136

Pitchford, J. D. (1974) Population in Economic Growth, Amsterdam-London-New York

Samuelson, P. A. (1958) An Exact Consumption-Loan Model of Interest with or without the Social Contrivance of Money. In: The Journal of Political Economy: 467-482

Samuelson, P. A. (1975) The Optimum Growth Rate for Population. In: International Economic Review: 531-538

Schmitt-Rink, G. (1983) Bevölkerungswachstum und gesamtwirtschaftliche Sparquote. In: Schmitt-Rink, G. (Ed.) Probleme der Bevölkerungsökonomie, Bochum: 60-71

Schmitt-Rink, G. (1984) Population Growth and Income Distribution. In: Steinmann, G. (Ed.), Economic Consequences of Population Change in Industrialized Countries, Berlin-Heidelberg-New York-Tokyo: 59-67

Singer, S. F. (Ed.) (1973) Is There an Optimum Level of Population? New York

Wander, H. (1971) Der Geburtenrückgang in Europa wirtschaftlich gesehen. Kieler Diskussionsbeiträge zu aktuellen wirtschaftspolitischen Fragen. Nr. 9. Institut für Weltwirtschaft, Kiel

Wander, H. (1975) Wirtschaftliche und soziale Konsequenzen des Geburtenrückgangs. In: Mitteilungsblatt der österreichischen Gesellschaft für Statistik und Informatik, Nr. 18, Wien: 72-90

II. Technical Progress and Social Security

Technological Change and Population Growth[1]

Manfred Neumann

1.

In the Malthusian and Ricardian tradition, economic development is viewed as a race between population and technical improvements. Technological change is envisaged as an outward shift of the production possibility frontier which opens new space to be filled with a growing population. Upon technical improvements, population size increases until the enlarged consumption possibilities are exhausted and consumption per head has come down to a stationary subsistence level again. Hence, according to this view, technical improvements elicit accelerated population growth. It will be shown in this paper that, from a neoclassical point of view, technical progress under quite reasonable assumptions lowers population growth.

In contrast to the classical view which focussed on discrete changes in technology, I shall envisage technological change as a continuous phenomenon proceeding at a constant rate. That rate will be considered to be exogenously given. Instead of looking for an optimal size of population which can be sustained by a given technology, the present paper will be concerned with the rate of growth of population sustainable at a given rate of technological change. As a matter of simplification, I shall disregard the presence of scarce resources which give rise to diseconomies of scale. Thus technical progress is presumed to occur at a rate that swamps any diseconomies. Hence constant returns to scale are assumed to obtain.

The determinants of population growth will be investigated from the point of view of optimal growth theory. The usual interpretation adopted within that approach is a normative one (see for example Dasgupta 1969). I should, however, suggest that this approach can also be utilized to derive hypotheses about actual behavior of men. That is done by employing the model of an eternal family which is concerned with utility of a representative member of that family and all descendents. The family is assumed to control both capital accumulation and the rate of growth of the family given production possibilities and their rate of increase due to technological change.

The basic notion to be used is that rearing children can be considered as a kind of capital formation. Raising children affects the future size of the family and thus total utility, appropriately discounted. Similarly, accumulation of physical capital affects the sustainable level of consumption per head. Hence, both rearing children and expending part of the annual output for capital accumulation can be viewed

---

[1] I am indebted for constructive comments of a referee. Responsibility for any errors remains with the author.

Microeconomic Studies
K. F. Zimmermann (Ed.)
Economic Theory of Optimal Population
© Springer-Verlag Berlin Heidelberg 1989

as contributing to future utility of the family. In the past, in many instances, children used to be valued as part of a family's work force and as such contributed to providing the means available for consumption and capital accumulation, respectively. Children were also expected to provide old age support for their parents. Since these reasons for having children have largely disappeared in modern industrialized societies they will be disregarded in what follows. Children began to be considered as a kind of consumer good; expenditures incurred by rearing children compete with present consumption of commodities in a similar way as capital accumulation, and for that matter, future consumption, competes with present consumption. From that point of view it appears reasonable to expect a high rate of time preference, at which future consumption is being discounted, to exert a depressing influence on both the demand for capital accumulation and children. Obviously, along these lines, only the demand for children can be explained. Thus the hypotheses, regarding population growth, to be developed are incomplete in so far as controlling fertility and mortality remains imperfect.

The main results will be that, first, there is an inverse relationship between the rate of time preference that is used for discounting future utility on one hand and both capital formation and population growth on the other hand. Secondly, we find that the rate of population growth is adversely affected by technological improvements.

The rest of the paper is organized as follows: In section II the assumptions of the model are stated and briefly discussed. In section III existence of an optimal rate of population growth is established. Section IV is devoted to a comparative static analysis which yields the results mentioned above. Finally, section V outlines some reservations and gives some hints regarding fields of further research.

2.

The model to be used can be described by the following assumptions:

A1 Technology

Production of a single all-purpose commodity is governed by a strictly quasi-concave production function $Y = F(K, AL)$ where K and L denote capital and labor, respectively. All variables are time dependent. F is linearly homogenous, exhibiting positive and diminishing marginal productivities. Technological change, proceeding at the exogenously given rate $a(t) := \dot{A}/A$, is purely labor augmenting.

In view of linear homogeneity the production function can also be written as $y = f(x)$ where $y := Y/AL$ and $x := K/AL$. Furthermore, $f'(x) > 0$ and $f''(x) < 0$.

Total production is devoted to both consumption and capital accumulation. As a matter of simplification, physical capital is assumed to last forever. The result of the analysis would not be changed qualitatively if instead "radioactive decay" of capital were assumed. Hence $Y = C + \dot{K}$. That can alternatively be written as

$$\dot{x} = f(x) - \tilde{c} - (n+a)x \qquad (1\ a)$$

where $\tilde{c} := c/AL$ is total consumption per efficiency unit of labor. The rate of population growth is given by

$$\dot{L} = nL . \qquad (1\ b)$$

Total consumption is used to support workers and both children and retired members of the family. The decision process concerning consumption is envisaged to proceed in two steps. First, it is decided which part of the annual output shall be used for consumption and capital accumulation, respectively. In a second step, total consumption is distributed between workers, children and retired persons, respectively. The first decision is governed by a utility function

$$U = \int_0^\infty L(t)u(c(t))e^{-\varrho t}dt$$ where ϱ is a constant rate of pure time preference, and

$c := C/L$ is total consumption per worker. The second decision, which is concerned with distributing consumption between the respective subgroups of the family, shall remain outside the scope of the present paper. Instantaneous utility $u(c)$ is thus assumed to depend on the consumption possibilities per worker.

Using the utility function U entails applying Bentham's principle of "the greatest happiness of the greatest number". It should be pointed out that it implies equal treatment of all individuals living at present and in the future. If alternatively a utility function $\int_0^\infty u(c)e^{-\varrho t}dt$ would have been used, as it is most popular in the literature on optimal capital accumulation, the well-being of all individuals living in the future would have been disregarded. That is, of course, totally inappropriate in a model of optimal population growth. Therefore, the Benthamite utility function appears to be most appealing. (Meade 1955, pp. 82-83).

Regarding the utility function the following assumptions will be adopted:

A2 Utility Function

The utility function is finite. Instantaneous utility, $u(c)$, exhibits positive and diminishing marginal utility. The elasticity of marginal utility, $\epsilon := -cu''(c)/u'(c)$, is constant. There is some subsistence level of consumption, c_0, at which instantaneous utility is zero.

The implied class of utility functions

$$u(c) = \frac{1}{1-\epsilon}(-c_0^{1-\epsilon} + c^{1-\epsilon}),\qquad(2\ a)$$

seems to be fairly broad. The assumption of a constant elasticity of marginal utility can be justified by taking into account that unless ϵ is constant, a steady state solution does not exist. Thus the desire to keep the analysis manageable and derive unambiguous results of a comparative static analysis requires the simplifying assumption of a constant ϵ.

Additionally we adopt assumption:

A3 Aspiration Level and Rational Expectations

Individuals are concerned with consumption per head deflated by their respective level of aspiration which is raised according to the anticipated growth of consumption possibilities. People possess perfect foresight and thus rationally expect consumption per worker to increase at the rate $a(t)$ in the long run. The subsistence level, c_0, is raised in accordance with a changing level of aspiration.

This assumption is supported by a host of empirical evidence showing that individuals feel better off only if their actual achievement exceeds some level of aspiration which, in turn, is raised upon success and lowered upon failure, respectively. (Helson 1964, Easterlin 1974). Furthermore, the level of subsistence consumption varies according to the level of economic achievement, as documented by grossly diverging poverty lines adopted in various countries.

Assumption $A3$ implies that $\tilde{c} := c/A$ should be treated as the relevant control. The instantaneous utility function can thus be rewritten as

$$u(\tilde{c}A) = \frac{1}{1-\epsilon} (- (\tilde{c}_0 A)^{1-\epsilon} + (\tilde{c}A)^{1-\epsilon}). \tag{2b}$$

3.

The problem to be solved can be stated as

$$\max_{(\tilde{c},n)} \int_0^\infty Lu(\tilde{c}A)e^{-\varrho t}dt$$

subject to equations (1a) and (1b), given some initial levels $L(0)$, $x(0)$, $A(0)$.

A steady state solution to that problem is characterized by the set of equations,[2]

$$f(x) - \tilde{c} - (n+a)x = 0 \tag{3}$$
$$f'(x) = \varrho + \epsilon a \tag{4}$$
$$\tilde{c}((\tilde{c}_0/\tilde{c})^{1-\epsilon} - \epsilon) - (1-\epsilon)(f(x) - xf'(x)) = 0. \tag{5}$$

To prove existence equation (5) is restated as

$$h(\tilde{c}) := \tilde{c} ((\tilde{c}_0/\tilde{c})^{1-\epsilon} - \epsilon) = (1-\epsilon) (f(x) - xf'(x)) =: g(x) .$$

Functions $h(\tilde{c})$ and $g(x)$ are depicted in Figure I where $\epsilon \leqq 1$ is assumed.[3]

Note that $h'(\tilde{c}) = \epsilon((\tilde{c}_0/\tilde{c})^{1-\epsilon}-1) \gtreqless 0$, as $\tilde{c} \lesseqgtr \tilde{c}_0$. Furthermore, $h(\tilde{c}) = 0$ at $\tilde{c} = 0$ and some $\tilde{c} > \tilde{c}_0$. That gives the graph of $h(\tilde{c})$, as depicted in Figure 1. The position of $g(x)$ is determined by the steady state value of x which, in turn, is uniquely given by equation (4). The optimal value of $\tilde{c}$ is given by the intersection of the graphs of $h(\tilde{c})$ and $g(x)$ where $\tilde{c} \geqq \tilde{c}_0$. Since $h(\tilde{c})_{\tilde{c}=\tilde{c}_0} = (1-\epsilon) \tilde{c}$, an intersection exists

---

[2]   Applying Pontryagins's Maximum Principle yields

(i) $- \epsilon \dot{\tilde{c}}/\tilde{c} = \varrho + \epsilon a - f'(x)$

(ii) $u(\tilde{c}) - (\partial u/\partial \tilde{c}) [\tilde{c} - \{f(x) - xf'(x) \}] = 0 .$

Employing equation (2b) gives equation (5). Equation (ii) is known as the Meade-rule (Meade 1955, p. 91) of optimal population (Dasgupta 1969, p. 299). The proof of sufficiency can be adopted from Dasgupta (1969) by assuming, without loss of generality, $A = 1$. It needs not be repeated here. The proof rests on the fact that $Lu (C/L)$ is concave in L and C. It should be emphasized that concavity does not depend on whether ϵ exceeds, or falls short of, unity.

[3]   The proofs follows the lines suggested by Dasgupta 1969. Nothing essential is lost by assuming $\epsilon \leqq 1$. It can be left to the reader to show that in the case $\epsilon > 1$ one obtains $h'(\tilde{c}) > 0$ at the relevant equilibrium point.

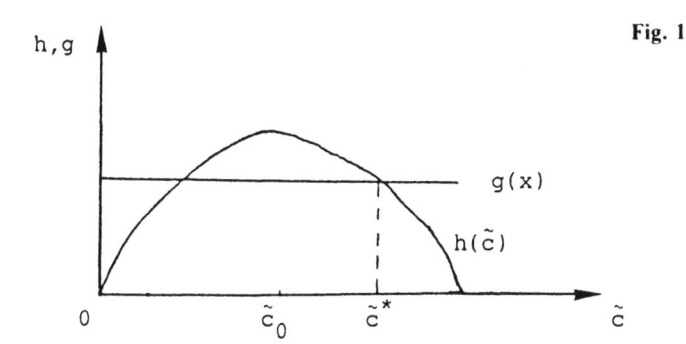
Fig. 1

if $\tilde{c} \geqq f - xf'$. Given $\varrho > 0$, clearly $\tilde{c} > f - xf'$. Once an optimal $\tilde{c}$ has been found, equation (3) yields the optimal rate of population growth,

$$n^* = \frac{f(x) - \tilde{c}}{x} - a.$$

This results in:

Lemma: Given assumptions *A1–A3* an optimal rate of population growth exists where $\tilde{c} > c_0$ provided $\varrho > 0$.

4.

A comparative static analysis can be conducted by using the differential of equations (3) − (5),

$$\begin{pmatrix} f'-n-a & -1 & -x \\ f'' & 0 & 0 \\ (1-\epsilon)xf'' & h' & 0 \end{pmatrix} \begin{pmatrix} dx \\ d\tilde{c} \\ dn \end{pmatrix} = \begin{pmatrix} 0 \\ d\varrho \\ 0 \end{pmatrix} + \begin{pmatrix} 0 \\ \epsilon \\ 0 \end{pmatrix} da$$

where $h'(\tilde{c}) \lessgtr 0$, as $\epsilon \lessgtr 1$.

Since

$$\frac{\partial x}{\partial \varrho} = \frac{1}{f''} < 0$$

$$\frac{\partial n}{\partial \varrho} = \frac{f'-n-a}{xf''} + \frac{(1-\epsilon)}{h'} < 0$$

one obtains:

Proposition 1

Given assumptions *A1-A3*, the higher the rate of time preference the lower will be the stock of capital per efficiency unit of labor and the optimal rate of population growth.

This result confirms the hypothesis that accumulation of physical capital and rearing children are similar phenomena.

Note that the savings ratio $s = 1 - \tilde{c}/f(x)$ and hence

$$\frac{\partial s}{\partial \varrho} = - \frac{f\partial\tilde{c}/\partial\varrho - \tilde{c}f' \, \partial x/\partial\varrho}{f^2}.$$

Since $\partial c/\partial\varrho = -(1-\epsilon)x/h' > 0$ and $\partial x/\partial\varrho < 0$, as shown above, $\partial s/\partial\varrho < 0$. Raising the rate of time preference thus yields a lower savings ratio.

The effect of technical progress on x and n is given by

$$\frac{\partial x}{\partial a} = \frac{\epsilon}{f''} < 0$$

$$\frac{\partial n}{\partial a} = \{-(f'-n-a)\epsilon h' + xf''(h' - \epsilon(1-\epsilon)) \}/\Delta < 0,$$

as $\Delta := - xh'f'' < 0$.

The impact of technological change on the savings ratio can be ascertained by looking at

$$\frac{\partial s}{\partial a} = \frac{f\partial\tilde{c}/\partial a - \tilde{c}f' \, \partial x/\partial a}{f^2}.$$

Noting that $\partial\tilde{c}/\partial a = -x\epsilon(1-\epsilon)h' > 0$ and $\partial x/\partial a < 0$, clearly $\partial s/\partial a < 0$.

Summarizing, one obtains:

Proposition 2

Given assumptions *A1-A3*, an increase in the rate of technological change yields a decline in optimal population growth, a lower stock of capital per efficiency unit of labor and a reduced savings ratio.

This result contrasts strongly with the classical notion of technical progress giving leeway to accelerated population growth.

It appears noteworthy that time preference and technological change exert a similar influence on both capital accumulation and population growth. The expectation of faster growth of consumption per head, due to technical progress, thus works into the same direction as a rise of impatience, as reflected in the rate of pure time preference. That may be interpreted as follows. The expectation of accelerated technological change gives rise to higher aspirations and a concomitant increase in consumption per worker. Just as rising impatience, such an increase in aspirations reduces the desire for further population growth.

5.

Although the results of the foregoing analysis are rather interesting, a couple of shortcomings remain. First of all, the analysis is silent about the distribution of consumption as between the various subgroups of the family. Secondly, it does not touch the problem of the optimal labor force participation ratio. To include that into the analysis additional assumptions regarding the utility function would have been necessary. Finally, technological change itself might be treated as an endogenous variable (see Neumann 1985), which would open the way to analysing the determination of technical change and population growth simultaneously.

References

Dasgupta, P. S. (1969) On the Concept of Optimal Population, Review of Economic Studies 36: 295-318

Easterlin, R. A. (1974) Does Economic Growth Improve the Human Lot? Some Empirical Evidence. In: P. A. David and M. W. Reder (Eds.) Nations and Households in Economic Growth, New York and London: Academic Press

Helson H. (1964) Adaptation-Level Theory. An Experimental and Systematic Approach, New York: Harper & Row

Meade, J. E. (1955) Trade and Welfare, London: Oxford UP

Neumann, M. (1985) Redistributive Income Taxation and Productivity Growth, mimeo

The Serendipity Theorem Reconsidered:
The Three-Generations Case Without Inheritance

Klaus Jaeger

1. Introduction

In his article on the optimum growth rate for population Samuelson (1975) proved within a two-generations model (individuals live and consume for two periods, but provide labor in the first period only) his famous so-called Serendipity Theorem: "At the optimum growth rate g*, private lifetime saving will just support the most golden golden-rule lifetime state". The underlying theory of optimum growth rate for population was criticized mainly on two partly-related grounds: (i) Deardorff (1976) pointed out that Samuelson's solution for the optimum population growth rate g*, derived only from necessary conditions for optimality, is in fact not optimal in general. In the special case in which both utility and production functions are Cobb-Douglas, Samuelson's solution, for those parameter values for which it exists, provides a global *minimum* of steady-state utility. Moreover, Deardorff proved that for CES production functions with substitution elasticity (σ) greater than unity, steady-state utility can be made arbitrarily large by taking g sufficiently close to $-\delta$ (the depreciation rate). In his reply to Deardorff's note, Samuelson (1976) agreed with Deardorff's analysis and results. In addition he mentioned an argument first brought up by Mirrlees: If σ remains bounded above zero as the capital intensity k approaches infinity, for most reasonable forms of the utility function, the solution $g^* = -\delta$ must be a local boundary maximum with finite utility. (ii) Arthur/ McNicoll (1978) evaluated within a neoclassical setting the implications of a change in the growth rate for population (being always equated to the (net) interest rate $r-\delta$) assuming that production and consumption are spread over a continuous-age lifecycle and that people are treated as individuals from birth, with a welfare criterion that reflects their expected lifetime utility of consumption. The main result of this comparative-dynamic analysis of golden rule steady-state paths is that under typical demographic schedules the net intergenerational transfer effect of population growth is in fact negative. Hence the optimum growth rate for population would again occur at the minimum feasible rate, i.e. theoretically at $g = -\delta$.

The general conclusion that can be drawn from (i) and (ii) is that the most critical point of the theory of optimum growth rate for population and thus of the Serendipity Theorem is the question of the existence of an optimal growth rate $g^* > -\delta$ for technologies with $\sigma > 0$. In his comment on Deardorff's criticism, Samuelson, however, stated many good reasons for *not* assuming $\sigma > 0$ as k runs from 0 to ∞ when dealing with the question of optimal population growth rates. Furthermore, in an appendix to his comment, Samuelson analysed the two-genera-

Microeconomic Studies
K. F. Zimmermann (Ed.)
Economic Theory of Optimal Population
© Springer-Verlag Berlin Heidelberg 1989

tions case with fixed-coefficient specifications of the utility and the production functions and showed that under these assumptions, depending on the values of the various parameters, an optimum growth rate for population $g^* > - \delta$ may exist. It is then an easy task to demonstrate that the Serendipity Theorem holds too, if the exonously given interest rate is set at its optimal level $r^* - \delta = g^*$.

Thus the state of the arguments in the debate could now be summarized as follows: Depending on the exact specifications of both the utility *and* the production functions concerning their respective elasticities of substitution an optimum population growth rate $g^* > - \delta$ may or may not exist; accordingly the Serendipity Theorem holds or doesn't hold or, strictly speaking, is significant (if at all) or of little importance because with $r^* - \delta = g^* = - \delta \leqq 0$ the optimal (gross) interest rate would have to be zero. This issue is a little bit unsatisfactory for it can hardly be expected that the controversy about the "right" specifications will be settled within a short time; furthermore the Serendipity Theorem stands or falls with the existence or non-existence of an optimum population growth rate $g^* > - \delta$.

In order to appraise the significance of the whole discussion, however, one has to remember two key assumptions which are made in this kind of two-age groups framework regardless of the assumed kind of utility and production functions: First, household utility does not depend on who consumes the family basket of goods; it is indifferent to the child-adult composition of the family. Second, children do not impose any costs, such as food and clothing, paid for by their parents.

2. Main Assumptions and Principal Results

In the following analysis the two key assumptions just mentioned are modified. It is assumed that each consumer lives and consumes for three periods, but provides labor in the second period only. Individuals in the second year of their life (as workers) take care of their children's (the first generation's) consumption by intergenerational transfers. The well-being of the representative person who works in the second period and retires in the third period of his life when old depends upon the per-capita real consumption of his children and upon his own consumption in the second and third periods of his life, respectively but not on the number of his children. Population growth rate g is exogenously given but changeable by an "authority" looking for a utility maximizing (optimal) growth path. Throughout the paper comparative-dynamic analysis is employed, i.e. only steady-state paths are considered. Finally, the two-factor technology with capital and labor as inputs is supposed to be specified by fixed-coefficients, i.e. $\sigma = 0$; thus the factor prices, especially the interest rate is exogenously determined and, like the growth rate g, a policy variable for the "authority". As usual two different scenarios are considered: a planning and a laissez-faire system (to be defined below). In the first one the "authority" controls all quantity variables including g, in the second one only g and r; in both systems the utility function is identical and the respective optimal steady-state allocation is to be looked for and analysed. The difference between the two systems lies in the fact that in the planning system the "authority", acting for private households so to say, controls all quantities, whereas in the laissez-faire system private housholds decide about their optimal consumption plans for given g and r which are themselves in some sense optimally controlled by the "authority". Any bequests from the retirees to their children or grand-children as well as gifts from children to parents (or grandparents) are excluded in the laissez-faire system. Within this briefly outlined setting, it is shown that:

(i) Depending on the values of various parameters, even in the three-generations case, an optimum growth rate $g^* > -\delta$ at which we are in the most golden golden-rule state of all maximizing lifetime well-being of each generation, does exist;

(ii) For arbitrarily given g falling between certain limits, there is an optimal interest rate $\bar{r}$, at which the utility of each generation in a steady-state is maximized; setting $g = \tilde{g} = \bar{r} - \delta \neq g^*$ this maximum is provided for by voluntary life-cycle personal savings in a laissez-faire system of old-age security, in which workers only save in order to form capital that is exactly consumed during retirement; thus we have a kind of "Modified Serendipity Theorem" stating a second-best solution for population growth rate at $\tilde{g}$ in a laissez-faire system;

(iii) Even if $g^* > -\delta$ does exist, the Serendipity Theorem does *not* hold in this three-generations case, i.e. with $r = g^* + \delta$ it will *not* turn out to be the case that voluntary life-cycle personal savings will just suffice to support the most golden golden-rule steady-state equilibrium without recourse to social security alterations of life-cycle consumption patterns;

(iv) As a corollary of (ii) and (iii), one has the following: By introducing a pay-as-you-go system of old-age security, which taxes each worker α and pays benefits to each retiree of β, optimal values of α^*, $r^* - \delta = g^*$ can be found, assuring in such a mixed system of old-age security the most golden golden-rule steady-state eqilibrium; the optimal value of α^* is equal to the optimal total children's consumption per worker. In other words, an additional pay-as-you-go system is necessary to secure in an otherwise privately organized capital-reserve system of old-age security the bliss-point of well-being.

These four statements clarify that we do not intend to solve the problem of the existence of an optimum population growth rate $g^* > -\delta$ by introducing an additional generation in the well-known two-age groups model; the solution still depends on the specification, especially of the production function. Rather, we want to show that even if an optimal $g^* > -\delta$ exists, the Serendipity Theorem does not hold in more general cases, e.g. in a model with three generations. Hence, the significance of this Theorem is questionable in any case, and not only if $g^* > -\delta$ does not exist. In other words, the existence of an optimal $g^* > -\delta$ is necessary but in general not sufficient for the validity of the Serendipity Theorem. On the other hand, our Modified Serendipity Theorem is theoretically always applicable in a laissez-faire system, if an optimal $g^* > -\delta$ exists. Moreover, introducing a suitable social security program in an otherwise laissez-faire organized old-age security system leads to the most golden golden-rule steady-state allocation of resources. Thus, if at all then only a mixed system and not a strict privately organized capital-reserve system without inheritance can generate such an optimal allocation. Being fair, the social security system does not influence the wealth or income constraint of the private households. Consequently, by manipulating α the "authority" can internalize the external effects induced by children's consumption ("too low" private savings for old-age security), thus enforcing the "optimum optimorum".

The rest of the paper is organized as follows: In Section 3 the formal model is set up and statement (i) is substantiated. The laissez-faire system is analysed in Section 4 and statements (ii) − (iv) are proved in Section 5 with reference to Sections 3 and 4; some short final remarks are given in Section 6.

3. The Planning System

Let[1]

$$u = u(x,y,z) \text{ with: } u_i > 0, u_{ii} < 0, u_{ij} \geq 0 \ (i \neq j \text{ and } i,j = x, y, z) \qquad (1)$$

or

$$u = \text{Min} [x/a, y, z/b] \qquad a, b > 0 \qquad (1\text{ a})$$

be an indicator of ordinal well-being, where x, y and z are per capita consumption as child, worker and retiree, respectively. At time t, there are L_t children, L_{t-1} workers and L_{t-2} retirees. Assuming that all individuals live exactly for three periods and further assuming a constant population growth rate g, i.e. $L_t = L_{t-1} (1+g)$ and $L_{t-1} = L_{t-2} (1+g)$, then at time t total consumption of the young (children), the workers and the elderly are given respectively by

$$X = xL_{t-1} (1+g); \quad Y = yL_{t-1}; \quad Z = zL_{t-1}/(1+g) \qquad (2)$$

The technology is a fixed-coefficient production function as in Samuelson (1976):

$$f(k) = \text{Min} [\lambda, k/\overline{k}] \qquad 1/\overline{k} > \delta > 0 \qquad (3)$$

where $\overline{k}$ is the gross capital-output ratio, $1/\lambda$ is the technical labor-output ratio (L_{t-1}/F), and k is the capital intensity (K/L_{t-1}); total gross output F (gross output per worker f) includes depreciation δK (δk).

With gross output being equal to the sum of total consumption (C = X+Y+Z) and gross investment, i.e.

$$\frac{F}{L_{t-1}} L_{t-1} = C + K_{t+1} - K_t + \delta K_t \qquad (4)$$

one yields from (4) by using (2):

$$F/L_{t-1} = x(1+g) + y + z/(1+g) + (1+g)k_{t+1} - (1-\delta)k_t \qquad (5)$$

Assuming a steady-state ($k_{t+1} \equiv K_{t+1}/L_t = k_t \equiv K_t/L_{t-1}$), eq. (5) reduces to when the capital-labor ratio is technically determined to the production-possibility restriction:

---

[1] Regarding mainly steady-states the time index t is omitted where no misunderstanding is expected. Furthermore the (eventual) pleasure of having children is excluded from (1) or (1a). Including these effects on the optimal program is another story (see e.g. the analysis by Pestieau (1989)).

$$\lambda(1-(g+\delta)\overline{k})-x(1+g)-y-z/(1+g) = 0 \tag{6}$$

Clearly eq. (6) only makes sense, if for x,y,z > 0 the following restriction holds:

$$1/\overline{k}-\delta>g>-1 \tag{7}$$

As Samuelson (1976) pointed out, the value of $\overline{k}$ might be a very small fraction because the length of time of one period in this model is not measured in calendar years but in decades. Thus, with $1/\overline{k}-\delta>0$ (see eq. (3)), g might well be greater than zero.

To find the optimum growth rate g*, at which the most golden golden rule steady-state is attained, one must maximize (1) subject to (6) with respect to x,y,z, and g. The optimal values of these variables (denoted by a star*) satisfy

$$u_1/u_2 = (1+g^*) \tag{8}$$
$$u_2/u_3 = (1+g^*) \tag{9}$$
$$z^*/(1+g^*)^2 = \lambda\overline{k}+x^* \tag{10}$$
$$\lambda(1-(g^*+\delta)\overline{k})-x^*(1+g^*)-y^*-z^*(1+g^*) = 0 ; \quad 1/\overline{k}-\delta>g^* \tag{11}$$

Eqs. (8) and (9) are the "biological interest rate" relations of Samuelson (1958) for the three-part golden rule and (10) is the corresponding implicit condition for optimal g*.

The necessary conditions of (8) $-$ (10) must be supplemented by second-order conditions in order to be sufficient for a true maximum. Define for optimal x*, y*, z* and g*:

$$G_1: = u_{11} - 2(1+g^*)u_{12}+(1+g^*)^2u_{22}< 0 ; \quad g^* > - 1 \tag{12}$$
$$G_2: = (1+g^*)u_{22} - u_{21} +(1+g^*)u_{31} - (1+g^*)u_{32} \gtrless 0 \tag{13}$$

but $G_2 < 0$ if $u_{31} \to 0$

$$G_3: = - u_{12}/(1+g^*)+u_{13}+u_{22} - (1+g^*)u_{23} \gtrless 0 \tag{14}$$

but $G_3 < 0$ if $u_{13} \to 0$

$$G_4: = u_{22}/(1+g^*) - 2u_{23}+(1+g^*)u_{33} < 0 \tag{15}$$

Second-order conditions for a maximum are then given by:

$$G_1 < 0 \tag{16}$$
$$G_1G_4 - G_2G_3 > 0 \tag{17}$$
$$- 2z^*(G_1G_4 - G_2G_3) - u_2 \cdot \sum_{i=0}^{3} (1+g^*)^iG_{i+1} < 0 \tag{18}$$

According to the exact specification of the utility function (1) and the respective strengths of the parameters $[\overline{k},\delta]$, conditions (16) $-$ (18) might hold for $- \delta< g^* < 1/\overline{k} - \delta$ and $\overline{k} < 1$. Consider as a special case the objective function (1a). As a matter of fact, this Leontief-like utility function implies, that for any given F or f, equation (1a) must hold with equality signs for all arguments because otherwise utility could be *ceteris paribus* raised by merely redistributing the given total (or per worker) consumption among the three generations. Then with:

$$x/a = y = z/b \tag{19}$$

maximizing utility from (1a) is tantamount to maximizing y (or x or z). Employing (6) yields:

$$y = \lambda(1 - (g + \delta)\overline{k}) [1 + a(1 + g) + b/(1 + g)]^{-1} \tag{20}$$

With low values for a, which means society attaches little importance to children's consumption, and with high values for b, which means that great importance is attached to consumption during retirement, an optimal g^* lying between $-\delta < g^* < 1/\overline{k} - \delta$ ($\overline{k} < 1$) that maximizes (20) and thus $u = u^*$ from (1a) might exist. This can easily be seen as follows: The numerator of (20) is a linear function in g with slope: $-\lambda\overline{k}$. The denominator has the slope $a - b/(1 + g)^2$. Thus, one can always find values of a and b, respectively, which are low and high enough, so that $-\lambda\overline{k} > a - b/(1 + g)^2 < 0$ and $g > -\delta$ as well as $-\lambda\overline{k} < a - b/(1 + g)^2$ and $g < 1/\overline{k} - \delta$. If this is the case, y in (20) (and u in (1a)) must first increase and then decrease with rising g in a certain range of $-\delta < g < 1/\overline{k} - \delta$ and a truly optimizing $g = g^* > -\delta$ must exist. Then, by differentiating (20) with respect to g, setting $dy/dg = 0$ and using (19) one gets (10) or:

$$z^* = \lambda b\overline{k}(1 + g^*)^2 [b - a(1 + g^*)]^{-1} ; \quad b > a(1 + g^*) \tag{21}$$

Together with (19) and (20) the optimal values of the variables x^*, y^*, z^* and g^* can be determined. In what follows, it is assumed that such an optimum does in fact exist.

4. The Laissez-Faire System Without Social Security

In a laissez-faire system without bequests, each worker starts with zero wealth and maximizes (1) or (1a) subject to a wealth or income constraint. With exogenously given [r,g], this constraint is for a technically determined capital-labor ratio analogous to (6):[2]

$$\lambda(1 - r\overline{k}) - (1 + g) x - y - z/(1 + r - \delta) = 0 ; \quad 1/\overline{k} > r > -1 + \delta \tag{22}$$

In (22) it is assumed that the expenditures for rearing children are fully provided by their parents (the workers), and $z/(1 + r - \delta)$ is today's (in period t) voluntary saving of the representative worker for his own old-age security. It must be stressed that the constraint (22) implies no repayment of the rearing costs by the children, e.g. one period later when they are workers; this again is in line with our assumption (see Section 2) that in the discussed version of the laissez-faire system there are no intergenerational transfers ("gifts" or bequests) except those from parents to children according to the unrepaid expenditures for rearing them. The modifications due to a total or partial repayment of the rearing costs are briefly discussed below (see Section 5).

---

[2] In the following analysis, r always denotes the *gross* interest rate including the depreciation rate δ. Thus $r-\delta$ is the *net* interest rate.

Using (1),[3] the optimizing process with given r and g yields the necessary conditions:

$$u_1/u_2 = 1+g \tag{23}$$
$$u_2/u_3 = 1+r-\delta \tag{24}$$

However, a laissez-faire steady-state equilibrium without intergenerational transfers between workers and retirees requires the following additional equilibrium condition, stating the equality of workers' savings with the system's productive capital (out of which, (net) interest and principal, the retirees consume):

$$z/(1+g) = (1+r-\delta)\lambda\bar{k} \tag{25}$$

Thus, either with given (r,g) z is exogenously determined by (25) and is thus in general not the solution to a utility maximizing process according to (23) und (24), or r and g may not be arbitrarily fixed (within the limits given by (22) and (7)). The formal reason for that is, of course, that the system (22) − (25) for arbitrarily given r and g is over-determined. What then can be done to assure the existence of a steady-state with utility-maximizing behavior of workers and a privately organized capital-reserve-system of old-age security? Assume that the "authority" first sets r in a sort of *tâtonnement* process at its optimal level ($\bar{r}$), at which (1) subject to (22) is maximized with given g, and then equates g with $\bar{r} - \delta$ to satisfy both the old-age security condition (25) of the laissez-faire system and the steady-state condition (6).

The optimal values of the endogenous variables, denoted by $\tilde{x}, \tilde{y}, \tilde{z}$ and $\tilde{r}$, satisfy with *arbitrarily given* $g < 1/\bar{k} - \delta$ (22) − (24) and[4]

$$\tilde{z}/(1+\tilde{r}-\delta) = (1+\tilde{r}-\delta)\lambda\bar{k} \tag{26}$$

By straightforward differentiation of (22) − (24), (26) and solving for $d\tilde{r}/dg$ one yields

$$d\tilde{r}/dg \gtrless 0 \quad \text{if } \tilde{G}_2(u_2 - (1+g)\tilde{x}) - G_1(u_{32}(1+\tilde{r}-\delta) - u_{22}\tilde{x}) \lessgtr 0 \tag{27}$$

assuming that the second order conditions are satisfied. With an appropriate objective function a negative relationship between $\tilde{r}$ and g may exist. Hence, for $\tilde{r} - \delta > g$ the "authority" can equate $\tilde{r} - \delta$ with g by raising g (and vice versa). If g happens to equal $\tilde{r} - \delta$, conditions (25) and (26) are identical and thus private lifetime saving in a laissez-faire system will just support a steady-state equilibrium with maximum $u = \tilde{u}$ at $\tilde{r} - \delta = \tilde{g}$. If such an equilibrium exists, it is unique and indicates for $\tilde{g} \neq g^*$ a kind of second-best solution when compared to $g = g^*$ and $u = u^*$.

---

[3] (1) being perhaps a little bit more general than (1 a) the latter utility function is only occasionally used to get more concrete or explicit results.

[4] Define: $\tilde{G}_2: = (1+g)u_{22} - u_{21} + (1+\tilde{r} - \delta)u_{31} - (1+\tilde{r}-\delta)(1+g)u_{32} < 0$ if
$u_{31} \to 0$ and $g > -1, \tilde{r} > -1 + \delta;$
$\tilde{G}_4: = u_{22} / (1+\tilde{r}-\delta) - 2u_{23} + (1+\tilde{r}-\delta)u_{33} < 0 \quad (\tilde{r} > -1+\delta)$
Then the second-order conditions for a true maximum are:
$G_1 < 0; G_1\tilde{G}_4 - \tilde{G}_2G_3 > 0; -2\tilde{z}[G_1\tilde{G}_4 - \tilde{G}_2G_3] - u_2G_1 < 0.$ Depending on the property of the objective function these conditions might hold. It can easily be demonstrated that this is the case for (1 a). For then one has using (19) and (22):
$x/a = y = z/b = \lambda(1 - r\bar{k})(1+r-\delta)[1+r-\delta+a(1+g)(1+r-\delta) + b]^{-1}$
Sufficient low and high values of a and b respectively yield a true maximizing $r = \tilde{r}$ falling between 0 and $1/\bar{k}$ if $\bar{k} < 1$.

Regarding again (1a) and (19), then using (26) one obtains from (22):

$$d\tilde{r}/dg = - a (1+\tilde{r}-\delta)^2 [2(1+\tilde{r}-\delta)(1+(1+g)a)+(b\overline{k} / \lambda]^{-1} < 0;$$
$$g > - 1; \tilde{r} > \delta - 1 \tag{28}$$

Now, with $\tilde{r} - \delta = \tilde{g}$ and using (26) in the utility maximizing steady-state, equation (22) can be written as:

$$1/\overline{k} - (\tilde{g}+\delta) - a(1+\tilde{g})^3/ b - (1+\tilde{g})^2 / b - (1+\tilde{g}) = 0 \tag{29}$$

For low and high values of a and b respectively this may be approximated by:

$$1 - 2\tilde{g}\overline{k} - (1+\delta) \overline{k} \approx 0 \tag{30}$$

so that:

$$\tilde{g} = \tilde{r} - \delta \approx (1/\overline{k} - 1 - \delta) / 2 \tag{31}$$

Thus, $1+2\tilde{g} < 1 / \overline{k} - \delta$ or $1+2\tilde{r} < 1/\overline{k} + \delta$ are necessary conditions for the existence of a second-best steady-state equilibrium in a laissez-faire system, being somewhat more restrictive than (7) and (22). But nevertheless, depending on $u(\cdot)$ and $f(\cdot)$ such an equilibrium might exist with $- \delta < \tilde{g} = \tilde{r} - \delta$.

5. The Serendipity Theorem Reconsidered and Social Security

Proposition (iii) of Section 2 can now easily be proved. Comparing the optimal conditions for the most golden golden-rule steady-state (8) — (10) with those of the optimal solution of the laissez-faire system (23) — (24) and (26) with $\tilde{r} - \delta = \tilde{g}$ and assuming uniqueness of the respective equilibria one immediately has: $g^* \neq \tilde{g} = \tilde{r} - \delta$ if $x^*, \bar{x} > 0$. Thus, equalizing the net interest rate with g^* violates some or all of the optimal or equilibrium steady-state conditions (22) — (25) or (26) of the laissez-faire system of old-age security because for $g = g^*$ conditions (8) — (11) with $x^* > 0$ must hold; and enforcing the equality of g with the optimal net interest rate of the privately organized capital-reserve-system only guarantees a second-best steady-state equilibrium, i.e. $\bar{u} < u^*$ (essentially (22) — (24) and (26) with $\tilde{g} = \tilde{r}-\delta$). Therefore, the Serendipity Theorem does not hold in the discussed three-generations case without bequests even if an optimal $g^* > - \delta$ exists.[5] Instead, a "Modified Serendipity Theorem" can now be discerned:

With a fixed-coefficient technology at the optimum interest rate $\tilde{r}$ maximizing utility in a laissez-faire system for any given g within its range of definition, private lifetime saving will just support the second-best and not the most golden golden-rule lifetime state, if the growth rate for population is equated to the optimal (net) interest rate, i.e. if $\tilde{g} = \tilde{r} - \delta$; thus $\tilde{g}$ might be termed the second-best population growth rate.

Now the natural question arises, if by adding a social security program to the system, laissez-faire's $\bar{u}$ could be converted to the higher u^* (regarding only steady-

---

[5]   As a matter of fact, the Serendipity Theorem is valid with $x = 0$, i.e. in a simple two-age model (workers, retirees). This can easily be seen by comparing the respective optimal conditions.

state solutions and not the transient paths to such equilibria). The budget identity of the steady-state social security program is given by:[6]

$$\alpha(1+g) = \beta > 0; \quad 0 < \alpha < 1 \tag{32}$$

Using (32) to eliminate β, the generalized income constraint (22) can now be written as:

$$\lambda(1 - r\bar{k}) - (1+g) \, x\text{-}y\text{-}z/(1+r - \delta) + \alpha \, [(1+g) / (1+r - \delta) - 1] = 0 \tag{33}$$

With exogenously given g and r, two cases may at first be distinguished:

(i) $g < r - \delta$. Clearly, in this case it does not pay to introduce a social security program with $\alpha > 0$, as the last term in the brackets of (33) would be negative and thus, the income constraint would be more binding with $\alpha > 0$ than with $\alpha = 0$. Consequently, steady-state utility must always be lower with $\alpha > 0$ than with $\alpha = 0$.

(ii) $g > r - \delta$. This is a Ponzi-like or chain-letter situation. The higher α, the less binding is the income constraint and thus the greater is steady-state lifetime well-being of the representative man or generation. This is so because with the system's growth rate being greater than the (net) interest rate, the present value of a worker's payments to and his benefits from the social security when old is positive. This again indicates that each generation benefits on a lifetime basis be indebting itself to the next generation (the more, the higher the initial debts) making the same with the future generations and so on. In a steady-state this implies an ever increasing (net) stock of debts (with growth rate $g - r + \delta > 0$) which is bequeathed from generation to generation.

Having excluded any (positive or negative) inheritance from the analysis, case (ii) can be also omitted. It remains the case when $g = r - \delta$, where the social security program has no influence on the income constraint (33), i.e. it is fair in the sense that the payments per worker to social security equal the present value of all benefits paid per retiree by the social security sytem. The generalized steady-state condition (25) for such a mixed system of old-age security can then be written as:

$$z /(1+g) = (1+r - \delta) \lambda\bar{k} + \alpha; \quad g = r - \delta \tag{34}$$

stating the equality of total consumption of the retirees with the sum of total transfer payments by workers and the system's capital and interest.

To find the optimal steady-state values of r, g, and α satisfying (34), first assume arbitrarily *given* g and α (within their respective limits) and maximize (1) subject to (33) with respect to x, y, z and r. This process yields the first-order conditions (23) and (24) with $r = \tilde{r}$ and:[7]

$$\tilde{z} /(1+\tilde{r} - \delta) = \lambda\bar{k}(1+\tilde{r} -\delta) + \alpha(1+g) / (1+\tilde{r} - \delta) \tag{35}$$

---

[6] We exclude $\alpha, \beta < o$ for in this case the retired should have to pay transfers to the workers — a not very realistic siutation.
Remember: α: = taxes paid by each worker to finance the pay-as-you-go social security system: β: = benefits received by each retiree from the social security system.

[7] Second-order conditions for a true maximum are assumed to hold (see above).

Now, the "authority" can again equate the population growth rate g with the optimal (net) interst rate just like it was shown above, and then it can choose the optimal α. Looking at (8) — (10) the result of such a procedure is

$$\bar{r} - \delta = r^* - \delta = g^* \tag{36}$$

and

$$\alpha^* = (1+g^*)\, x^* > 0 \tag{37}$$

with a maximum at u = u*. This result is not surprising. Comparing (10) with the general laissez-faire equilibrium condition (25) with $g^* = r - \delta$, it immediately follows that the equilibrium condition of the privately organized capital-reserve system implies z < z* (x* > 0). Thus, introducing a fair social security system (with α^*) leaving the income constraint (22) unaltered and setting $g^* = r - \delta$ two ends can simultaneously be attained: (i) laissez-faire's z is raised to the optimal level z* and (ii) this z* is compatible with the optimal conditions of the individual utility maximizing process in the laissez-system ((23), (24)) leading to x* and y*. Thus statement (iv) of Section 2 is proved. It can be summarized as follows: With a fixed-coefficient technology at the optimum growth rate g* and optimal interest rate $r^* - \delta = g^*$, private lifetime saving will just support the most golden golden-rule lifetime state (u = u*) in a three-age group model with children depending on their parents, if a pay-as-you-go system of old-age security is added taxing each worker $\alpha^* = (1+g^*)x^*$, i.e. setting the contribution per worker equal to optimum total children's consumption per worker.

There is at least one objection which may be raised to the above analysis. If one assumes that the children repay their rearing costs, including net interest, to their parents one period later (when they are workers) the Serendipity Theorem is again valid even in the three-generations case. This can easily be seen as follows: The (expected) present value of the repayments (per worker) is simply given by x(1+g) (1+r— δ) / (1+r —δ) = (1+g) x; a worker has to repay his own rearing costs (including net interest) to his (retired) parents or exactly to one retiree, i.e. each worker has to pay in the assumed steady-state: $(1+r -\delta) X_{t-1}/L_{t-1} = (1+r - \delta) x$. Thus, instead of (22), the budget constraint of a worker deciding about his lifetime consumption had now to be written as:

$$\lambda(1 - r\bar{k}) - (1+r - \delta)x-y-z \,/\, (1+r - \delta) = 0 \tag{22'}$$

because the expected present value of the repayments (per worker) exactly equals the rearing costs (per worker) and thus the term (1+g) x vanishes. Maximizing (1) subject to (22') yields with given r (and g) the necessary condition:

$$u_1/u_2 = (1+r -\delta) \tag{23'}$$

and (24) remains as before. Instead of (25) the laissez-faire equilibrium condition for old-age security *with* this sort of intergenerational transfers would now be given by

$$z \,/(1+g) = (1+r - \delta)\, \lambda\bar{k} + (1+r - \delta)\, x \tag{25'}$$

Hence, by setting $r - \delta$ equal to g* one obtains the "optimum optimorum" in a laissez-faire system, i.e. essentially the conditions (8)-(11) of the planning system.

We have excluded from our analysis any "gifts" from children to parents or bequests but it should be emphasized once more that our results do depend critically on the non-existence of such intergenerational transfers. In our opinion, however, there are at least two reasons for *not* assuming such transfers: (i) the repayment of the rearing costs by the children in the way shown above is tantamount to the assumption that people are treated *as individuals from birth* maximizing their (expected) lifetime utility of consumption by borrowing and lending as e.g. in Arthur/McNicoll (1978). This is not a very realistical view because total rearing costs (including net interest) are never exactly repaid or financed by borrowing and rearing costs are in general regarded by the parents as lost expenditures. (ii) if only a fraction of the rearing costs would be repaid, the Serendipity Theorem is again not valid in the three-generations case. Assume γ to be that fraction. From the above argument, it immediately follows that a pay-as-you-go system of old-age security with an optimal $\alpha^* = (1 - \gamma)(1+g^*)x^*$ has to be introduced to secure the "optimum optimorum" in a laissez-faire system with $r^* - \delta = g^*$. Thus in general one cannot expect the Serendipity Theorem to be valid.

On the other hand, regarding γ as a policy variable $(0 \leq \gamma \leq 1)$ the "optimum optimorum" in a laissez-faire system can be supported by an infinity of different (α^*,γ) combinations with $d\alpha^* / d\gamma = -(1+g^*)x^*$, i.e. the social security system and the *individual* bearing of the rearing costs are substitutes. It is really indifferent in this most golden golden-rule steady-state whether the society decides to tax each worker high or low (high or low values of α^*) in order to finance a pay-as-you-go social security if the *individual* burden of bearing the own rearing costs are simultaneously reduced or increased (low or high values of the "self-financing ratio" γ). In other words, if the intergenerational transfers according to unrepaid rearing costs from parents to children are increased, taxes per worker must also be increased in the "optimum optimorum" and vice versa. This is so, because lowering γ (increasing these intergenerational transfers) means increasing "external financing" of the "private" rearing costs and thus an increasing α^* must internalize these external effects.

6. Final Remarks

Generalizing the original two-age groups model by introducing an additional generation dependent on its parents (the workers), it has been shown that the existence of an optimum population growth rate $g^* > -\delta$ is, as usual, conditioned by the specification of the production function (and in a smaller degree by that of the utility function) but that the existence of $g^* > -\delta$ by no means implies the validity of the Serendipity Theorem as stated by Samuelson. Instead, a Modified Serendipity Theorem has been proved showing a sort of second-best solution for the population growth rate in a laissez-faire system. However, by supplementing the privately organized capital-reserve system of old-age security by a fair pay-as-you-go social security system, the best of all steady-states can be reached in such a mixed system, if g, r and α are accordingly manipulated (by a benevolent "authority").

On the other hand, this "optimum optimorum" can also be obtained in a laissez-faire system without any social security program ($\alpha = 0$), i.e. the Serendipity Theorem is valid even in the three-generations case, if the "self-financing ratio"' γ indicating the fraction of the rearing costs *paid for by the children* when they are workers is set equal to one. Otherwise, for $0 \leqq \gamma < 1$ taxing each worker an amount equal to his unrepaid rearing costs in order to finance a pay-as-you-go social security system is a necessary condition for the "optimum optimorum" in a laissez-faire system. As a consequence, the Serendipity Theorem is not valid in general even if $g^* > - \delta$ exists.

The assumptions underlying the foregoing analysis have been heroically over-simplified. Some of these simplifications could be remedied without altering the essential quality of the results. But the most critical point of the present argument should be again explicitly mentioned, that is the exclusive concentration on steady-state paths. Neither stability problems which are more serious in a fixed-coefficient technology than with production functions with substitution elasticity greater than zero, nor the welfare implications of going from one steady-state to another one have been analysed. Thus, even if the stability of the steady-states is assumed, just because a laissez-faire system is observed in a second-best steady-state equilibrium [$\bar{u}, \bar{r} - \delta = \bar{g}$] this does not mean that society necessarily wishes to move to the higher most golden golden-rule state u^* (with or without an additional social security program), as doing so would necessarily imply a transient sacrifice of consumption (and thus of utility) by some generations. To decide if such a transition would be preferable to society, one would have to know its systematic time preference and this might prove the changing of the second-best solution to be intertemporally ineffi-cient.

Bearing these caveats in mind, the results of the present analysis are not very surprising. A fully-informed "authority" can always plan *all* quantities (including g and thus L) such that society is in the best of all steady-states (u^*) and (assuming uniqueness) the corresponding dual (shadow) price system can to the trick as well with exogenously given optimal $g = g^*$ where individuals maximize utility over their own lifetimes under perfect competition if *no* externalities are present. In other words: fixing all exogenously given quantities at their respective optimal levels, a perfectly competitive price system without externalities will lead to satisfaction of all optimal equilibrium conditions of the planning system (assuming stability and uniqueness of the equilibrium). Having proved this for a growing economy in a steady-state is the merit of Samuelson's analysis and this, in fact, is in our opinion the essential meaning of his original two-part Serendipity Theorem. But in our case, in which workers maximize only over their own lifetimes *and* plan optimal present consumption for their own children, an exogenous (changeable) growth rate g ($\neq 0$) acts like an externality, for a varying g has a threefold influence (one positive, two negative) on consumption (and u), the gain and the loss in utility being just equated at optimal $g = g^*$: the higher the rate of population growth g, the more the need to "waste" resources on the "widening" of capital to assure a constant (steady-state) capital intensity $\lambda\bar{k}$ *and* on the rearing of children with constant per capita consumption x; on the other hand, a high population growth rate gives retired peo-ple many workers to rely on, i.e. every retired person stands on the shoulders of more workers. The first and the third effect might be internalized by an optimal price system in a two-age model ($g^* = r^* - \delta$), but the second is not in the three-generations case. This is so because a changing g alters the current composition of familiy's consumption and thus *society's* exchange ratio $(1 + g)$ between per capita consumption of children and parents (workers), respectively, without having any influence on the (relative) price of the respective present consumption goods which are always exchanged on a one to one basis. This discrepancy between society's and individuals' exchange ratios is neglected by the parents (the workers) optimizing over their own lifecycle only for exogenously given g (and r). Thus, for $g^* = r - \delta$ and $0 \leq \gamma < 1$ either the individual optimizing process violates the equilibrium condition of the privately organized capital-reserve-system or the optimal conditions do not hold leading to voluntary "under-saving" per worker, i.e. a "too low" per capita consumption of the retirees if the rearing costs are not fully repaid by the children when they are workers. In any case, this situation requires direct intervention by the state to redistribute consumption by lump-sum taxation ($\alpha^* L_{t-1}$) in an amount equal to children's consumption unrepaid $[(1 - \gamma)(1 + g^*) x^* L_{t-1}; 0 \leq \gamma < 1]$, in order to guarantee the best intertemporal steady-state allocation (u^*) in an otherwise privately organized laissez-faire system. Another possibility to internalize these external effects might be to assume an endogenously determined population growth rate g with inheritance by introducing the number of children or the growth rate g as explicit arguments in the utility function. However, this is reserved for explicit analysis elsewhere.

References

Arthur, W. B. and McNicoll, G. (1978) Samuelson, Population and Intergenerational Transfers. International Economic Review 19: 241-246

Deardorff, A. V. (1976) The Optimum Growth Rate for Population: Comment. International Economic Review 17: 510-515

Pestieau, P. (1989) Endogenous Population and Fixed Input in a Growth Model with Altruism, in this volume

Samuelson, P. A. (1958) An Exact Consumption-Loan Model of Interest with or without the Social Contrivance of Money. Journal of Political Economy 66: 467-482

Samuelson, P. A. (1975) The Optimum Growth Rate for Popualtion. International Economic Review 16: 531-538

Samuelson, P. A. (1976) The Optimum Growth Rate for Population: Agreement and Evaluations. International Economic Review 17: 516-525

III. Limited Resources

Endogenous Population and Fixed Input in a Growth Model With Altruism[1]

Pierre Pestieau

1. Introduction

Analyses of economic growth may treat population as an independent variable or as an endogenous one. To each of these two approaches may be associated a certain theoretical view of growth. Modern growth theories in the tradition of Ramsey and Solow are based on a constant proportional rate of population growth as the essential driving force of the mechanism with perhaps some aid from technological progress. The classical economists, especially Ricardo, rely on the idea that in the presence of fixed inputs per capita consumption tends eventually to fall and to reach a floor at which population stops growing. Dividing these two views, there is not only the question of whether population is independent of economic considerations but also that of whether there is a natural resource constraint that cannot be removed by substitution with reproductible inputs or by technological progress.

The latter issue is an important one although neglected for many years by economists. There are various reasons for this neglect and one of the most important is that so far there has been no real resource constraint which has not been solved in some way or another and there seems little likelihood of such a constraint becoming effective in the near future. Whether this situation will be maintained in the far future is controversed and largely outside the realm of economic analysis. What can be said is that there are no sufficiently persuasive reasons to conclude there is no limit to economic expansion. Thus, to base a long-run theory on some input scarcity is at least as valid as to brush the problem away. As Goodwin (1978) puts it: "If we cannot predict disaster, we cannot predict its avoidance either".

As to the population issue, the evidence for there being some simple set of economic determinants of fertility and mortality is not very strong. Nevertheless to assume constant population growth is not realistic and the classical idea that the effects of resource scarcity ought to be incorporated in the analysis of population growth cannot be denied.

Indeed the two basic Ricardian assumptions, endogenous population and fixed inputs, are usually discussed and objected to separately[2] whereas they are in fact inseparable : it is the fixed supply of inputs which makes population dependent on per capita income. This is the thesis adopted in this paper.

---

[1] I wish to thank Helmuth Cremer, Steve Slutsky and a referee for helpful comments.

[2] The traditional literature on the optimum population does not deal with the possibility of a fixed factor and inversely most analyses of limits to growth do not consider population as an endogenous variable. See however Dasgupta (1969) section 3.

Microeconomic Studies
K. F. Zimmermann (Ed.)
Economic Theory of Optimal Population
© Springer-Verlag Berlin Heidelberg 1989

The argument is presented in an intergenerational model of consumption in which the utility of each generation depends on the level of its consumption, the size of the following generation and some index of altruism towards future generations. Though the Ricardian stationary state cannot be avoided, it is shown that the path of population growth and the stationary level of per capita income depend on the degree of altruism towards future generations. It is also shown that if within each generation individuals are not alike, they might behave "demographically" as free riders and thus lead to a growth of population which could be considered as not socially optimal.

The viewpoint taken in the paper is positive rather than normative. In contrast to the literature on optimal population, here we try to find the population growth that would actually take place rather than that which ought to take place.

The paper is organized as follows: In section 2, both neo-classical and Ricardian models of growth, stripped to the basics, are compared. Section 3 sets up the intergenerational model. Sections 4 and 5 discuss the cases corresponding to various degrees of altruism between and within generations respectively.

2. Ricardian Versus Neo-Classical Growth Model[3)]

The framework is very simple. The economy possesses three inputs: a fixed flow of input (E), capital (K) and labour (L). Output (Y) is produced from these inputs under conditions of constant returns to scale and can be either consumed or invested to augment the stock of capital services which depreciates exponentially at the rate μ. Population and labour force grow at the percentage rate n to be defined later.

The constant returns to scale production function can be written as:

$$Y = F(K, L, E)$$

or, in per-head terms,

$$y = f(k, e)$$

One has also:

$$\frac{\dot{Y}}{Y} = W_K \frac{\dot{K}}{K} + W_L n$$

where $\dot{Y} = \dfrac{dY}{dt}$ and $\dot{K} = \dfrac{dK}{dt}$, W_K and W_L denote the factor share of capital and labor respectively. By assumption $W_K + W_L + W_E = 1$, W_E being the fixed input's share. In per capita terms,

$$\frac{\dot{y}}{y} = W_K \frac{\dot{k}}{k} - W_E n \tag{1}$$

[3)] For similar presentation, see Johansen (1967) and Pichford (1974).

Table 1.

Model	Population growth (n)	Share of natural resources (W_E)
Neo-classical	fixed	$0^{a)}$
Classical	h (y − m)	positive
	h′ > 0, h (0) = 0	
	m = constant	

a) W_E could be positive with E being non essential.

Table 1 summarizes the main distinctions between the two models. In the neo-classical one, the rate of change in the capital-labor ratio is, by definition and assumption:

$$\dot{k} = sy - (n + \mu) k \qquad (2)$$

where s is the constant savings ratio.

One can easily show the existence of a positive capital-labor ratio to which the system would converge; in the long run capital and output both grow at the same rate as labour. There is nothing to prevent population from growing at that given rate. Of course, assuming away the fixed input is the essential reason for this.

In the Ricardian model, both labor and capital growth can be represented by the following two differential equations:

$$n \equiv \frac{\dot{L}}{L} = h (y - m) \qquad m > 0 \qquad (3)$$

$$\frac{\dot{K}}{K} = s \frac{Y}{K} - \mu \qquad \mu > 0, \qquad (4)$$

where m is Ricardo's natural price of labor, a minimum level of subsistence and h(.) is the population growth function.

We can draw some conclusions from this by implicit differentiation of (3):

$$\frac{F_L}{L} dL + \frac{F_K}{L} dK - \frac{Y}{L^2} dL = 0 \qquad (5)$$

where:

$$F_L \equiv \frac{\delta F}{\delta L} \quad \text{and} \quad F_K \equiv \frac{\delta F}{\delta K}$$

Rearranging (5) yields:

$$\frac{dK}{dL}\frac{L}{K} = \frac{Y - F_L \cdot L}{F_K \cdot K} = \frac{W_E + W_K}{W_K} > 1 \tag{6}$$

Similarly, differentiating (4) yields:

$$\frac{dK}{dL}\frac{L}{K} = \frac{F_L L}{Y - F_K K} = \frac{1 - W_K - W_E}{1 - W_K} < 1 \tag{7}$$

Using (6) and (7), one easily shows that whatever the initial values of L and K the economy tends to a stationary state L*, K*, at which point the return to labor and capital will be at fixed levels:

$$\frac{F(K^*, L^*, E)}{K} = \frac{\mu}{s} \quad \text{and} \quad y = m$$

and all economic variables will stop growing.

From this quick review, it appears that the two Ricardian assumptions are necessary to achieve the stationary solution. Without fixed input, population could grow at a fixed rate. Without the endogenous population, the economy would tend to an unbearable zero per capita income. In the remainder of this paper, rather than taking population growth as some function of per capita income, we will deduce it from the behavior of a society which facing a fixed input chooses a rate of reproduction which maximizes a given utiltiy function.

3. The Basic Model

1. *Individuals.* Let L_t be the number of identical individuals of generation t born at $t - 1$. Each generation lives one period and then chooses the number of its children n_t so that $L_{t+1} = L_t n_t$. The parameter n_t is thus the gross rate of population growth.

2. *Consumption.* The output to be consumed in time t is a function of two factors: the number of people L_t and some fixed flow of input E. In the absence of capital, the introduction of which would not add anything to the argument, consumption and output are equivalent. We have in per capita terms:

$$y_t = f(e_t) \tag{8}$$

where $f' > 0$ and $f'' < 0$; y_t is the per capita consumption and e_t the per capita fixed input.

It will be assumed that individuals starve below a certain level m of consumption; with that constraint, if f(.) is a C.E.S. production function:

$$f(\cdot) = [a + b \, e_t^{-\beta}]^{-\frac{1}{\beta}} \tag{8'}$$

where $a + b = 1$ and $\beta \geq -1$, there can be an upper limit to population growth. Indeed,

$$L < L^* = \left(\frac{m^{-\beta} - a}{b}\right)^{\frac{1}{\beta}} E$$

For $\beta = 1$ (perfect substitution):

$$L^* = \infty \qquad \text{if } m \leqslant a$$

$$L^* = \frac{b\,E}{m - a} \qquad \text{if } m > a$$

For $\beta = 0$ (Cobb-Douglas):

$$L^* = m^{-1/b}\,E$$

For $\beta = \infty$ (perfect complementarity):

$$L^* = \frac{E}{b\,m}$$

The implication of a maximum level of population is quite clearly that population cannot grow forever. If the rate of population growth is positive, and there is some fixed input, the classical law of decreasing returns leads to a level of population beyond which people starve. Thus the question to be dealt with is twofold: What is the path of the population growth rate and can there be an equilibrium for which individuals' consumption would be above the subsistence level. Answers to these questions will depend on the degree of altruism of individuals towards future generations and towards their contemporaries.

3. Utility Function. Let u_t be the utility indicator of people in generation t. We assume that each individual's welfare depends upon his own consumption and the number of his children; it can also reflect some concern for the future. The way such concern is expressed will determine an explicit formulation of the utility function. This can range from mere egotism to concern for all future generations[4].

— egotist utility :

$$u_t = u\,(y_t,\, n_t) \tag{9}$$

— concern for one's children's consumption:

$$u_t = u\,(y_t,\, n_t,\, y_{t+1}) \tag{10}$$

— concern for one's children's utility[5]:

$$u_t = u\,(y_t,\, n_t,\, u\,(y_{t+1},\, n_{t+1},\, u\,(\dots)))$$

with such a function, generation t lives forever through its offspring. Assuming that the function is additive, that is, $u_t = u\,(y_t,\, n_t) + \lambda\, u_{t+1}$, one has:

---

[4]   The assumption that there is a positive utiltiy in having children is traditional in the literature on optimum population. See, for example, Votey (1969). As to the altruism towards future generations, see Razin and Ben-Zion (1975) and Nerlove et al. (1987).

[5]   Function (11) is sometimes called nonpaternalistic whereas function (10) would be paternalistic. The term paternalism is used to emphasize the fact that generations care about what others actually consume and not the utilities they derive from the act of consumption. See Ray (1985).

$$u_t = \sum_{s=t}^{\infty} u(y_s, n_s) \lambda^{s-t} \tag{11}$$

where $\lambda < 1$ is the subjective rate of time preference.

— limited concern for one's children's utility:

$$u_t = u(y_t, n_t) + \delta \lambda \sum_{s=t+1}^{\infty} u(y_s, n_s) \lambda^{s-t} \tag{12}$$

where λ has the same meaning as above and δ is a measure of the degree towards the present generation t values future generations' consumption and fertility relative to its own.

With $\delta = 1$, one has perfect altruism as in (11); with $0 < \delta < 1$, one has imperfect altruism. Another way to express imperfect altruism is by using a utility function in which the altruistic concern is restricted to the next generation:

$$u_t = u(y_t, n_t) + \delta u(y_{t+1}, n_{t+1}) \tag{13}$$

These utility functions have the standard quasi-concavity properties with two particularities: utility is zero for per capita income below the subsistence level m and beyond a certain number of children $\bar{n}$, marginal utility of having children is zero. It is assumed that both m and $\bar{n}$ are constant over time, and that $m > 0$ and $\bar{n} > 1$.

4. Altruism Between Generations

We now show that the stationary level of income and the equilibrium population size, if any, are closely dependent on the degree of altruism between generations.

4.1 Egotist Utility

At time t, y_t is given. Individuals alive at that time choose to have the number of children n_t which will maximize the utility (9). They will choose $\bar{n}$. After r periods, the minimum of subsistence is reached, where r is such that:

$$L_t \bar{n}^r \leqslant L^* < L_t \bar{n}^{r+1}$$

Assuming for simplicity that $L_t \bar{n}^r = L^*$, two things can happen after r periods: Either individuals choose $\bar{n}$ leading to $(\bar{n} - 1) L^*$ deaths of starvation or if total production is equally divided, doomsday is unavoidable.[6]

---

[6]   This conclusion is at odds with of Eckstein et al. (1989) who show that selfish and short-sighted individuals can induce a non-subsistence steady state. In their model however the consumption cost of children enters individuals' budget constraint.

4.2 Altruism Limited to Next Period Consumption

Again in period t, generation t only controls its rate of growth n_t and chooses it in order to maximize (10) subject to (8). One of the problems with this maximization is that both the indifference curve and the transformation curve in the plane y_{t+1}, n_t are convex towards the origin; thus a necessary condition for an interior maximum is that the slope of the indifference curve diminishes faster than the slope of the transformation curve as n_t increases. Such a restriction is not really serious to the extent that one can reasonably assume that y_{t+1} and n_t are not substitutable in each individual preferences. On Figure 1, for the case where $y_t = e_t$ which is assumed throughout this section, we illustrate this point.

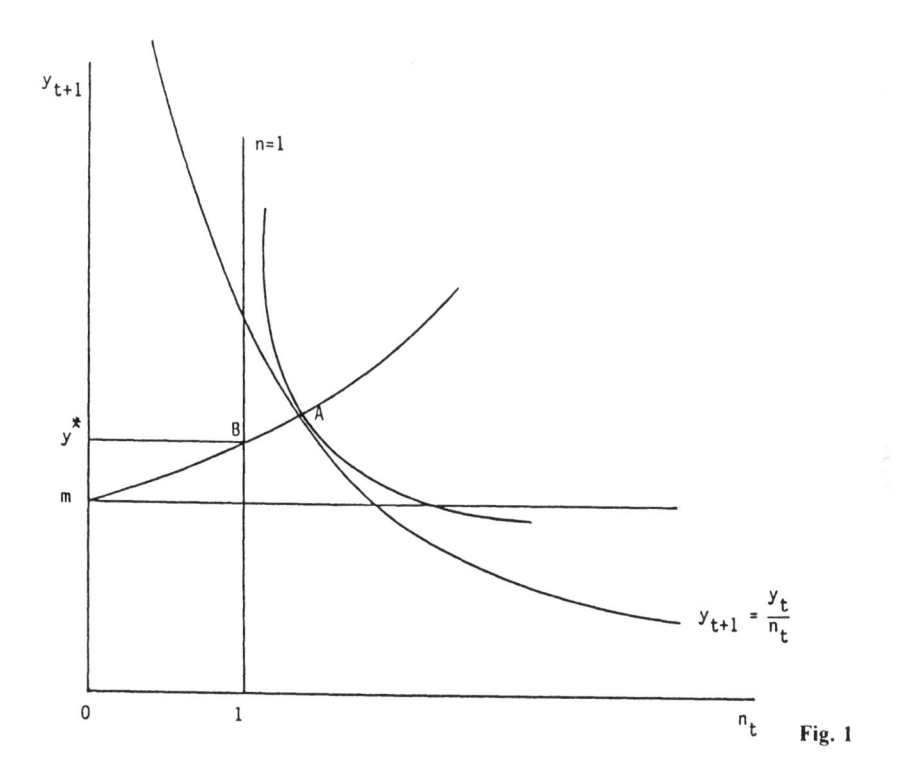

Fig. 1

For any value of y_t at time t, there is a rectangular hyperbola and an equilibrium point A such as depicted on Figure 1. If one connects all these equilibrium points, one gets an expansion path m B A. The stationary point is B but it is not clear that the economy converges smoothly to that point. Also, the stationary per capita income y^* can be more or less above the subsistence level m depending on the utility function.

To see that more clearly, we maximize (10) subject to the constraint:

$$y_{t+1} n_t = y_t \tag{14}$$

The first and second-order conditions for a maximum are respectively:

$$u_2 - u_3 \, y_t \, n_t^{-2} = 0 \tag{15}$$

and

$$\frac{u_2}{n_t} \left(\frac{u_{22}}{u_2} n_t + \frac{u_{33}}{u_3} y_{t+1} + 2 \right) < 0 \tag{16}$$

where u_i and u_{ii} are the first and second order partial derivatives with respect to the i_{th} argument and where the cross-derivatives are assumed to be zero (separability).

Rewriting (15) gives:

$$n_t = \frac{u_3}{u_2} y_{t+1} \tag{17}$$

Equation (17) may be interpreted as describing at any point in time t the optimum rate of population growth as a function of the trade-off between the desire of having children and the satisfaction of having them "well-fed".

Combining (17) and (14), one gets the following first-order non linear difference equation:

$$y_t = \left(\frac{u_2}{u_3} y_{t-1} \right)^{1/2} \tag{18}$$

One would like to show that it converges towards the steady-state solution:

$$y^* = \frac{u_2^*}{u_3^*} \tag{19}$$

Note first that the level of the equilibrium value of per capita consumption is thus equal to the marginal rate of substitution between next generation's average income and current fertility. In other words, it decreases with the degree of altruism towards next generation.

With respect to convergence, the necessary and sufficient condition for local stability, i.e. stability around the equilibrium value y^*, is:

$$-1 \leqslant \left. \frac{dy_t}{dy_{t-1}} \right|_{y_t = y^*} = \frac{R_2 - 1}{R_2 + R_3 - 2} \leqslant 1 \tag{20}$$

where $R_2 \equiv -\dfrac{u_{22}}{u_2}$, $R_3 = -\dfrac{u_{33}}{u_3}$ and $R_2 + R_3 - 2 > 0$ from (16)

Hence, the conditions for local stability are that either $R_2 > 1$, $R_3 > 1$ or $R_2 < 1$ and $R_3 + 2 R_2 > 3$. This amounts to saying that the indifference curves in the (n_t, y_{t+1}) space ought to be strongly convex. If conditions (20) holds everywhere, one then has global stalibility as well.

4.3 Perfect Altruism

Let us now assume that the utility of each generation is a function of the level of its consumption and the number and the utility of the newly born children. Hence, one is led to consider the utility of an infinite number of generations as in (11). One can easily show that the stationary relation of this problem (max (11) subject to (8)) is simply given by:

$$u_n \frac{1-\lambda}{\lambda} = u_y \, y^* \tag{21}$$

where $u_n \equiv \dfrac{\delta u \, (y, n)}{\delta n}$ and $u_y \equiv \dfrac{\delta u \, (y, n)}{\delta y}$. Again, one can show that if the degree of concavity of the utility function is high enough, then the stationary income y^* increases with λ $(0 < \lambda < 1)$. One may add that if λ is also equal to the social rate of time preference, the solution obtained here can be viewed as socially optimal.

4.4 Imperfect Altruism

When turning to utility functions (12) or (13) such that each generation displays a limited degree of altruism towards future generations, it is no longer true that the population growth pattern expected by generation t is going to be implemented by subsequent generations. In other words, in the present setting intertemporal consistency does not hold anymore, and a new notion of equilibrium has to be introduced.

There is an analogy between this problem and that of choosing the rate of saving in the growth literature. In that respect, Phelps and Pollak (1968) using a utility function such as (12) assume that generation expects each succeeding generation to choose the saving ratio that is best from its own viewpoint. This leads to a game-theoretic equilibrium sequence of saving ratios having the property that no generation acting alone can do better and all generations act so as to warrant the expectations of the future ratios. Kohlberg (1976) has later taken the same approach but restricted the altruism of each individual to his immediate successor as in (13). In the growth context with reproducible capital, there is an infinite number of long run equilibrium savings ratio. However, with a fixed input, the problem is by far more complex. At time t, an individual will choose n_t in order to maximize (13); he would like his heirs to choose the highest possible n_{t+1}; yet he realizes that these heirs, out of their altruism for their own heirs, would not do so. The first-order condition for an interior maximum (assumed to exist) is:

$$n_t \frac{\delta u \, (y_t, n_t)}{\delta n_t} - \lambda \, y_{t+1} \frac{\delta u \, (y_{t+1}, n_{t+1})}{\delta y_{t+1}} = 0 \tag{22}$$

From (22) one has an implicit relationship between n_t, y_t and n_{t+1} denoted by:

$$n_t = \psi \, (y_t, n_{t+1}) \tag{23}$$

The long-run solution of this process is simply given by:

$$n = \psi\, (\hat{y}, n) = 1 \tag{24}$$

with $\hat{y} \geqslant m$. $\hat{y}$ can be viewed as an equilibrium for all subsequent generations in the game theoretic sense; no generation acting alone could increase its total utility given the decisions of the other generations. Phelps and Pollak have used the term "Cournot-Nash equilibrium" to label this particular type of solution, however the question of how can this equilibrium be reached, still remains unanswered.

To illustrate the problem at hand, let us use the following utility function:

$$u_t = (y_t^{-\beta} + n_t^{-\beta})^{-\frac{1}{\beta}} + (y_t^{-\beta}\, n_t^{\beta} + n_{t+1}^{-\beta})^{-\frac{1}{\beta}} \tag{25}$$

where β is positive and such that the second-order condition for a maximum is satisfied. The first-order condition is:

$$y_t = n_t^2\, \lambda^{\frac{1}{\beta}} \left\{ \frac{y_t^{-\beta} + n_t^{-\beta}}{y_{t+1}^{-\beta} + n_{t+1}^{-\beta}} \right\}^{\frac{1+\beta}{\beta^2}} \tag{26}$$

From (26), one obtains a relation between n_t and n_{t+1} for a given y_t, as in (23). The dynamic path is going to depend on both the nature of this relation and on the nature of expectations. Suppose that individuals expect n_{t+1} to be equal to n_t. It is far from being certain that eventually that stationary solution will be attained. That is,

$$\hat{y} = \lambda^{1/\beta} \quad \text{and} \quad n = 1 \tag{27}$$

In fact, it can easily be shown that if the individuals expect $n_{t+1} = (n_t)^{1/2}$, then y_t converge towards $\lambda^{1/\beta}$ and n_t towards 1 but clearly this is quite a particular kind of expectation.

5. Altruism Within a Generation

In the previous section the rate of population growth towards its stationary state as well as the stationary state itself have been shown to depend on the degree of altruism between generations. In this section, it is argued that within each generation the degree of altruism does matter as well. So far individuals of a given generation were assumed to be identical. If they are not, each of them may be tempted to have more children than he ought optimally, hoping that the others will not follow and thus his children will not suffer from overpopulation. This problem has clearly the same structure as that of the "free rider" in the public good literature[7].

At time t, total income is Y_t, population L_t and each individual i = 1, ..., L_t has a utility function:

---

7) Buchanan (1968)

$$u_t^i = u(y_t, n_t^i, y_{t+1})$$ (28)

where:

$$y_{t+1} = \frac{y_t L_t}{L_{t+1}} \equiv \frac{y_t}{n_t}$$ (29)

If he considers the number of children n_t^j of the other agents j as given, the i_{th} individual tries to choose n_t^i so as to maximize (28); in view of (29); this requires:

$$n_t^i = \frac{u_3^i}{u_2^i} \frac{y_{t+1}}{L_t}$$ (30)

The optimality condition comes from the following Pareto maximization:

$$\underset{n_t^i, y_{t+1}}{\text{Max}} \quad \sum_i \lambda^i u_t^i$$

subject to the constraint (29). It is simply:

$$n_t^i = \frac{y_{t+1}}{L_t} \sum_i \frac{u_3^i}{u_2^i}$$ (31)

Comparing (30) and (31) shows that in an economy where each individual is concerned only with the advantages that he personally will gain from his decision, regardless of the gain to others, the number of children is too high. Clearly, such an equilibrium is properly speaking a non-cooperative equilibrium for the game corresponding to the economy. Obviously, it is to the mutual advantage of everyone in this game to favor a state that is attainable only by concerted agreement, but this requires some altruism among individuals.

This "free rider" scenario is similar to that first sketched in 1833 by the mathematician William Forster Lloyd and recently revisited by the biologist philosopher Garnett Hardin (1968) under the name the Tragedy of Commons[8]. It is interesting to read the way a non-economist envisions the free rider problem.

"The tragedy of the commons develops in this way. Picture a pasture open to all. It is to be expected that each herdsman will try to keep as many cattle as possible on the commons. Such an arrangement may work reasonably satisfactorily for centuries because tribal wars, poaching and disease keep the numbers of both man and beast well below the carrying capacity of the land. Finally, however, comes the day of reckoning, that is, the day when the long-desired goal of social stability becomes a reality. At this point, the inherent logic of the commons remorselessly generates tragedy.

As a rational being, each herdsman seeks to maximize his gain. Explicitly or implicitly, more or less consciously, he asks, "What is the utility to me adding one

---

[8] I am indebted to Serge Feld for bringing this article to my attention.

more animal to my herd ?" This utility has one negative and one positive component.

1) The positive component is a function of the increment of one animal. Since the herdsman receives all the proceeds from the sale of the additional animal, the positive utility is nearly + 1 .

2) The negative component is a function of the additional overgrazing created by one more animal. Since, however, the effects of overgrazing are shared by all the herdsman, the negative utility for any particular decisionmaking herdsman is only a fraction of − 1.

Adding together the component partial utilities, the rational herdsman concludes that the only sensible course for him to pursue is to add another animal to his herd. And another; and another . . . But this is the conclusion reached by each and every rational herdsman sharing a commons. Therein is the tragedy. Each man is locked into a system that compels him to increase his herd without limit − in a world that is limited. Ruin is the destination toward which all men rush, each pursuing his own best interest in a society that believes in the freedom of the commons. Freedom in a commons brings ruin to all." (Hardin 1968, p. 1244).

Conclusion

The results of this paper can now be summarized. First it is either in the absence of altruism between generations or in case of unstable dynamics that the population growth depends on and is eventually stopped by an exogenously given per capita consumption : subsistence level for some, natural price of labor for others. Second, when there is some altruism between generations the rate of population growth and stationary per capita income are normally a function of the degree of altruism. Third, the absence of cooperation within each generation is likely to lead to a rate of population growth that is above the level that is optimal from each individual's viewpoint.

To put it differently, one can say that the laissez-faire solution is likely to lead to a higher population than the Benthamite criterion except when individuals are perfectly altruistic and share the same rate of time preference as the government.

These results have been obtained within a somewhat restrictive model. It should however be noted that the introduction of technical progress, capital, and discovery of new natural resources would not affect the main conclusions of this paper as long as the fixed input remains a binding constraint in the long-run.

References

Buchanan, J. (1968) The Demand and Supply of Public Goods. Rand McNally, Chicago

Dasgupta, P. (1969) On the Concept of Optimum Population. Review of Economic Studies 36

Eckstein, Z., Stern, S., and Wolpin, K. I. (1989) Fertility Choice, Land, and the Malthusian Hypothesis. This volume

Goodwin, R., (1978) Wicksell and the Malthusian Catastroph. Scandinavian Journal of Economics 80

Hardin, G., (1962) The Tragedy of the Commons Science. Vol. 162: 3859

Johansen, L., (1967) A Classical Model of Economic Growth in Socialism, Capitalism and Economic Growth. (Ed.) C. H. Feinstein, Cambridge University Press

Kohlberg, E., (1976) A Model of Economic Growth with Altruism Between Generations. Journal of Economic Theory 13

Nerlove, L., Razin, A., and Sadka, E. (1987) Household and Economy : Welfare Economics on Endogenous Fertility. Academic Press, New York.

Phelps, E. S. and Pollak, R. A. (1968) On the Second Best National Savings and Game Equilibrium Growth. Review of Economic Studies 35

Pichford, J. D. (1974) Population and Economic Growth North-Holland, Amsterdam

Ray, D. (1985) Non Paternalistic Intragenerational Altruism. IMSSS Technical Report 470, Stanford University

Razin, A. and U. Ben-Zion (1975) A Intergenerational Model of Population Growth American Economic Review 65: 5

Votey, H. L., (1969) The Optimum Population and Growth : A New Look. Journal of Economic Theory 1

On the Malthusian Hypothesis and the Dynamics of Population and Income in an Equilibrium Growth Model With Endogenous Fertility

Zvi Eckstein, Steve Stern, and Kenneth I. Wolpin

1. Introduction

In this paper we analyze two positive issues regarding population and economic growth. The first issue concerns the pessimistic conjecture of Malthus that the existence of a fixed amount of land leads to the eventual decline in per-capita consumption and capital.[1] The second issue concerns the observed positive association between population growth and income growth in developed countries (Kuznetz (1966)). To analyze these issues we use a version of the overlapping generations growth framework in which fertility is subject to individual choice.[2]

Starting with Malthus' postulates on decreasing marginal productivity, due to a fixed supply of land, and exogenous exponential population growth, we demonstrate the Malthusian result that the competitive economy converges in finite time to zero consumption per-capita. The dynamic allocation of this Malthusian economy is unavoidable and no non-optimality (externality) elements exist.[3] However, we also show, by an example, that even if individuals care *only* about the number of their children and not about their children's welfare, there exists an equilibrium in which they would eventually choose to have only one child for each adult. Hence, by endogenizing their fertility decision, the equilibrium with indefinite population growth is ruled out. Given a land market and fertility choice, the Malthusian result no longer necessarily follows. This result is in contrast to the result of Pestieau (1989) who claims that we can avoid the Malthusian (Ricardian) world only if parents behave sufficiently altruistically toward their children. In his model, there is no land market and, hence, the entire future of the economy affects current decisions mainly through direct welfare consequences. In a perfect-foresight land market, the current value of land is a function of the present value of land rents in the infinite future. Hence, the existence of a steady state solution is guaranteed only if the fertility rate is eventually consistent with zero population growth.

Kuznets (1966) defines economic growth as a sustained increase in both income per capita and population size. The rates of population growth vary across countries

---

[1] The discussion of this topic here is based partially on Eckstein, Stern, and Wolpin (1988).

[2] For a survey of endogenous fertility in overlapping generations growth models see Schwödiauer and Wenig (1989).

[3] This result is compatible with that of Nerlove, Razin, and Sadka (1986) who show the efficiency of competitive markets in a Malthusian economy with endogenous fertility and perfect altruism.

Microeconomic Studies
K. F. Zimmermann (Ed.)
Economic Theory of Optimal Population
© Springer-Verlag Berlin Heidelberg 1989

and over time in a manner that seem to be systematically connected to the level and rate of growth in per-capita income. In particular, richer countries have lower fertility rates and countries where per-capita income is growing, at the same time, have declining population growth rates.

In the second part of this paper we analyze the equilibria of a Diamond (1965) overlapping generations growth model in which, fertility, again, is subject to choice, but in which there is no essential fixed factor. We show that if offspring are assumed to consume time of adults before they reach adulthood, then the stylized facts associated with the demographic transition can be duplicated by the mode. Further, we show that the economy may cycle or converge smoothly to the steady state. Our goal is to show that neoclassical growth theory with endogenous fertility is consistent with existing aggregate observations on population and income growth over long periods of time in many countries.

The paper is organized as follows: In the next section we describe the general model. Section 3 discusses the Malthusian economy and in section 4 we analyze the dynamics of the growth model with endogenous fertility. In section 5 we conclude the paper.

2. The Environment

We consider a standard overlapping generations growth model (Diamond, 1965) with land and endogenous population (Eckstein and Wolpin, 1985). The technology is represented by a constant returns to scale aggregate production function $F(K, L, R)$ where K is capital, L is labor, and R is land, such that: $f(k, r) = F(\frac{K}{L}, 1, \frac{R}{L})$ where $k = \frac{K}{L}$ and $r = \frac{R}{L}$. The single good can either be consumed or stored as capital for next period consumption. Capital depreciates at a rate δ in storage and production. Land cannot be directly consumed and does not depreciate in production. Individuals live for three periods, as infants who make no decisions in the first period, as workers ("young") in the second period, and finally as retired ("old") in the third period. In the second period, individuals supply one unit of labor and decide upon life-cycle consumption (savings) and the quantity of own children. Individuals are assumed to enjoy parenthood and children are costly to bear and rear; each child born at time t consumes $e(t)$ units of the good.

The representative individual of generations t has lifetime utility function:

$$V[C_1(t), C_2(t), n(t+1)] \tag{1}$$

where $C_i(t)$ is the consumption of a member of generation t at period $i+1$ of the individual's life $(i=1, 2)$, and $n(t+1)$ is the number of children (fertility) of each member of generation t.[4] The utility function satisfies the usual concavity and differentiability conditions with respect to all variables, and to assure positive consumption we assume that $V_1/V_2 \to \infty$ (0) as $C_1/C_2 \to 0$ (∞), where $V_i > 0$

---

[4]   Alternatively one can view $n(t+1)$ as the number of surviving children given a fixed and known child mortality rate, i. e., as the net fertility rate. Assuming that the utility of parents directly depends on the number of surviving offspring, given the ability to control fertility, the results that follow would be trivially true by assumption.

($i=1,2,3$) are the partial derivatives with respect to the i_{th} argument in (1). We restrict the utility function not to include the utility of children so as to emphasize the independence of our result from the assumption of altruistic behavior.[5]

At time t the economy consists of $N(t+1)$ infants, $N(t)$ young, and $N(t-1)$ old. The economy begins at $t=1$ with $N(0)$ old and $N(1)$ young as initial conditions. Each of the initial old is endowed with $K(1)$ units of capital and $\dfrac{R}{N(0)}$ units of land, where R is the aggregate fixed stock of land. Since all individuals are assumed to be alike, there are $N(t) = n(t)N(t-1)$ young at each period $t \geq 1$. Each of the old at time t owns $K(t)$ units of capital and $R(t) = \dfrac{R}{N(t-1)}$ units of land. Since each young worker supplies one unit of labor, the number of workers at time t is $N(t) = L(t)N(t-1)$ with $L(t) = n(t)$ the number of workers per old person at time t.

3. The Malthusian Hypothesis

In this section we discuss some implications of the model with respect to the Malthusian hypothesis, i.e., the exponential growth of population and the eventual decline in per-capita consumption.

Following the standard interpretation of Malthus with respect to production, we make three assumptions: (a) the marginal product of labor is decreasing; (b) land is an essential factor of production and its quantity is fixed; and (c) population growth is exponential and cannot be directly reduced by individual choice.[6] The conventional definition of essentiality in the literature (Solow (1974)) implies that production converges to zero as land per worker approaches zero, for any positive level of capital per-capita.[7] We interpret assumption (c) as saying that $n = \min \{n(t)\}_{t=0}^{\infty} > 1$.[8] And without loss of generality we let $e(t) = 0$. Then, we hav a Malthusian economy that satisfies the following proposition:[9]

---

[5] The exclusion of children's utility from parents preferences equation (1) eases considerably the mathematics of characterizing the allocation of the economy.

[6] This interpretation is the same as that of Pestieau (1989) and are the precise assumptions made by Malthus himself (1798, 1970 edition p. 70-71).

[7] Since Solow (1974), most of the literature on limited growth in the case of essential exhaustible resources has used the Cobb-Douglas technology as their main framework of anlysis (e. g., Mitra, 1983).

[8] One can extend the model with exogenous fertility to make n(t) a function of endogenously determined variables or some other exogenous checks on population (death rates). However, the results presented here would hold as long as n(t) is not part of the individual choice set and $n(t) > 1$ for all t.

[9] These assumptions reduce the technical difficulty of the proof. The reader should be aware that they represent an extreme case that, however, should work against the intended result that $n_t = 1$ as $t \to \infty$. $\delta = 1$ implies *less* gain from capital accumulation and so a greater likelihood of eventual subsistence. The Cobb-Douglas production function is the standard example for an economy with essential fixed inputs (Solow, 1974 and Mitra, 1983, among others). The log additive utility function implies that savings are proportional to current income alone, as in the standard Solow growth model, and so also reduces the impact of the future on the current fertility decision. For a general characterization of the allocation over time for Diamond model with a fixed asset see Tirole (1985).

Proposition 1: In the Malthusian economy that satisfies assumption (a), (b), and (c) consumption per capita approaches or reaches zero (subsistence). If capital per-capita monotonically decreases, consumption per-capita approaches zero; otherwise consumption is zero in a finite time.

Proof: For positive consumption the dynamic feasibility constraint of the economy is given by:

$$C_1(t) + \frac{C_2(t-1)}{n} = f\left(k(t), \frac{R}{N(0)n^t}\right) - n\,k(t+1) + (1-\delta)\,k(t) > 0 \tag{2}$$

From (2) it is clear that if $k(t+1) < \frac{1-\delta}{n} k(t)$ then consumption is positive for $k(t) > 0$. However, if $k(t) \to 0$ then since $f(\cdot,\cdot) \to 0$ as $t \to \infty$, per-capita consumption must also go to zero. If $k(t) \to k > 0$, then eventually $k(t+1) > \frac{1-\delta}{n} k(t)$ and consumption is negative (given the essentiality of land). Thus, $f(\cdot,\cdot)$ approaches zero unless $k(t)$ is monotonically increasing. Given that $n > 1$ and $0 < \delta < 1$ so that $n + \delta - 1 > 0$, it is sufficient to prove that:

$$f\left(k(t), \frac{R}{N(0)n^t}\right) - k(t)\,(n + \delta - 1) < 0 \text{ for some } t > 1. \tag{3}$$

For constant returns to scale of $F(\cdot,\cdot,\cdot)$ we know that for any $\lambda > 1$, $f(\lambda k(T),r) < f(\lambda k(T),\lambda r) < \lambda f(k(T),r)$. Hence, for any $t > T$ letting $\lambda = \frac{k(t)}{k(T)}$, and $r = \frac{R}{N(0)n^t}$, it follows that:

$$f\left(k(t), \frac{R}{N(0)n^t}\right) / k(t) < f\left(k(T), \frac{R}{N(0)n^t}\right) / k(T) \tag{4}$$

Since the right hand side of (4) approaches zero as $t \to \infty$ given the essentiality of land, the left hand side must also approach zero. Then, there must exist a time T^* at which for all $t > T^*$, $f(k(t), \frac{R}{N(0)n^t}) / k(t) < (n + \delta - 1) k(t)$. *Q.E.D.*

It is important to note that the result is derived from the feasibility constraint and has nothing to do with the way allocation is achieved. It is also useful to recognize that there exists a somewhat stronger version of the proposition which permits an interaction between the net fertility rate and economic activity, as some might argue, is closer to Malthus' intentions.

Malthus defined subsistence consumption to be that level at which population was stable. Although as just noted, we have simplified by assuming that population growth is independent of consumption, it is easy to accommodate this notion of subsistence. To do so, define subsistence consumption to be a value, $\epsilon > 0$, such that for all levels of consumption per-capita below ϵ, population is constant. Our proposition would then imply that the economy will reach this subsistence level of consumption in a finite time and will remain there as long as population is constant.

The proposition stated above is non-trivial given the existence of capital in the model. If there is no capital, then the Malthusian result follows even if land is not essential, i. e., $\lim_{R \to 0} F(0,L,R) > 0$, as long as the marginal product of labor is, after some point, declining. The above proposition shows that even with endogenous capital accumulation, the economy converges to subsistence consumption if land is fixed in quantity and is essential for production, and fertility is exogenously given at greater than the replacement rate. Malthus' pessimism is not necessarily due to a misunderstanding of the process of capital accumulation not to an inability to foresee technical change, for even costless technical change has to be sustained at an average rate which is higher than the *exogenous* rate of population growth in order to prevent the eventual decline in consumption. Furthermore, note that if land is not essential in production, as in case of the CES production function with an elasticity of substitution greater than 1, the Malthusian result does not follow since $\lim_{r \to 0} f(k,r) > 0$. For example, if land and capital are perfect substitutes in production the model is asymptotically equivalent to the standard growth model. Observe that given that land is essential in production, altruism *per-se* (e. g., Pestieau 1989) would not prevent the Malthusian result. However, if fertility is *endogenous*, regardless of whether individuals are perfectly selfish in their preferences as in equation (1), there exists an equilibrium path for the decentralized economy in which the steady state coincides with zero population growth. This result is given next by way of an example, emphasizing the necessity of condition (c).

3.1 Endogenous Fertility in a Competitive Malthusian Economy

In the competitive economy the problem of a young person at generation t who is born at t-1 is to maximize (1) subject to:

$$C_1(t) = W(t) - \bar{k}(t+1) - P(t)R(t+1) - en(t+1), \quad e > 0 \tag{5}$$

$$C_2(t) = F\big(\bar{k}(t+1), L(t+1), R(t+1)\big) - W(t+1)\, L(t+1) \\ + (1-\delta)\bar{k}\,(t+1) + P(t+1)\, R(t+1) \tag{6}$$

by choice of $\bar{k}\,(t+1)$, $R(t+1)$, $n(t+1)$ and $L(t+1)$, where now $e(t) = e$ for all $t \geq 0$, is cost per child. Each of the young of generation t saves $\bar{k}(t+1) = \dfrac{K(t+1)}{N(t)}$ units of the single consumption good for use in production at time $t+1$ and purchases $R(t+1)$ units of land for the same purpose at price per unit $P(t)$. Each supplies exactly one unit of labor, receives as a wage $W(t)$ units of consumption good and decides about their fertility level. At time $t+1$ each of the old of generation t hires $L(t+1)$ units of labor for production using the accumulated capital $\bar{k}(t+1)$ and purchases land $R(t+1)$, and consumes the net of labor cost production, the non-depreciated quantity of capital, and the revenues from selling the non-depreciated land.

The first-order necesarry conditions for a maximum are:

$$
\begin{array}{lll}
-V_1 + [F_1 + (1-\delta)]\, V_2 \leq 0 & \text{with} = \text{if } \bar{k}(t+1) > 0 & (7) \\
[F_2 - W(t+1)]\, V_2 \leq 0 & \text{with} = \text{if } L(t+1) > 0 & (8) \\
-P(t)V_1 + [F_3 + P(t+1)]\, V_2 \leq 0 & \text{with} = \text{if } R(t+1) > 0 & (9) \\
-V_1 e + V_3 \lesseqgtr 0 & \text{with} = \text{if } n(t+1) > 0 & (10)
\end{array}
$$

As is standard, the rates of return on capital and land are equal (equations (7) and (9)), and from (8) the marginal product of labor is equal to the wage rate.

In addition to the existence of non-negative values of $\bar{k}(t+1)$, $L(t+1)$, $R(t+1)$, $n(t+1)$, $W(t)$ and $P(t)$ which satisfy (8) - (11), a perfect-foresight competitive equilibrium requires that land and labor markets clear, i. e.,

$$L(t)N(t-1) = N(t) \qquad \text{and} \qquad (11)$$
$$R(t+1)N(t) = R \qquad (12)$$

We consider the Cobb-Douglas example where capital is fully depreciated in production ($\delta = 1$), where the utility function is log additive:

$$V(C_1(t), C_2(t), n(t+1)) = \beta_1 \ell n C_1(t) + \beta_2 \ell n C_2(t) + \beta_3 \ell n n(t+1) \qquad (13)$$

and where production is Cobb-Douglas:

$$F\big(K(t+1), L(t+1), R(t+1)\big) = AK(t+1)^{\alpha_1} L(t+1)^{\alpha_2} R(t+1)^{1-\alpha_1-\alpha_2} \qquad (14)$$

$$= AL(t+1)k(t+1)^{\alpha_1} r(t+1)^{1-\alpha_1-\alpha_2}$$

with $k(t) = \dfrac{K(t)}{L(t)}$ and $r(t) = \dfrac{R(t)}{L(t)}$. Algebraic manipulations of the first-order conditions, the budget constraints and market clearing relationship yield the following equations:

$$n(t+1)k(t+1) + P(t)R(t+1) = \left(\frac{\beta_2}{\beta_1+\beta_2+\beta_3}\right) A\alpha_2 k(t)^{\alpha_1} r(t)^{1-\alpha_1-\alpha_2} \qquad (15)$$

$$= sW(t)\, n(t+1) = \frac{1}{e}\left(\frac{\beta_3}{\beta_1+\beta_2+\beta_3}\right) A\alpha_2 k(t)^{\alpha_1} r(t)^{1-\alpha_1-\alpha_2} = \frac{\beta_2}{\beta_2 e} sW(t) \qquad (16)$$

where $s = \dfrac{\beta_2}{\beta_1+\beta_2+\beta_3}$ is the marginal rate of savings and $W(t)$ is the equilibrium wage rate.

The fertility rate is thus seen to be a constant fraction of first period income. Fertility, and thus population growth, is greater the lower is the cost of children and the greater their psychic benefit. Notice that these two equations contain three unknowns, $n(t+1)$, $k(t+1)$, and $P(t)$.[10] Substituting (16) into (15) yields:

$$\frac{\beta_3}{\beta_2 e} sW(t)k(t+1) + P(t)\frac{R}{N(t)} = sW(t) \qquad (17)$$

An equilibrium for this economy consists of a time path for $[P(t), k(t+1),$

---

10 Recall that $R(t+1) = \dfrac{R}{N(t)}$ and $N(t) = n(t)n(t-1)n(t-2)...n(1)N(0)$.

$n(t+1)]_{t=1}^{\infty}$ that satisfied (15) and (16) and the initial conditions.[11] Suppose that $P(t)$ is conjectured to be of the form:

$$P(t) = \theta sW(t) \frac{N(t)}{R} \tag{18}$$

Then for a constant θ the solution for $k(t)$ is:[12]

$$k(t) = (1-\theta) \frac{\beta_2}{\beta_3} e \quad 0 < \theta < 1 \tag{19}$$

and that for the population growth rate:

$$n(t+1) = \frac{1}{e}\left(\frac{\beta_3}{\beta_1 + \beta_2 + \beta_3}\right) A_{\alpha 2}\left[(1-\theta)\frac{\beta_2}{\beta_3} e\right]^{\alpha_1} r(t)^{1-\alpha_1-\alpha_2} = C r(t)^{1-\alpha_1-\alpha} \tag{20}$$

We have thus found an equilibrium path for the economy characterized by constant capital per capita.

Further, rewriting (20) as:

$$n(t+1) = C\left(\frac{R}{N(0)}\right)^{1-\alpha_1-\alpha_2}\left[\frac{1}{n(1)n(2)...n(t)}\right]^{1-\alpha_1-\alpha_2}$$

by recursive substitutions it can be shown that:

$$n(t+1) = n(2)^{(\alpha_1+\alpha_2)^{t-2}} \tag{21}$$

It is apparent that since $\alpha_1 + \alpha_2 < 1$, population growth or the fertility rate converges to unity. Thus, the competitive equilibrium is characterized by *zero* population growth in the steady state. If $n(2)$ is bigger than unity then convergence is from above while if $n(2)$ is less than unity convergence is from below. Whether $n(2)$ is above or below unity depends upon the given level of $n(1)$ and the other parameter values. For example, the lower the cost of children (e) the higher will be the fertility rate at each point along the path. Hence, if initially the cost of children is low, then along the competitive equilibrium path capital per-capita is constant, population declines and income per capita ($W(t)$) decreases. Since in the stationary equilibrium $n=1$, consumption per-capita has a positive finite steady state level. Thus, when fertility is subject to choice, there exists a competitive equilibrium which avoids the Malthusian outcome.

---

[11] It is quite possible that multiple equilibria exist, particularly since there is no initial condition for the price of land (See Tirole (1985)).

[12] Using (8) and (10) it can be shown that there exists a unique θ that satisfies $s\alpha_2\theta^2 + (1-\alpha_1-\alpha_2 s)\theta - (1-\alpha_1-\alpha_2) = 0$.

4. On the Dynamics of Population and Income

In this section, we consider the extent to which the implications of an overlapping generations growth model with endogenous fertility conforms to cross-country and time-series observations on fertility and economic growth. We deviate from the Malthusian economy in two ways. First, we do not assume that land is essential in production. Second, fertility (population) is determined endogenously in the model.

In order to simplify the discussion we assume that the production function has constant returns to scale in capital and labor. In order to illustrate the dynamics of population and income we adopt the assumption that each child born at t costs $e(t) = e_0 + e_1 W(t)$ units of the good where e_0 is the good cost of a child and e_1 is the fraction of time required to raise a child (See also Razin and Ben Zion (1975)).

Formally, the problem of a young person of generation t who is born at time t-1 is to maximize (1) subject to:

$$C_1(t) = W(t) - \bar{k}(t+1) - e(t) n(t+1) \tag{22}$$

$$C_2(t) = F[\bar{k}(t+1), L(t+1)] - W(t+1) L(t+1) + (1-\delta) \bar{k}(t+1) \tag{23}$$

by choice of $C_1(t)$, $C_2(t)$ $\bar{k}(t+1)$, $n(t+1)$ and $L(t+1)$.

The first order necessary conditions for a maximum can be written as:

$$\frac{V_1[C_1(t), C_2(t), n(t+1)]}{V_2[C_1(t), C_2(t), n(t+1)]} = F_1 [\bar{k}(t+1), L(t+1)] + (1-\delta) \tag{24}$$

$$\frac{V_1[C_1(t), C_2(t), n(t+1)]}{V_3[C_1(t), C_2(t), n(t+1)]} = e(t) \tag{25}$$

$$F_2[\bar{k}(t+1), L(t+1)] = W(t+1) \tag{26}$$

where the subscript i $(i=1,2,3)$ refers to the derivative with respect to the i_{th} variable of the function. Equation (24) implies that the net marginal return on capital equals the marginal rate of substitution between consumption over the two periods of life. Equation (25) says that the cost per child is equal to the marginal rate of substitution between current parent's consumption and utility from children, and the last condition equates wages to the marginal product of labor.[13]

A perfect foresight competitive equilibrium consists of non-negative values of $W(t)$, $n(t+1)$, $\bar{k}(t+1)$, and $L(t+1)$ for all $t \geq 1$, that are consistent with the necesarry conditions for the maximum problem of the young, $N(t+1) = [1+n(t+1)] N(t)$ and $L(t) N(t-1) = N(t)$.

Having described the structure of the model, in the next section we explore the positive features of the model. In particular, empirical regularities with respect to economic growth, population growth, and per-capita income across countries and over time should be explicable in the context of the model.

---

[13] It is known that if the steady state of this economy exhibits $f'(k) < n + \delta$, then a fixed stock of a paper asset would be valued in equilibrium. Eckstein and Wolpin (1985) analyze this model including the case of valued paper assets.

5.1 Fertility and Population Growth

In most countries, as income and capital per capita grow, the net growth rate of population declines. This demographic transition is primarily due to the decline in birth rates. Hence, we focus our discussion on fertility alone, assuming no deaths and no migration. We interpret the trend in the time-series observations as an outcome of the non-steady state equilibrium path of the model economy. It is not necessary to solve completely for the decentralized equilibrium in order to derive some basic results. In particular, if the utility function is contemporaneously separable, it is easy to see from (25) that fertility and first-period consumption must move together.[14] If first period consumption is normal, then fertility will also be positively correlated with income per capita along the equilibrium path. Since in the path $k(t)$ is predetermined at $t+1$, higher levels of $k(t)$, and therefore of per-capita income at t, could only produce lower levels of fertility if children were inferior. In the steady state, however, since $k(t)=k(t+1)$, income per capita is predetermined and this difference between the steady state and the path is crucial.[15]

In order to consider a multi-period path from any initial conditions to a steady state, we assume a utility function of the form:

$$V = C_1(t)^{\beta_1} + C_2(t)^{\beta_2} + n(t+1)^{\beta_3} \qquad (28)$$

The production function is assumed to be Cobb-Douglas with $F[k(t)] = Ak(t)^{\alpha}$.

Table 1. Path Simulations

Case	Parameters				Period(t)					
	e_0	e_1	β_3		1	2	3	4	5 ... ∞	
A.	.9	0	.7	$k(t)$	.001	4.51	1.06	1.35	1.29	1.30
				$n(t+1)$	.022	4.86	2.02	2.33	2.28	2.28
B.	.3	0	.4	$k(t)$	.001	.618	.909	.930	.931	.932
				$n(t+1)$	.016	2.84	3.38	3.42	3.42	3.42
C.	.05	.15	.7	$k(t)$	.001	.055	.198	.401	.615	1.35
				$n(t+1)$	1.21	2.66	2.66	2.56	2.47	2.25
D.	0	.20	.7	$k(t)$	.001	.013	.079	.272	.647	6.24
				$n(t+1)$	3.49	2.90	2.42	2.05	1.78	1.05

$\beta_1 = \beta_2 = .5, \alpha = .5, A = 10, \delta = 1$

---

[14] Differentiating (5), $-V_{11} e(t)dC_1(t) + V_{33} d[1+n(t+1)] = 0$ which implies that $dC_1(t) = \dfrac{V_{33}}{e(t)V_{11}} d[1+n(t+1)]$.

[15] If leisure is an argument in the utility function, income would no longer be predetermined.

Table 1 reports several simulations of the model for alternative values of e_0 and e_1. It turns out that the difference between β_3 and β_2 is important to the shapes of the equilibrium paths so that β_3 is also varied in some of the simulations. The first two simulations assume only a goods-cost of children ($e_1 = 0$) for two values of β_3, one larger and one smaller than β_2. In case A where β_3 is larger than β_2, n and k cycle in the same direction, while in case B, where β_3 is smaller than β_2, n and k move in the same direction, which depends on the initial value of k. In case C, e_0 is lowered and e_1 is raised, and the propensity for n and k to move in opposite directions increases. In this case capital per worker increases throughout the equilibrium path while fertility first increases, reaches a plateau and then decreases until the steady state is reached. This example seems to be broadly consistent with the observations on fertility and economic growth as they are summarized by Kuznets. [16] In the final example, case D, there is only a time cost in raising children, where per-capita income rises and fertility falls throughout. These examples demonstrate that almost any set of equilibrium paths of fertility and income per-capita, including cycles, are consistent with a perfect foresight competitive equilibrium. Hence, no general propositions are feasible for this model.

Given the time cost of children in this model, as capital accumulates and the wage rate then rises, there is a substitution away from children and towards goods consumption. At the same time, as income per-capita grows, the demand for children increases given the structure of preferences in this example. The path that actually arises depends upon the relative strengths of these two effects which are directly related to the relative magnitudes of the fixed goods cost and the time cost of raising children. [17]

The steady state solutions of the four examples show that economies with higher capital per-capita have lower population growth rates. This result is independent of the time cost for raising children. Hence, the steady state solution of the four examples are consistent with the cross-country differences of income per-capita and population growth rates as they are described by Kuznets (1966). [18]

---

[16] Obviously some elements of the demographic transition are still missing in this model, e. g., child mortality (Schultz, 1976), but can be incorporated in straightforward fashion.

[17] This can be shown for any separable utility function. Differentiating (25) and using (26) yields

$$\frac{d[1+n(t+1)]}{dk(t)} = \frac{-k(t)f''[k(t)]}{V_{33}} \{e_1 [1 + n(t)]V_1 + [e_0 + e_1(1+n(t))W(t)]V_{11}\}.$$

The first term inside the brackets corresponds to the substitution effect and the second to the income effect.

[18] The reader should be aware of the fact that with different parameter values it is possible to generate examples where higher capital per-capita is associated with higher fertility rates. Note that if we consider the case where a valued asset is competitively traded in this economy, then the steady state would be characterized by the golden rule. Then, since $f'(k) = n + \delta$ we get the result that higher k is always associated with lower n in the steady state.

5. Concluding Remark

In this paper we have showed the significance of endogenizing the fertility decision on the dynamics of capital accumulation and consumption. First, the endogenity of fertility enables a competitive economy to sustain positive consumption per-capita in the face of a fixed and essential factor of production, and so the Malthusian hypothesis is not necessarily realized. Second, with endogenous fertility, if the cost of raising children is very time consuming, then the equilibrium growth path of capital per-capita is associated with declining fertility. The model, thus, can generate endogenously characteristics of the economy associated with the demographic transition.[19]

References

Diamond, P. (1965) National Dept in a Neoclassical Growth Model. American Economic Review 5,5

Eckstein, Z. and Wolpin, K. I. (1985) Endogenous Fertility and Optimal Population Size. Journal of Public Economics 27: 93-106

Eckstein, Z., Stern, S. and Wolpin, K. I. (1988) Fertility Choice, Land and the Malthusian Hypothesis, International Economic Review 29: 353-361

Kuznets, S. (1966) Modern Economic Growth. New Haven: Yale University Press

Malthus, R. (First Published 1798) An Essay On The Principle of Population, Antony Flew (Ed.) (Penguin Books, England, 1970)

Mitra, T. (1983) Limits On Population Growth Under Exhaustible Resource Contraints. International Economic Review 24: 156-168

Nerlove, M., Razin, A. and Sadka, E. (1986) Endogenous Population with Public Goods and Malthusian Fixed Resources: Efficiency and Market Failure, International Economic Review

Nerlove, M., Razin, A. and Sadka, E. (1989) Social Optimal Population Size and Individual Choice. This Volume

Pestieau, P. (1989) Endogenous Population And Fixed Input in A Growth Model With Altruism. This Volume

Razin, A. and Ben-Ziron, U. (1975) An Intergenerational Model of Population Growth. American Economic Review: 923-933

Schultz, T. P. (1976) Interrelationship Between Mortality and Fertility. In Population and Development. (Ed.) Ronald G. Ridker. Baltimore: Johns Hopkins University Press

Schwödiauer, G. and Wenig, A. (1989) Choice of Fertility and Population Pressure in Traditional Rural Societies, This Volume

Solow, R. M. (Symposium 1974) Intergenerational Equity and Exhaustible Resources, Review of Economic Studies

Tirole, J. (1985) Asset Bubbles and Overlapping Generations Econometrics, Vol. 53: 6

---

[19] In an economy with a single type of agent born at each period no new non-optimality emerges due to endogenous fertility (see Nerlove et. al. 1989). However, heterogeneity of individuals with respect to their preference for children and their cost of raising them may generate some new welfare and public policy implications due to the fact that children cannot be directly traded.

Choice of Fertility and Population Pressure in Traditional Rural Societies

Gerhard Schwödiauer and Alois Wenig

1. Introduction

Since Malthus's "Essay on Population" (1798) classical economics regarded the theory of population as an integral part of political economy. Neoclassical economics maintained the interest in the question of population but, under the influence of utilitarianism, gave it a somewhat different direction. Level and growth of population took on more and more the character of exogenous variables which influence the outcome of the economic process but are no longer explained by means of the same analytical apparatus that was employed to understand the behavior of the endogenous economic variables. If the level or growth of population was considered the subject of rational choice, it was in the context of normative analysis where the choices are made by a fictitious benevolent dictator but not by the people themselves (see, e. g., Lane, 1977). In the non-normative long-run equilibrium models of neoclassical growth theory population was just assumed, with some remarkable exceptions (e. g., Meade, 1968), to grow at a constant exogenously given rate. Moreover, growth theorists did not, as demographers have been used to, pay attention to the different age cohorts of which the total population is made up. Mainly two developments in economic theory changed the picture completely: One was the explicit introduction of age cohorts or overlapping generations into models of long-run economic equilibrium by Samuelson (1958) which, though still treating population growth as an exogenous variable, revolutionized the analysis of intertemporal equilibria of economies with an infinite time horizon made up of finitely lived individual agents. The other important theoretical development was Becker's (1960, 1981) uncompromising application of economic choice analysis to fertility behavior and the theory of the family. In most of the recent contributions to the theory of population by economists these two strands of thinking play a major role.

In section 2 of this paper we present a somewhat general framework for the analysis of endogenous population along these lines and offer some comments on the recent literature. In section 3 we study a specific model of a traditional rural society characterized by a fixed supply of land, a productive role for children, and a fixed non-market institution for the distribution of social product. We show that a stable generative tradition of such a society will under empirically plausible assumptions produce a continual pressure of population growth on the supply of food. We also show that old-age social security may help to prevent progressive impoverishment of such a society. Some concluding remarks interpret these analytical results in the light of recent historical research on population growth and its relationship to technological and institutional change.

Microeconomic Studies
K. F. Zimmermann (Ed.)
Economic Theory of Optimal Population
© Springer-Verlag Berlin Heidelberg 1989

2. Endogenous Fertility: A General Framework of Analysis

Following Samuelson's (1958) model of overlapping generations we divide time into discrete periods during each of which three generations of people, children, young adults (parents), old adults (grandparents), coexist. All plans are assumed to be made at the beginning of a period, children are born then, and deaths occur at the end of a period. Let us denote the number of children living during period t, i. e. from point of time t to $t+1$, by $N_0(t)$, the number of young reproductive adults in period t by $N_1(t)$, and the number of old people, living till the end of period t, by $N_2(t)$. The net fertility rate for period t, n(t), i. e., the number of children per reproductive adult surviving infant age, is defined by the relationship

$$N_0(t) = n(t)N_1(t) , 0 \leqq n(t) \leqq \bar{n} .^{1)} \tag{1}$$

As is not uncommon in mathematical demography (Keyfitz, 1986; Feichtinger, 1979) we avoid the complications of sexual reproduction and marriage by confining our analysis to a one-sex model. Not all children reach the reproductive age:

$$N_1(t) = \beta N_0(t-1) , 0 < \beta \leqq 1 , \tag{2}$$

where β is the survival rate ($1-\beta$ the death rate) for children, which for our purposes is assumed to be constant over time. While n(t) is considered a control variable, β and the (net)fecundity rate $\bar{n} > \dfrac{1}{\beta}$ are exogenously given.[2] For the sake of simplicity we assume that all young adults survive till old age,

$$N_2(t) = N_1(t-1) , \tag{3}$$

and die at the end of their third stage of life. The total population N(t) is closed with respect to migration:

$$N(t) = N_0(t) + N_1(t) + N_2(t) . \tag{4}$$

From (1) − (3) follows that $N_0(t) = \beta n(t)N_0(t-1)$, $N_1(t) = \beta n(t-1)N_1(t-1)$, and $N_2(t) = \beta n(t-2)N_2(t-1)$. A steady-state development of population is generated by a time-invariant net fertility.

$$n(t) = n. \tag{5}$$

If in $t = 0$ the size and structure of population is given by the arbitrary initial conditions $N_0(0)$, $N_1(0)$, $N_2(0)$, and $n(t) = n$ for all $t = 1,2,...$, then

---

[1]   Since we assume, for the sake of simplicity, that deaths occur suddenly at the end of a period, $N_0(t) = n(t) N_1(t)$ is also the number of children raised and living during the period from t to $t+1$. Alternatively one might assume that children born at t die with a constant time rate of $(1-\beta)n(t)$ per parent, in which case the average stock of children per parent in period $(t, t+1)$ would be $\dfrac{1+\beta}{2} n(t)$. In particular, this formulation would make the size of a family's child labor force (in the model of section 3 of the paper) positively dependent on the survival ratio β but would not significantly change the main conclusions of the analysis.

[2]   The assumption $\bar{n} > \dfrac{1}{\beta}$ is made to assure at least the physical possibility of population growth at a rate of $\beta\bar{n} - 1 > 0$.

$$N(2) = \beta N_0(0)[\beta n^2 + \beta n + 1]$$

and

$$N(t) = (\beta n)^{t-2} N(2) \text{ for } t = 2,3,\dots;$$

thus, in the three-generations model with time-invariant mortality and fertility-rates it takes just two periods to reach the so-called stable population that grows at a constant population growth rate of $\beta n - 1$ in constant proportions

$$N_0(t) : N_1(t) : N_2(t) = 1 : \frac{1}{n} : \frac{1}{\beta n^2} .$$

The production possibilities of the society are described by a production function

$$X(t) = H(R(t) , N_0(t), N_1(t) - b(n)N_1(t)) , \tag{6}$$

where $X(t)$ denotes the quantity of output (a homogeneous consumption-cum-investment good), $R(t)$ stands for the effective input of non-human resources, $N_0(t)$ is the labor input provided by children, and $N_1(t) - b(n)N_1(t)$ measures the labor input available from the parent generation. While, for the sake of simplicity, we assume the marginal productivity of members of the old generation to be zero, we do not exclude the possibility of a positive marginal productivity of child labor. Parents cannot devote their whole labor time to the production of output: $b(n(t))$ is the share of their time absorbed in the rearing of $n(t)$ children[3], where

$$b(0) = 0, b(\bar{n}) < 1 , b' \geqq 0 , b'' < 0 \text{ if } b' > 0. \tag{7}$$

As to non-human inputs we make the simplifying assumption that capital stock $K(t)$, being the result of accumulation of saved output, and land $L(t)$, representing the available flow of exogenously given natural resources, are strictly complementary,

$$R(t) = \min(K(t) , L(t)). \tag{8}$$

This particular assumption is as such not crucial to the analysis but is convenient, and is made here for this purpose only, for juxtaposing clearly modelling differences found in the literature concerning the effective scarcity of material factors of production. The production function H satisfies the usual conditions, in particular it is assumed to be homogeneous of degree one and to possess positive first-order and negative second-order partial derivatives.[4]

---

[3]   Here, as everywhere in this paper, we approximate the discrete number of children by a continuous variable. This analytically most convenient assumption may be justified to some extent by pointing out that we describe the behavior of an average, representative parent.

[4]   In order to assure, without recourse to strong concavity conditions on the utility function, interior optimum solutions for n in spite of the (plausible) assumption $b'(n) > 0$, $b''(n) < 0$ we may impose the condition

$$H_{22} - 2b'(n)H_{23} + [b'(n)]^2 H_{33} < b''(n) H_3 ,$$

i.e. $\partial^2 H / \partial n^2 < 0$ (H_{ij} are the respective second-order partial derivatives).

The behavior of adults who are young in period t is described as maximizing a lifetime utility function

$$U_t(c_1(t), c_2(t+1), n(t)) = U(c_1(t), c_2(t+1), n(t)), \qquad (9)$$

where $c_1(t)$ denotes the per-capita consumption of the representative young adult, $c_2(t+1)$ the per-capita consumption he plans for his old age, subject to constraints depending upon further assumptions about technology and socioeconomic institutions to be discussed below. Adults who are old (i. e., in the last stage of their lives) in period t choose their consumption $c_2(t)$ so as to maximize a utility function $V_t(c_2(t))$ observing the relevant constraints, where V_t is assumed to be consistent with U in the sense that

$$V_t(c_2(t)) \equiv U(c_1(t-1), c_2(t), n(t-1)). \qquad (10)$$

The utility function U satisfies the usual conditions, in particular it is assumed to be quasi-concave, twice continously differentiable, and increasing in consumption levels; $\partial U / \partial n(t)$ may be > 0, reflecting a net enjoyment of parenthood, or ≤ 0 if the loss of leisure due to the time devoted to raising children outweighs the joy of parenthood. Children are not assumed to take any decisions: Their material consumption $c_0(t)$ is fixed at a conventional level[5], the extent to which they work is decided upon by their parents.

If we are interested in normative analysis, and in particular in the question of optimal population growth, we may now ask what behavior a benevolent (as well as omniscient and, apart from technological and other physical constraints, also omnipotent) social planner would under these circumstances impose on the members of society, provided that the exogenous supply of natural resources L(t) is semi-stationary,

$$L(t) = g^t L, g \geq 1, \qquad (11)$$

where g-1 represents the rate of resource-augmenting technical progress. The obvious policy of a benevolent planner accepting individual preferences would be to choose a steady-state sequence

$$\{c_1(t) = c_1, c_2(t) = c_2, n(t) = n, k(t) = k\}_{t = 0,1,...} \qquad (12)$$

of consumptions per capita for young and old adults, numbers of children, and per-capita capital stocks

$$k(t) = \frac{K(t)}{N_1(t)}, \qquad (13)$$

which is Pareto-optimal with respect to the set of utility functions

$$\{U_t, V_t\}_{t = 0,1,...}, \qquad (14)$$

where the population N(0) is assumed to possess already a stable structure. Contrary to models with exogenous fertility, the intergenerational Pareto criterion does not

---

[5] Again, this assumption is made to simplify matters. One might, alternatively, put $c_0(t)$ into the parents' utility function − $U(c_0(t), c_1(t), c_2(t+1), n(t))$ − without changing the analysis fundamentally.

lead to ethical difficulties if fertility is endogenous (Lane, 1977; Nerlove-Razin-Sadka, 1989).

Because of the time-consistency requirement (10), a Pareto-optimal program (c_1^o, c_2^o, n^o, k^o) maximizes

$$U(c_1, c_2, n) \tag{15}$$

subject to

$$nc_o + c_1 + \frac{1}{\beta n} c_2 + s \leq H(\min[k, (\frac{g}{\beta n})^t \lambda], n, 1 - b(n)), \tag{16 a}$$

$$s = (\beta n + \delta - 1)k , \tag{16 b}$$

$$\lambda = \frac{L(0)}{N_1(0)} , \tag{16 c}$$

$$c_1, c_2, k \geq 0; \bar{n} \geq n \geq 0 , \tag{16 d}$$

for all $t = 0,1,...$, where δ is the constant rate of depreciation of capital stock ($0 \leq \delta \leq 1$). We observe that any steady-state program requires

$$\beta n \leq g . \tag{17}$$

For an interior solution the first-order conditions are

$$\frac{U_1^o}{U_2^o} = \beta n^o, \tag{18 a}$$

$$\frac{U_3^o}{U_1^o} = c_o - [H_2^o - b'(n^o)H_3^o] - \frac{1}{\beta(n^o)^2} c_2^o , \tag{18 b}$$

$$\beta n^o = \begin{cases} 1 + H_1^o - \delta \text{ for } k^o < \lambda , \\[2mm] 1 - \delta \qquad \text{for } k^o \geq \lambda , \end{cases} \tag{18 c}$$

$$n^o c_o + c_1^o + \frac{1}{\beta n^o} c_2^o = H^o - (\beta n^o + \delta - 1)k^o , \tag{18 d}$$

where by $U_i^o, H_i^o, i = 1,2,3$, we denote the respective first-order partial derivatives of U and H at (c_1^o, c_2^o, n^o, k^o). The interpretation of these conditions is straightforward: The optimal rate of population growth equals both the marginal rate of time preference (18 a) and the net marginal product of capital (18c); (18 d) is a material balance condition stating that total consumption across generations equals output minus the amount of net investment necessary for keeping the per-capita stock of capital constant; (18 b) equates the parents' subjective marginal rate of substitution between present consumption and number of children with the marginal cost (in terms of present consumption) of an increase in fertility, where this (net) marginal cost of an increase in the steady-state number of offspring equals a child's consumption c_o minus the (possibly negative) net marginal product $H_2 - b'H_3$ of the child's labor (taking into account the corresponding reduction in the parents' labor time), minus the decrease of the burden of feeding the old generation, $c_2^0/\beta(n^0)^2$, due to the more favourable age composition of the population.

The model outlined so far displays the features common to most of the models recently studied in the literature on endogenous fertility in an overlapping generations context. In contrast to the earlier welfare analysis of population growth the modern analysis does not stop at the solution to the benevolent planner's problem. The latter is rather taken as a standard for judging institutional arrangements on their ability to provide the correct signals to individuals who not only have control over production, current consumption and old-age provision but also choose the number of their offspring according to their own preferences. The question usually posed in the literature is whether and under which conditions a system of competitive markets for output, labor and assets, i.e. the corresponding perfect foresight competitive equilibrium price system, would support a Pareto-optimal allocation. Crucial modelling assumptions are (a) whether children's net marginal productivity is positive or not, (b) whether there are durable factors of production and associated property rights that provide a source of income for the generation of no longer productive, retired people, and (c) whether there are exogenously given natural resources the fixed supply of which effectively limits the growth of output.[6]

---

[6] Meltzer and Richard (1985), e. g., assume $H_1 \equiv 0$ (in which case (18 c) takes on the corner solution $\beta n^0 \geqq 0$, $\beta n^0 k^0 = 0$), $H_2 - b'(n)H_3 < 0$ (in fact, they put $H_2 \equiv 0$), and $U_3 \equiv 0$, and show that in such a world, where there is no possibility for saving, the upbringing of children involves increasing marginal costs, and adults do not enjoy parenthood as such, a perfect foresight competitive equilibrium will yield the Pareto-optimal steady state only if the working generation maximizes $U(c_1(t), c_2(t+1)) V_t(c_2(t))$. Otherwise, i. e., if no such filial obligation towards the grandparents is internalized in the parents' preferences, the Pareto-optimal allocation will emerge in competitive equilibrium only in the presence of government social security financed by taxation of parents and government subsidies payed to parents for having children. Market failure in achieving a Pareto-optimum may, of course, also be the result of externalities. Nerlove, Razin and Sadka (1989) study such externalities resulting from marriage and bequests if the consumption of grown-up children (or their, i. e. the future parent generation's, utilities) are an argument of the present parent generation's utiltiy function. Some recent contributions allow for an accumulation of capital, following Diamond's (1965) overlapping-generations growth model and amending it for an endogenous choice of fertility (Razin-Ben Zion, 1975; Eckstein-Wolpin, 1985). They implicitly make an assumption like $g > \bar{n}$ and λ sufficiently large, meaning that the prospects for capital accumulation are not impeded by the existence of a scarce original factor of production, which together with the retention of the assumption $H_2 \equiv 0$ reduces the production function (6) and (8) to $H(\cdot) \equiv G(K(t), N_1(t) - b(n)N_1(t))$. In this "great-American-dream model" (Marglin, 1984) young adults work, bring up children, and save enough both to purchase the existing stock of capital from the old generation and to add sufficient net investment for keeping the capital-labor ratio constant. Again, the perfect foresight competitive equilibrium supports the Pareto-optimal steady-state allocation. Eckstein-Stern-Wolpin (1989) argue that this model might also be given a descriptive interpretation in the light of time-series evidence on developed countries and of international cross-sectional evidence. Only recently (Pestieau, 1989; Eckstein-Stern-Wolpin, 1989) the time-honored Malthusian theme of a fixed supply of land putting a limit to further growth — in our terms: $\lambda \leqq k$ and $g = 1$ — has been taken up again in the framework of an overlapping generations model with choice of fertility. The major conclusion seems to be that also in this case, the competitive equilibrium is capable of generating a Pareto-optimal steady-state, viz. that with zero population growth ($\beta n^0 = 1$), thus preventing a Malthusian catastrophe.

The model of traditional rural society presented in the next section of this paper is a special case of the more general model outlined in this section, which departs on several points from the models in the literature discussed. While the structure of the latter seems to offer an acceptable though highly idealized approximation to the conditions of a capitalist industrial society, it is probably less adequate for capturing the technology and social organization of a traditional agrarian society which preceded the industrial market economy in Western Europe and can presently still be observed in many of the underdeveloped nations suffering under the pressure of fast population growth. Since our aim is to give a positive, explanatory analysis of the forces behind this population pressure we try to preserve in our model some of the stylized facts about a traditional rural economy.

An outstanding characteristic, perhaps the most important one in this context, of a traditional rural economy is that children are productive. In contrast with a modern industrial economy the comparatively complicated technology of which demands rather long education and training, and accordingly leaves little room for a significant productive employment of children[7], child labor is a pervasive phenomenon of traditional rural societies. Moreover, the time cost incurred by the parent generation and invested in the children's human capital is small in traditional rural societies compared with urbanized industrial ones. We therefore not only assume

$$H_2 - b'(n)H_3 > 0$$

but set also $b(n(t)) \equiv 0$ and, for the sake of simplicity, $H_2(\cdot) \equiv H_3(\cdot)$. Thus, the special form of the production function (6) chosen to describe the technology of a traditional agrarian economy is

$$H(\cdot) \equiv F(R(t), N_0(t) + N_1(t)). \tag{6'}$$

Secondly, we take it as a stylized fact that the most important natural resource of an agricultural economy, arable land, is given in a fixed amount L, i. e., $g = 1$ in (11) or, equivalently,

$$L(t) = L. \tag{11'}$$

Furthermore, it seems to be typical of a traditional rural economy that most of its capital is not invested in tools and other short-lived instruments of production but in the amelioration of land, in water supply systems, dams, drainage facilities, etc. Thus, we may characterize a not yet fully developed agricultural economy by $K(t) < L$, which leaves room for capital accumulation for some time but not for steady-state growth. In our model we deal with a "mature" traditional agricultural economy where $K(t) \geqq L$ and $\delta = 1$, i. e. in which all investment opportunities are

---

[7] The child labor quite common during the early stages of industrialization of Western Europe or Japan (Boserup, 1981) was an heritage of the agrarian society into which the first, still rather primitive methods of industrial production were introduced. In many parts of the Third World children are an important part of the labor force. To quote Ester Boserup (1981, p. 180): "Rural women in Africa need many children to help them in their double role as agricultural workers and housewives under primitive conditions. Moreover, if they fail to produce any children, or stop childbearing at a young age, they risk being divorced and therefore having no support in old age."

exhausted (and all existing capital appears as a stock of permanent "rent" goods). Therefore, the non-human factor of production in the production function (6') is according to (8)

$$R(t) = L .$$ (8')

Lastly, from a descriptive-explanatory point of view studying the competitive equilibrium of an economy of the traditional rural type does not seem overly relevant. In a traditional rural society the appropriation of the social product is not organized mainly via competitive markets for output, labor, and land, but through rather rigid institutional rules of ownership and distribution.

3. A Model of Generative Equilibrium for a Traditional Rural Society

3.1 Social Structure, Production, and Consumption

The society we consider consists of families and clans. A family is made up of a father, a mother, and their children. A clan is defined as the set of all those families whose fathers are brothers. The grandparents who are the parents of the fathers in the clan also belong to the clan. For the sake of analytical convenience we may think of all children being born as twins with every pair of twins consisting of a boy and a girl; girls are married out and join the clans of their husbands. Since under this assumption in every family and every clan the number of men equals the number of women, we can fall back on our simple one-sex model.

The land is assumed to be equally distributed among the clans of the society, and within the clans among the families.[8] The parents own the land which may not be sold. When the parents become grandparents they bequeath their land to their sons in such a way that each son gets an equal share in his parents' estate.

The production possibilities of a clan with $N_1(t)$ married couples and $N_0(t) = N_1(t)n(t)$ sons (pairs of twins) is described by

$$X(t) = N_1(t)F(\lambda(t), 1 + n(t)) ,$$ (19)

where F is the familiy production function, which here is, *a priori*, not required to be linearly homogenous, $\lambda(t)$ is the land per family, and $1 + n(t)$ the family's labor input (measured in pairs of family members). All members of the clan share equally in the net output $X(t)$ so that the consumption per couple in each cohort is

$$c_0(t) = c_1(t) = c_2(t) = c(t) ,$$ (20)

---

[8] In systems of this type existing in reality the rules are often somewhat less rigid: "Under the system of tribal tenure, which still predominates in large parts in Africa, all members of the local tribe have access to clear land for long-fallow cultivation. If such land is controlled by the local chief, he traditionally assigns more to large families... Thus, as long as this system persists, a man obtains more land by marrying more wives and getting more children." (Boserup, 1981, p. 180) Taking into account this flexibility would not weaken our main conclusion about the inherent tendency towards overpopulation in traditional rural societies which rests on the incentive to procreate provided by productivity of children.

and per-capita consumption proper is $c(t)/2$. Suppose the grandparents of a clan of the current period t had $n(t-1) = n$ sons of which βn survived. Since we assume every son to get married, we have βn families in the clan of period t. Furthermore, let $n(t) = m$ be the number of sons per family in the clan. Together with the grandparents the whole clan has $1 + \beta n (1+m)$ pairs of members. Let $\lambda(t) = \lambda$ be the size of the land per family the parents of the current generation are endowed with. Then

$$c(t) = \frac{\beta n F(\lambda, 1+m)}{1 + \beta n(1+m)} =: \Phi(\beta n, m) . \tag{21}$$

In the following period all parents of the clan of period t become grandparents and members of the respective βn clans of period $t+1$ each of which consists of βm families endowed with plots of land of size $\dfrac{\lambda}{\beta m}$ per married couple. Let $n(t+1) = k$ be the number of sons per family in period $t+1$, which is assumed to be the same for all families in the clan. Then consumption per capita of a member of a clan of period $t+1$ is $c(t+1)/2$, where

$$c(t+1) = \frac{\beta m F(\frac{\lambda}{\beta m}, 1 + k)}{1 + \beta m(1+k)} =: \Psi(\beta m, k). \tag{22}$$

In particular, $\Phi(\beta n, m)$ is the consumption of a father and a mother in period t while $\Psi(\beta m, k)$ is their consumption in period $t+1$ when the same people have become grandparents.

3.2 Optimal Fertility Choice in the Absence of Uncertainty

We assume parents to maximize the utility function

$$U(c(t), c(t+1)) = c(t) + \frac{1}{1+r} c(t+1) , \tag{23}$$

which is a special case of a separable version of the more general utility function (9); r is the parents' individual time discount rate. We have left out $n(t)$ as a separate argument of the utility function (23). This simplification does not mean that we assume parents in traditional rural societies not to enjoy parenthood, it is just an application of Occam's razor: Due to their productivity and the rule of distribution the number of children influences parents' consumption in a way to provide sufficient incentives to have children (incentives that would be absent in an industrial society) so that we need not base our conclusion concerning overpopulation on an additional, subjective element. If we insert (21) and (22) into (23),

$$U(\cdot) = \Phi(\beta n, m) + \frac{1}{1+r} \Psi(\beta m, k) , \tag{24}$$

we see that, given the numbers n and k of children in the preceding and following generations, the mortality rate $1 - \beta$ and the subjective time discount rate r, it is via the choice of the number m of their offspring that the parents of the current generation can shape their lifetime stream of consumption so as to maximize their utility.[9]

A crucial assumption we make in this paper, in line with the existant literature on endogenous population in overlapping generations models, is that the time-invariant share β of children surviving to adulthood is known to the parents with certainty. In the absence of this deterministic feature, i. e. within a doubtlessly more realistic stochastic set-up of the model where β would be just the mathematical expectation of a random variable the realization of which is the number of children actually surviving, the parents would have to solve a decision-making problem under uncertainty.[10]

Let us now assume that n is the number of children conforming to the generative tradition of the society observed in the past. This tradition conditions the expectations of the reproductive adults so as to make them uniform and extrapolate the grandparents' generative behavior to the future behavior of the children, i. e. we set $k = n$ in (24). Then the goal function of parents the current period becomes

$$U(\cdot) = V(m, n) = \Phi(\beta n, m) + \frac{1}{1+r} \Psi(\beta m, n). \tag{25}$$

A reproductive tradition n will obviously only prove "stable", in the sense of being sustainable over time, if the number of children m chosen by the current parent generation confirms the past and anticipated generative behavior, i. e. if $m = n$.

---

[9] The fundamental tenet of the analyis is, of course, that also in traditional rural societies parents are able to control the number of their children sufficiently well. Contrary to widespread popular opinion historical research has shown that effective methods of birth control are not a recent achievement but have been known and practiced since prehistoric time. The ancient techniques may be less humane than the modern ones but not less effective in controlling the number of offspring surviving infancy (Thomas, 1984). Regarding the question of the current parents' egotistical versus altruistic behavior (Pestieau, 1989) it may be pointed out that the fixed rule of distribution we assume imposes a certain amount of solidarity since the parents' present consumption equals the grandparents' consumption, and the parents' future consumption equals their children's consumption in adulthood.

[10] If the number of children reaching adulthood is a random variable $\bar{\nu}(m)$ with possible realizations $\nu(m) = 0, 1, ..., m$ and mathematical expectation $E\bar{\nu}(m) = \beta m$, the problem of the parents in the current period would be to maximize a goal function
$$W(m, \nu(n), n) = \Phi(\nu(n), m) + \frac{1}{1+r} E u (\Psi(\bar{\nu}(m), n)) ,$$
where u with $u' > 0$ is a v. Neumann-Morgenstern utility function reflecting the parents' attitude towards risk ($u'' < 0$ being interpreted as risk aversion, $u'' \equiv 0$ as risk neutral behavior, etc.). Though in our model of a clan-based society, in which the current parents' future consumption depends exclusively on the number of their own children surviving (and not, as in a great society with society-wide competitve markets, on the future labor force as a whole), the introduction of uncertainty is analytically more significant than in the context of a great-society model (for which we could invoke a law of large numbers), we have good reasons t conjecture that at least under the simplifying assumption of $\bar{\nu}(m)$ being binomially distributed (with β as the fixed and independent survival probability of any child) our central conclusion concerning stable generative traditions would not be changed fundamentally. The inquiry into this problem will, however, be left to another paper.

Therefore, to judge the "stability" of a potential generative tradition n we have to find out whether it is in the interest of the current parents to deviate from n or not. For this purpose we calculate the parents' "best response" m^o to n by maximizing their goal function (25) with respect to m; this best response will be dependent upon n:

$$m^o = m^o(n) .\qquad (26)$$

The first-order necessary condition for m^o to maximize V for given n is

$$\frac{\partial V(m^o, n)}{\partial m} = \frac{\partial \Phi(\beta n, m^o)}{\partial m} + \frac{1}{1+r}\frac{\partial \Psi(\beta m^o, n)}{\partial m} = 0 ,\qquad (27)$$

provided that an interior solution exists (which is the case for this model). From (21) and (22) it follows that this equation can also be written as

$$\frac{1}{1+m^o}\,\Phi(\beta n, m^o)\,[\epsilon - \frac{\beta n/1 + m^o)}{1 + \beta n(1 + m^o)}\,] +\qquad (28)$$

$$\frac{1}{1+r}\frac{1}{m^o}\,\Psi(\beta m^o, n)\,[\frac{1}{1 + \beta m^o(1 + n)} - \eta] = 0,$$

where $\eta := \dfrac{F_L(L,N)L}{F(L,N)}$ and $\epsilon := \dfrac{F_N(L,N)N}{F(L,N)}$ are the production elasticities of the respective family inputs of land L and labor N. In what follows, we shall confine ourselves to that case where η and ϵ are independent of variations in the inputs of land and labor, i. e. to the case where the production function F is of the Cobb-Douglas type[11]

$$F(L,N) = L^\eta N^\epsilon\qquad (19')$$

with $0 < \underline{\epsilon} \leqq \epsilon \leqq \bar{\epsilon} < 1, 0 < \underline{\eta} \leqq \eta \leqq \bar{\eta} < 1.$

With this assumption (28) becomes

$$g(m^o,n)\,(1+r)\,\frac{m^o}{1+m^o}\,(\beta m^o)^\eta\,[\epsilon - \frac{\beta n(1 + m^o)}{1 + \beta n(1 + m^o)}\,] = \eta - \frac{1}{1 + \beta m^o(1 + n)},\qquad (29)$$

where $g(m,n) = \dfrac{1 + \beta m(1 + n)}{1 + \beta n(1 + m)}\,\dfrac{n}{m}\,\left[\dfrac{1+m}{1+n}\right]^\epsilon .$

---

[11] There is not much loss of generality from concentrating on this generalized Cobb-Douglas production function which captures reasonably well the notion of essentiality of the fixed factor. See on this, e. g., the comment by Eckstein, Stern and Wolpin (1989, footnote 9).

3.3 Existence, Uniqueness and Comparative Statics of Stable Generative Traditions

A fertility rate n* is said to represent a stable generative tradition if for the response function $m^o(\cdot)$ of any parent generation, it satisfies the nonco-operative (Nash) equilibrium condition

$$n^* = m^o(n^*).\tag{30}$$

Setting $n = n^* = m^o$ in (29) yields, since $g(n,n) = 1$, the equation determining the equilibrium fertility rate[12] n*:

$$(1+r)\,\frac{n^*}{(1+n^*)}\,(\beta n^*)^\eta\,[\epsilon - \frac{\beta n^*(1+n^*)}{1+\beta n^*(1+n^*)}] = \eta - \frac{1}{1+\beta n^*(1+n^*)}\tag{31}$$

Theorem 1

If $r > -1, 0 < \beta \leqq 1, 0 < \underline{\epsilon} \leqq \epsilon \leqq \bar{\epsilon} < 1$ and $0 < \underline{\eta} \leqq \eta \leqq \bar{\eta} < 1$ then there always exists an n* > 0 which solves (31), i. e. satisfies (30).

Theorem 2

A sufficient condition for n* to be unique is $\epsilon + \eta \leqq 1$ (i. e. that the production function (19′) exhibits non-increasing returns to scale).

Corollary 1

(A) If the production function exhibits constant returns to scale ($\epsilon + \eta = 1$), n* is the positive root of the equation

$$n^*(1+n^*) = \frac{\epsilon}{\beta\eta}\,.$$

(B) In the case of decreasing returns to scale ($\epsilon + \eta < 1$) we have $n_{G0} < n^* < n_{H0}$, where n_{G0} and n_{H0} are the positive roots of

$$n_{G0}(1+n_{G0}) = \frac{1}{\beta}\,\frac{\epsilon}{1-\epsilon}\quad\text{and}$$

$$n_{H0}(1+n_{H0}) = \frac{1}{\beta}\,\frac{1-\eta}{\eta}\,,$$

respectively.

Diagram 1 elucidates the situation described in the above corollary:

---

[12] It seems that Lane (1977, pp. 111 ff.) was the first to advocate the use of the Nash non-co-operative equilibrium concept in the analysis of endogenous fertility. He dealt, however, with a normative, ethical problem and employed the Nash equilibrium in the selection of "self-policing" Pareto-optimal steady states of a model with capital accumulation and without effectively scarce factors.

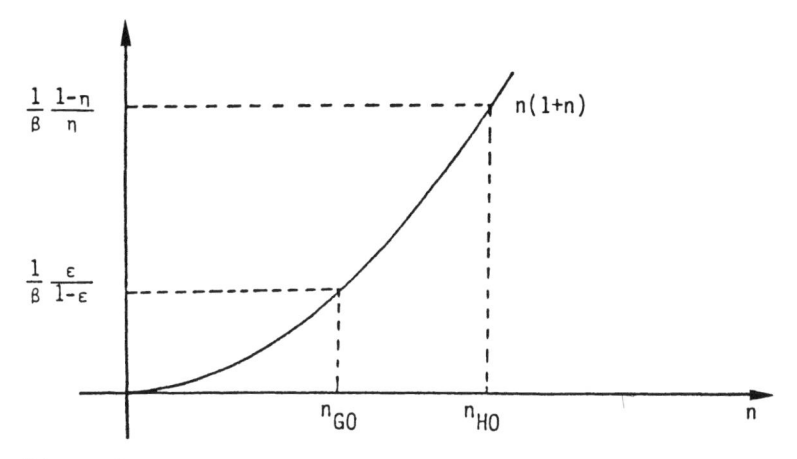

Diagram 1

It is of interest to know how the time-invariant rate of fertility, which in the case of a Cobb-Douglas production function with non-increasing returns to scale represents the unique stable generative tradition, would have to change in response to changes in the parameters ϵ, η, β, and r.

Theorem 3

Let $\epsilon + \eta \leqq 1$ so that n* is unique. Then

(A) $\quad \dfrac{\partial n^*}{\partial \epsilon} > 0 \;$ and $\; \dfrac{\partial n^*}{\partial \beta} < 0 \;$;

(B) $\quad \dfrac{\partial n^*}{\partial r} = 0 \;$ for $\epsilon + \eta = 1, \quad \dfrac{\partial n^*}{\partial r} < 0 \;$ for $\epsilon + \eta < 1$;

(C) $\quad \dfrac{\partial n^*}{\partial \eta} < 0 \;$ for $\epsilon + \eta = 1 \;$ or $\; \beta n^* \geqq 1.$

3.4 Impoverishing Stable Generative Traditions

As we have seen from the analysis of the more general model in section 2, only a rate of fertility $n = \dfrac{1}{\beta}$, i. e. a population growth rate of $\beta n - 1 = 0$, would allow a Pareto-optimal steady-state development of an economy endowed with a fixed amount of land. For the traditional rural society, $n = \dfrac{1}{\beta}$ implies $\Phi(\beta n,n) = \Psi(\beta n,n)$, i.e. a constant per-capita consumption over time for every generation, while $n > \dfrac{1}{\beta}$ is equivalent to $\Phi(\beta n,n) > \Psi(\beta n,n)$, i. e. a continual impoverishment of clans as time goes on, and $n < \dfrac{1}{\beta}$ with $\Phi(\beta n,n) < \Psi(\beta n,n)$ implies increasing per-capita con-

sumption for successive generations. The question we now address is whether a
stable generative tradition, i.e. the constant fertility rate n* possessing the (Nash)
equilibrium property that no parent generation has an incentive to deviate from it
as long as the other generations are observed or anticipated, respectively, to stick
to n* , would guarantee a Pareto-optimal steady state or, at least, prevent society
from impoverishing itself in the course of time. The result of our analysis is that a
stable generative tradition does not only not rule out impoverishment but even
makes it the likely outcome (for empirically plausible parameter constellations).
The following theorem gives sufficient conditions for the unique stable generative
tradition to be impoverishing or not to be impoverishing, respectively:

Theorem 4

Let $\epsilon + \eta \leqq 1$ so that n* is unique. Then

$$\frac{\epsilon}{1-\epsilon} > 1 + \frac{1}{\beta} \rightarrow \beta n^* > 1 \text{ , and} \tag{32}$$

$$\frac{1-\eta}{\eta} < 1 + \frac{1}{\beta} \rightarrow \beta n^* < 1 \text{ .} \tag{33}$$

In the case of constant returns to scale the following corollary offers a criterion
for impoverishing stable generative traditions:

Corollary 2

If $\epsilon + \eta = 1$ then

$$\beta n^* \mathrel{\substack{\geqq \\ <}} 1 \leftarrow \frac{\epsilon}{\eta} \mathrel{\substack{\geqq \\ <}} 1 + \frac{1}{\beta} \text{ .} \tag{34}$$

In Theorem 3, local comparative-static properties of the equilibrium fertility
rate n* with respect to small parameter variations have been given. Except for the
effect of a change in the survival rate β they imply unambiguously the local comparative-static properties of the equilibrium rate of population growth:

$$\frac{\partial(\beta n^*)}{\partial\epsilon} > 0 \text{ , } \frac{\partial(\beta n^*)}{\partial\eta} < 0 \text{ , } \frac{\partial(\beta n^*)}{\partial r} \leqq 0$$

(under the conditions specified in Theorem 3). Since the stable generative tradition
n* responds to a small increase in β, i.e. a small drop in the mortality rate, by a fall
of the fertility rate, it depends on the elasticity of n* with respect to β whether the
equilibrium rate of population growth $\beta n^* - 1$ will decrease or increase with a small
change in the mortality rate $1 - \beta$:

$$\frac{\partial(\beta n^*)}{\partial\beta} \mathrel{\substack{\geqq \\ <}} 0 \leftarrow \frac{\partial n^*}{\partial\beta} \cdot \frac{\beta}{n^*} \mathrel{\substack{\geqq \\ <}} - 1 \text{ .}$$

Theorem 4 and Corollary 2 allow somewhat more global (if only essentially
qualitative) conclusions about the effect of parameter variations on the rate of

population growth associated with a stable generative tradition: For any positive β there is a production elasticity of labor ϵ sufficiently close to 1 such that the stable generative tradition is impoverishing, and, on the other hand, for any ϵ and η with $\epsilon + \eta \leq 1$ there is a mortality rate $\beta - 1$ sufficiently close to 1 such that the stable generative tradition ceases to be impoverishing. E.g., for $\beta = 1$ (i.e., a mortality rate of 0) and $\epsilon + \eta = 1$ the production elasticity of labor just guaranteeing a stationary consumption level is $\frac{2}{3}$, any production elasticity of labor higher than $\frac{2}{3}$ results in an impoverishing stable generative tradition; for $\epsilon = \frac{3}{4}$ the mortality rate would already have to be 50 % in order to ensure a non-impoverishing stable generative tradition. We also observe that in the sufficient (and in the case of constant returns to scale also necessary) conditions for a stable generative tradition to be impoverishing or not the subjective element of the time discount rate r does not play any role.

3.5 Does Social Security Prevent Impoverishment?

It is often argued that loosening the bond of intergenerational solidarity by introducing a social security system of old-age provision would reduce the incentive to have children and thus the tendency towards long-run impoverishment. With some qualifications this conjecture turns out to be correct for our traditional agrarian economy.

Let us first assume that the old-age social security is organized on a clan-wide basis by taxing the families within a clan at a rate $\tau, 0 < \tau < 1$, and using the proceeds from this social security tax to finance the consumption of the old. If the net output after tax is shared equally among family members

$$c_0(t) = c_1(t) = \frac{(1-\tau) \beta n F(\lambda, 1+m)}{\beta n(1+m)} \quad , \tag{35 a}$$

$$c_2(t) = \tau \beta n F(\lambda, 1+m) \quad , \tag{35 b}$$

and

$$c_0(t+1) = c_1(t+1) = \frac{(1-\tau) \beta m F(\frac{\lambda}{\beta m}, 1+k)}{\beta m(1+k)} \quad , \tag{36 a}$$

$$c_2(t+1) = \tau \beta m F (\frac{\lambda}{\beta m}, 1+k) \quad . \tag{36 b}$$

Again, we assume parents to maximize the utility function

$$U(c_1(t), c_2(t+1)) = c_1(t) + \frac{1}{1+r} c_2(t+1) , \tag{23'}$$

given the anticipation $k = n$. The following theorem can then be proved:

Theorem 5

Let $r > -1$, $0 < \beta \leqq 1$, and F be of the generalized Cobb-Douglas type (19′) with $0 < \underline{\epsilon} \leqq \epsilon \leqq \bar{\epsilon} < 1$, $0 < \underline{\eta} \leqq \eta \leqq \bar{\eta} < 1$. Then there is always a social-security tax rate $\tau = \tau^*$, $0 < \tau^* < 1$, such that a stable generative tradition $n^* > 0$ exists for an exonomy with young adults maximizing (23′) subject to (35 a), (36 a), and $k = n$, and no stable generative tradition is impoverishing.

Corollary 3

Let τ be such that two stable generative traditions $n^+ < n^*$ exist. Then

$$\text{Then } \frac{\partial n^*}{\partial \tau} = -\frac{\partial n^+}{\partial \tau} < 0, \frac{\partial n^*}{\partial \epsilon} = -\frac{\partial n^+}{\partial \epsilon} < 0, \frac{\partial n^*}{\partial \eta} = -\frac{\partial n^+}{\partial \eta} > 0,$$

$$\frac{\partial n^*}{\partial \beta} = -\frac{\partial n^+}{\partial \beta} < 0, \frac{\partial n^*}{\partial r} = -\frac{\partial n^+}{\partial r} > 0.$$

Only the larger of the two equilibrium fertility rates, n^*, can be influenced by an appropriate choice of tax rate so as to yield stationary per-capita consumptions.

A last remark may be devoted to the possibility that the social security system is not restricted to the clan but is organized on a society-wide basis. If the society consists of so many clans that the old-age consumption parents can expect does no longer significantly depend on the number of their own children, then they are maximizing

$$(1 - \tau) \frac{\lambda^\eta (1+m)^\epsilon}{1+m} + \frac{1}{1+r} \bar{c}_2 \ ,$$

where $\bar{c}_2$ is their old-age income perceived as independent of m. In this case their optimal response will be $m^o = 0$. A stable generative tradition with $n^* > 0$ could only be sustained if n enters the utility function of the parents and/or there is a government not only collecting social security taxes but also subsidizing the upbringing of children.

4. Concluding Remarks

The results of our analysis of stable generative traditions in traditional rural societies, in particular the finding that such generative traditions are rather likely to lead to a progressive impoverishment of these societies, ought not to be understood as an unconditional prediction. In reality, impoverishment may be checked by technological advances and/or institutional changes, or it will eventually be checked, at a low level of per-capita consumption however, by an increase in mortality[13]. Some

---

[13] As we see from Theorem 3 and 4 just a slight decrease in β might not be sufficient to reduce βn^*, a dramatic deacrease in β will, however always do. It will not only be natural causes like diseases by undernourishment that bring about a fall in β, even more effective will be wars or emigration which particularly affect the share of children that reach reproductive adulthood in a given society.

modern economic historians seem even to regard the constant population pressure at work in traditional agrarian societies[14] as a necessary condition for the emergence of a process of endogenous industrialization (Clark, 1977; Boserup, 1981; Hesse, 1982). This does not, however, fit in well with the conventional neo-Malthusian view still "shared by most economic historians, according to which stagnant population should be the normal pattern in preindustrial societies, and sustained population growth an abnormal feature calling for a special explanation" (Boserup, 1981, p. 94). The model presented in this paper offers a theoretical clue to the understanding of the nature of permanent population pressure in traditional rural societies, which is possibly superior to the mechanistic short cut of viewing fertility as immediately causally related to per-capita incomes. In particular, the latter theory has its difficulties in reconciling the hypothesis that on some (low?) levels of income fertility is an increasing function of per-capita consumption (the neo-Malthusian view proper) with the hypothesis, on which many hopes concerning present underdeveloped countries seem to rest, that on other (higher?) levels of income fertility becomes a decreasing function of per-capita consumption (see, e.g., Pitchford, 1974, pp. 54 ff.). Our model explains both fertility and per-capita incomes as the joint consequences of the choices made by people within a certain technological and institutional environment. If we have some hope concerning the solution of the population predicament facing the Third World, our analysis suggests that we should base it on technological advances reducing the net productivity of child labor and on institutional changes like social security and/or competitive markets working in the same direction.

Appendix: Proofs of Theorems

Proof of Theorem 1

Let $G(n)$ and $H(n)$ respectively denote the left-hand and the right-hand side of (31).

The expression $g(n) = \epsilon - \dfrac{\beta n(1+n)}{1+\beta n(1+n)}$ is a strictly decreasing function of n with $g(0) = \epsilon$ and $g(\infty) = \epsilon - 1$. Thus G has the following properties:

---

[14] Colin Clark already is quite explicit about the impact of population pressure on traditional agrarian societies when criticizing "the simple Malthusian view that these technical or political changes lead to a population increase (or decrease, as the case may be) until a new equilibrium is reached. In the great majority of cases, however, it is population change which is the cause, and technical and political change the consequence. At any rate in the early stages of the development of agriculture, the need to support a larger population from a given area of land is going to call for an increased input of labor per unit of food produced" (Clark, 1977, p. 134). And: "It is rapid population growth which is the principal motive force bringing about, at certain periods in history, extensive clearings of uncultivated land, drainage of swamps, introduction of improved crops and manures, and the like, which historians tend to describe as 'agricultural revolutions' generally failing, however, to trace their origin to population increase... It is not permissible to say that things now are different from what they were. Many of the essential economic and political issues in the developing countries are similar to those of past centuries in Europe." (Clark, 1977, p. 137-138).

$$G(0) \quad\; = 0 \,,$$
$$G(\infty) \quad = -\infty \,,$$

$$G(n) \quad \begin{cases} > 0 \text{ for } n < n_{G0} \,, \\ = 0 \text{ for } n = n_{G0} \,, \\ < 0 \text{ for } n > n_{G0} \,, \end{cases}$$

where n_{G0} is the positive root of the equation $\epsilon = \dfrac{\beta n_{G0}(1+n_{G0})}{1+\beta n_{G0}(1+n_{G0})}$.

The function H has the following properties:

$$H(0) \quad\; = \eta - 1 < 0 \,,$$
$$H(\infty) \quad = \eta > 0 \,,$$
$$H'(n) \quad\; > 0 \,,$$

$$H(n) \quad \begin{cases} < 0 \text{ for } n < n_{H0} \,, \\ = 0 \text{ for } n = n_{H0} \,, \\ > 0 \text{ for } n > n_{H0} \,, \end{cases}$$

where n_{H0} is the positive root of the equation $\dfrac{1}{1+\beta n_{H0}(1+n_{H0})} = \eta$.

The following Diagram 2 shows the functions G and H under the assumption that $n_{G0} < n_{H0}$.

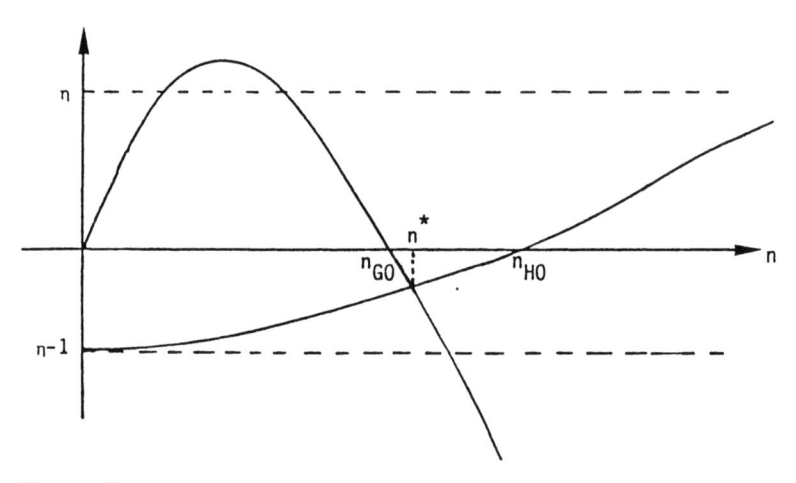

Diagram 2

From this diagram the existence of a positive n* follows immediately.

Q.E.D.

Proof of Theorem 2

It is easy to show that $G'(n) < 0$ for $n \geqq n_{G0}$. $H'(n) > 0$ holds everywhere. Thus $n_{H0} \geqq n_{G0}$ is a sufficient condition for the uniqueness of n^*. Since we consider only positive values of n_{H0} and n_{G0} our sufficient condition can also be written as

$$1 + \beta n_{H0}(1+n_{H0}) \geqq 1 + \beta n_{G0}(1+n_{G0}) .$$

By the definitions of respectively n_{H0} and n_{G0} we get

$$1 + \beta n_{H0}(1+n_{H0}) = \frac{1}{\eta} ,$$

$$1 + \beta n_{G0}(1+n_{G0}) = \frac{1}{1-\epsilon} ,$$

and hence $\dfrac{1}{\eta} \geqq \dfrac{1}{1-\epsilon}$ implies the uniqueness of n^*.   Q.E.D.

Proof of Corollary 1

Follows immediately from the proof of the above theorem.

Proof of Theorem 3

$\dfrac{\partial n^*}{\partial \epsilon} > 0$ and proposition (B) can be verified immediately by shifting appropriately the function $G(n)$ in equation (31) or, respectively, the corresponding curve in Diagram 1. That $\dfrac{\partial n^*}{\partial r} = 0$ for $\epsilon + \eta = 1$ can also be seen immediately from the above Corollary 1 (A).

In order to prove $\dfrac{\partial n^*}{\partial \beta} < 0$ and proposition (C) we make use of the equation

$$dG(n^*, \beta, \eta) = dH(n^*, \beta, \eta) ,$$

where $dG(\cdot)$ and $dH(\cdot)$ are the respective total differentials of the left and right-hand sides of equation (31). From the above equation it follows that

$$\frac{\partial n^*}{\partial \beta} = \frac{\dfrac{\partial H}{\partial \beta} - \dfrac{\partial G}{\partial \beta}}{\dfrac{\partial G}{\partial n} - \dfrac{\partial H}{\partial n}}$$

and

$$\frac{\partial n^*}{\partial \eta} = \frac{\dfrac{\partial H}{\partial \eta} - \dfrac{\partial G}{\partial \eta}}{\dfrac{\partial G}{\partial n} - \dfrac{\partial H}{\partial n}} .$$

Since the fulfillment of the second-order condition for individual optimization

implies $\dfrac{\partial G}{\partial n} - \dfrac{\partial H}{\partial n} < 0$,

$$\text{sign } \frac{\partial n^*}{\partial \beta} = -\text{ sign } \left(\frac{\partial H}{\partial \beta} - \frac{\partial G}{\partial \beta}\right)$$

and

$$\text{sign } \frac{\partial n^*}{\partial \eta} = -\text{ sign } \left(\frac{\partial H}{\partial \eta} - \frac{\partial H}{\partial \eta}\right) \quad \cdot$$

Let us first address the question of sign $\dfrac{\partial n^*}{\partial \eta}$:

From $\dfrac{\partial H}{\partial \eta} = 1$ and $\dfrac{\partial G}{\partial \eta} = G(n^*, \beta, \eta) \cdot \ln(\beta n^*)$ it follows that $\dfrac{\partial n^*}{\partial \eta} < 0$ if $\beta n^* \geqq$ 1 because $G(n^*, \beta, \eta) < 0$ and $\ln(\beta n^*) \geqq 0$ for $\beta n^* \geqq 1$.

For $\epsilon + \eta = 1, \dfrac{\partial n^*}{\partial \eta} < 0$ follows from Corollary 1 (A) to Theorem 2, regardless of the sign of $\beta n^* - 1$. To show that $\dfrac{\partial n^*}{\partial \beta} < 0$, which is equivalent to $\dfrac{\partial H}{\partial \beta} - \dfrac{\partial G}{\partial \beta} > 0$, is a matter of straigthforward computation of the partial derivatives involved.

Q.E.D.

Proof of Theorem 4

For non-increasing returns to scale we have shown (Corollary 1) that the inequalities

$$n_{G0} \leqq n^* \leqq n_{H0}$$

hold. Thus, $\beta n_{G0} > 1$ is a sufficient condition for $\beta n^* > 1$ while $\beta n_{H0} < 1$ implies $\beta n^* < 1$. The equations for n_{G0} and n_{H0} can also be written, respectively, as

$$\frac{\epsilon}{1-\epsilon} = \beta n_{G0} + \frac{1}{\beta} (\beta n_{G0})^2$$

and

$$\frac{1-\eta}{\eta} = \beta n_{H0} + \frac{1}{\beta} (\beta n_{H0})^2$$

For $\beta n_{G0} = 1, \dfrac{\epsilon}{1-\epsilon} = 1 + \dfrac{1}{\beta} ; \dfrac{\epsilon}{1-\epsilon} > 1 \dfrac{1}{\beta}$ obvioulsy implies $\beta n_{H0} > 1$. Likewise for βn_{H0}.

Q.E.D.

Proof of Corollary 2

Immediately from Corollary 1(A).

Q.E.D.

Proof of Theorem 5

By inserting (35 a) and (36 a) into (23′) and putting the partial derivative of the resulting expression

$$(1-\tau)\,\frac{\lambda^{\eta}(1+m)^{\epsilon}}{1+m} + \frac{1}{1+r}\,\tau\beta m\left(\frac{\lambda}{\beta m}\right)^{\eta}(1+n)^{\epsilon}$$

with respect to m equal to zero we obtain the equation

$$(1-\tau)\,\{1-\epsilon\}\,(1+m^{0})^{\epsilon-2} = \frac{1}{1+r}\,\tau(1-\eta)\,(\beta m^{0})^{-\eta}\,\beta(1+n)^{\epsilon}$$

satisfied by the optimal response m^{0}. Setting $n = n^* = m^0$ yields the equation

$$\frac{1-\epsilon}{1-\eta}\,\frac{1-\tau}{\tau}\,(1+r)\,\beta^{\eta-1}\,(n^*)^{\eta} = (1+n^*)^{2}$$

fulfilled by the (Nash)equilibrium fertility rate n^* if such a stable generative tradition exists. The above equation can also be written as

$$\frac{1-\epsilon}{1-\eta}\,\frac{1-\tau}{\tau}\,(1+r)\,x^{\eta} = \beta + 2x + \frac{1}{\beta}\,x^{2}\,,$$

where $x = \beta n^*$. The following diagram shows the graphs of the left-hand side, $A(x)$, and the right-hand side, $B(x)$, of this equation as functions of x:

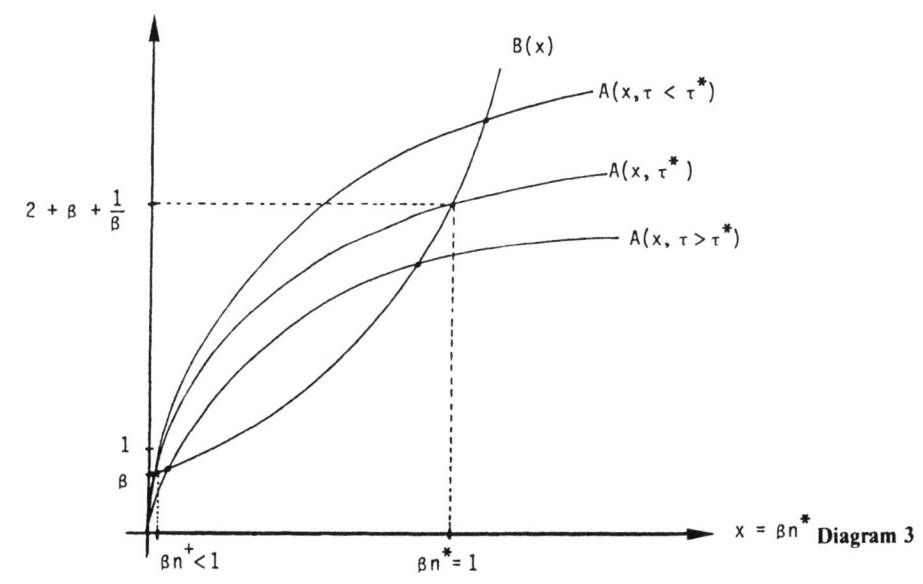

$$B(x)$$
$$A(x,\tau < \tau^*)$$
$$A(x,\tau^*)$$
$$2+\beta+\frac{1}{\beta}$$
$$A(x,\tau > \tau^*)$$
$$1$$
$$\beta$$
$$x = \beta n^* \quad \textbf{Diagram 3}$$
$$\beta n^+ < 1 \qquad \beta n^* = 1$$

We choose $\tau = \tau^*$, $0 < \tau^* < 1$, so that

$$\frac{1-\epsilon}{1-\eta} \frac{1-\tau^*}{\tau^*} (1+r) = 2 + \beta + \frac{1}{\beta} \, ,$$

which is obvioulsy always possible. For this $\tau^* x = \beta n^* = 1$ satisfies the equilibrium condition. Since $A(0) = 0$, $A' > 0$, $A'' < 0$, $B(0) = \beta > 0$, $B' = 2 + \frac{2}{\beta} x > 0$, $B'' = \frac{2}{\beta} > 0$, and $B'(1) = 2 + \frac{2}{\beta} \geqq 2 + \frac{1+\beta^2}{\beta} = A(1) > > \eta A(1) = A'(1)$, there is one and only one other stable generative tradition n^+; moreover, $\beta n^+ < \beta n^*$.

Q.E.D.

Proof of Corollary 3

Immediately from the inspection of Diagram 3.

Q.E.D.

References

Becker, G. S. (1960) An Economic Analysis of Fertility. In: R. A. Easterlin (Ed.) Demographic and Economic Change in Developed Countries, Princeton, N. J.: Princeton University Press, 209 − 231

Becker, G. S. (1981) A Treatise on the Family, Cambridge, Mass.: Harvard University Press

Boserup, E. (1981) Population and Technology. Oxford: Basil Blackwell Publ.

Clark, C. (1977) Population Growth and Land Use, London and Basingstoke: Macmillan Press (1st Edition 1967)

Diamond, P. A. (1965) National Debt in a Neoclassical Growth Model. American Economic Review 60:1126-1150

Eckstein, Z., Stern, S., and Wolpin, K. J. (1989) On the Malthusian Hypothesis and the Dynamics of Population and Income in an Equilibrium Growth Model With Endogenous Fertility. In this volume.

Eckstein, Z. and Wolpin, K. J. (1985) Endogenous Fertility and Optimal Population Size. Journal of Public Economics 27:93-106

Feichtinger, G.(1979) Demographische Analyse und populationsdynamische Modelle. Wien-New York: Springer-Verlag

Hesse, G. (1982) Die Entstehung industrialisierter Volkswirtschaften. Tübingen: J. C. B. Mohr (Paul Siebeck)

Keyfitz, N. (1968) Introduction to the Mathematics of Population. Reading, Mass.: Addison-Wesley Publ

Lane, J. S. (1977) On Optimal Population Paths. Berlin-Heidelberg-New York: Springer Verlag

Marglin, S. A. (1984) Growth, Distribution and Prices. Cambridge, Mass. and London: Harvard University Press

Meade, J. E. (1968) The Growing Economy, London: Allen & Unwin

Meltzer, A. H. and Richard S. F. (1985) Debt and Taxes with Endogenous Population, Or Why Public Social Security Systems Are Prone to Crises. Pittsburgh: Unpublished Paper, Graduate School of Industrial Administration, Carnegie-Mellon University

Nerlove, M., Razin A., and Sadka, E. (1989) Socially Optimal Population Size and Individual Choice. In this volume.

Pestieau, P. (1989) Endogenous Population and Fixed Input in a Growth Model With Altruism. In this volume.

Pitchford, J. D. (1974) Population in Economic Growth. Amsterdam-London: North-Holland Publ. Comp.

Razin, A. and Ben-Zion, U. (1975) An Intergenerational Model of Population Growth, American Economic Review 70:923 − 933

Samuelson, P. A., (1958) An Exact Consumption-Loan Model of Interest with or without the Social Contrivance of Money. Journal of Political Economy 66:467 − 482

Thomas, H. (1984) Geschichte der Welt, Stuttgart: Deutsche Verlags-Anstalt (English original: A Unfinished History of the World, 1979)

IV. International Economics

Economic Interdependence and Optimum Population: An Examination of Meade's Objection to the Individual Utility Criterion[1)]

John D. Pitchford

Meade (1955) devoted a chapter of his *Trade and Welfare* volume to optimum population and optimum saving. In this discussion he finds reasons for abandoning individual welfare as a criterion for optimum population in favour of the use of total utility. His objection to individual, or as he calls it "per caput" utility is worth quoting in full.

"But to the present author it would seem improper to take the maximization of welfare per head as the ultimate objective. A consideration of one of the more extreme implications of this objective should be sufficient to demostrate its inapplicability. Suppose two communities A and B exist. Suppose that neither has any appreciable economic dependence on the other so that the disappearance of A would not appreciably affect the standard of living in B nor the disappearance of B the standard of living in A. Suppose, further, that the standard of living in B is somewhat lower than in A, though both communities are prosperous and enjoy high standards. The strict application of the objective of maximizing welfare per head would lead to the conclusion that the world would be a better place if community B ceased to exist, since output per head for all citizens of A and B would certainly be increased if that section of the community with the somewhat lower standard were to cease to exist. It is true that when A and B exist together the richer citizens of A may be being taxed in order, in the interests of a utopian distributional policy, to supplement the lower incomes in B. In this case the citizens of A would enjoy an increase in their average real incomes if the citizens of B were all to cease to exist. But this distributional arrangement can be judged on its own merits. It can be removed without the removal of the citizens of B. Suppose the taxation of A to subsidize B is stopped. Is it really reasonable to conclude that a prosperous B should be blotted out in order to raise the arithmetical calculation of the average real consumption of the world citizen to the slightly higher figure enjoyed in A? Yet this is what the acceptance of the objective would involve." [p. 87]

The purpose of this paper is to re-examine Meade's objection to the individualistic criterion in order to see whether it is as substantial a criticism as Meade believed. In the quoted statement Meade assumes his two islands have no economic dependence on each other. By dependence he means that if one island disappeared welfare in the other island would be appreciably affected, presumably reduced. To go further into the points he makes it is necessary to be more specific about the nature of dependence. Two things which can give rise to economic dependence between countries are trade, and the possibility of sharing public goods such as a common language, currency, government, defence, and so forth. Presumably these dependencies will exist for most economies so that to assume them away would seem to bias the analysis against the per capita criterion. Moreover, to get an idea of how

---

[1)] I am indebted to Brian Ferguson and Neil Vousden for discussions on this topic.

Microeconomic Studies
K. F. Zimmermann (Ed.)
Economic Theory of Optimal Population
© Springer-Verlag Berlin Heidelberg 1989

far population would extend across regions, the nature of their dependencies needs to be examined. It would seem most likely that when two islands have fairly similar living standards they will be likely to trade and have other economic dependencies. Framed this way the question becomes, assuming there are economic dependencies when will these ensure that the less prosperous island B is populated according to the individualistic criterion? This issue is studied in section I and the conditions under which island B is and is not populated in the face of dependencies are elucidated. It is found that with respect to trade the populating of island B depends on the relation between its per capita production possibility curve and that of island A. The possibility of sharing the costs of provision of public goods can also lead to the populating of island B.

There are then circumstances in which, even in the face of economic dependencies, some less well endowed regions of the world are left unpopulated.[2] This seems damaging to the per capita criterion. However, in section II it is argued that if there is a relaxation of some of the conditions with which this criterion has been surrounded, its role for judging optimum population may still be significant. For instance, with more than one government in the world, island B could be populated.

While the analysis does not result in a complete rehabilitation of the individualistic criterion, it nevertheless may clarify some of its implications.

1.

Suppose two islands named A and B, distinguished by a star for island B and no star for island A, have different resource endowments and can each produce two goods, 1 and 2. The population of island A is represented by N and of B by N^* so that

$$N + N^* = L \tag{1}$$

where L is the total population on both islands. It is assumed that there is no difference between the population and the workforce. Defining employment in industry i in island A and B, respectively, as N_i, N_i^*,

$$N_1 + N_2 = N \tag{2}$$

$$N_1^* + N_2^* = N^* \tag{3}$$

Outputs are represented by F_i and F_i^* ($\epsilon\ C^{(2)}$) and average and marginal products by y_i and F_i', respectively. Production is assumed to take place with fixed resources in each island. As the concept of optimal population to be studied here involves the notion of an *endpoint* of an optimal growth process,[3] workers are assumed to be equipped with capital so that the net marginal product of capital is

---

[2] It is an empirical question as to whether these circumstances would leave large areas of fertile land unpopulated or merely the poorer more barren regions.

[3] Meade (1955) examined conditions for optimal population which would apply on the path to an optimal end point. However, his analysis did not fully encompass all optimal dynamic issues. Dasgupta (1969) elucidates these issues for Meade's model but does not fully take account of the dynamics of population growth.

zero.[4] Capital is thus an endogenous variable and can be omitted from the production functions without loss of generality. Production functions are then given by[5]

$$F_i = F_i(N_i), \quad F_i^* = F_i^*(N_i^*), \quad F_i, F_i^* \in C^{(2)}, \quad i=1,2. \tag{4}$$

A typical production function is taken to have the form shown in Figure 1, so that F has a unique maximum at $\overline{N}$, $y = F/N$ has a unique maximum at $\hat{N}$ and

$$F'(0) = y(0) > 0. \tag{5}$$

For sector i $y_i = F_i / N_i$.[6]

If the islands trade

$$\sigma_i = (F_i + F_i^*) / L \tag{6}$$

where σ_i is the average consumption of good i across both regions. There is nothing so far in the model which allocates total consumption between the two regions. To fix ideas take the case (mentioned by Meade) in which consumption per capita is equalized across islands. For this case per-capita consumption, $s_i = F_i / N$,[7] is such that

$$\sigma_i L = s_i N + s_i N^* = F_i + F_i^*, i = 1,2 \tag{6'}$$

and rearranging

$$F_i - s_i N = s_i N^* - F_i^*, i = 1,2 \tag{6''}$$

so that exports (imports) of country A are imports (exports) of country B.

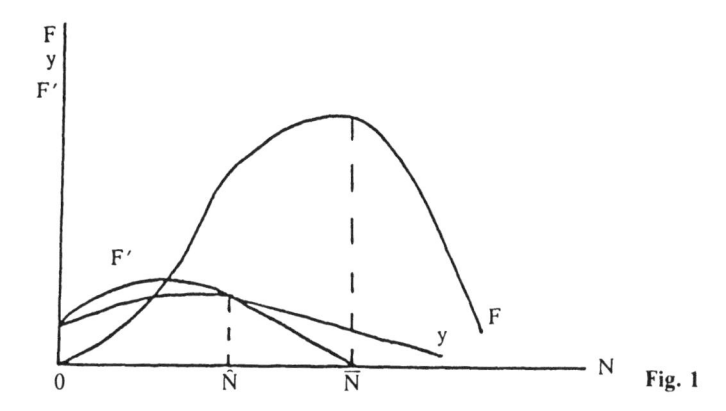

Fig. 1

---

[4] With a positive discount rate the gross marginal product of capital would be equated to the discount rate.

[5] $C^{(2)}$ is the class of twice differentiable functions with continuous second order partial derivates.

[6] In what follows some per capita concepts are defined as the ratio of a magnitude to the total population and others to the workforce in a particular sector. Definitions will be given for each concept to prevent possible ambiguity.

[7] For island B, $s_i^* = F_i^* / N^*$.

Reasonable uniformity of tastes across consumers is essential to the individualistic criterion and important for the total utility criterion. While the assumption of additive utility will ensure that total utility can still be defined, when tastes differ markedly the outcome is not a concept which has much appeal. Hence it will be assumed for the present that tastes are identical for consumers across both islands.

Suppose first that only one good exists and is represented by dropping the goods subscripts. This case involves no trade and so can be used to illustrate Meade's point. Output per head of total population across the two regions is given by

$$z = \{ F(N) + F^*(N^*) \} / L \tag{7}$$

which may be written

$$z = y(N) (N/L) + y^*(N^*) (N^*/L) \tag{7'}$$

Assume that $y(\hat{N})$ is greater than $y^*(\hat{N}^*)$ so that island A has the greater optimal value of per capita output and hence the greater utility. Now z is the weighted average of two numbers $y(N)$ and $y^*(N^*)$. It follows that a maximum of (7') is achieved when $N/L = 1$ and $N^*/L = 0$. This result is illustrated in Figure 2 where per-capita output for each island is plotted against its population with island B's population measured from the origin to the left. The line AB is the graph of linear combinations of y and y* given in (7'). It is clear that z is maximized when $N^* = 0$, $N = \hat{N}$. Island B is left unpopulated. Now what happens if there are two goods so that the possibility of trade is introduced?

When there are two commodities the problem is to maximize

$$u(\sigma_1,\sigma_2), \ \sigma_i = (F_i + F_i^*) / L, \ u \ \epsilon \ C^{(2)} \tag{9}$$

subject to (1), (2), (3), (4) and (6).

Necessary conditions for an interior optimum with both islands populated are

$$u_1\sigma_1 + u_2\sigma_2 = u_1 F_1' \tag{10}$$

$$u_1 F_1' = u_2 F_2' = u_1 F_1^{*'} = u_2 F_2^* \tag{11}$$

Now per capita consumption across the two islands can be written

$$\sigma_i = s_i \frac{N}{L} + s_i^* \frac{N^*}{L}, \qquad i = 1,2 \tag{12}$$

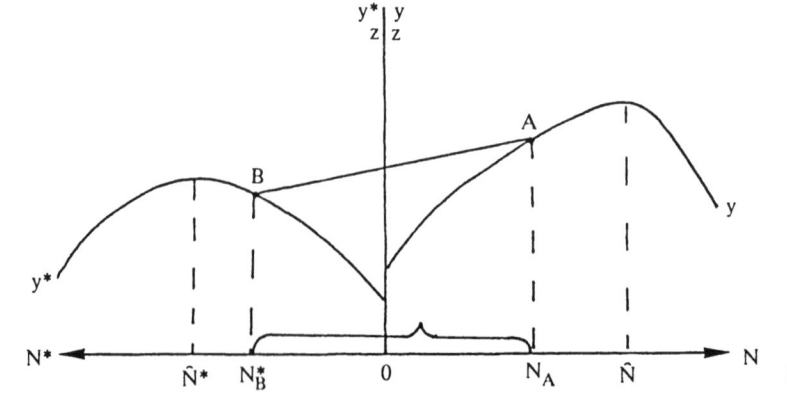

Fig. 2

Using (12) the above conditions can be reduced to the optimum population condition for each island separately, if the marginal productivity conditions for the other island are discarded, and N/L and $N*/L$ are set at unity and zero, respectively, to reflect which island is populated.[8] The complete necessary conditions, involving inequality constraints, are not given here for brevity, but are neutral with respect to whether one or both islands will be populated at an optimum. Further information must be added with respect to production conditions before this issue can be resolved. To start with note that production possibility curves can be constructed for each island relating $s_1 = F_1(N_1) / N$ to s_2 and s_1^* to s_2^*. The curve is defined for island A, for instance, by

$$\text{Max} \quad F_1(N_1) / N \qquad (13)$$
$$N, N_1, N_2$$

subject to

$$N_1 + N_2 = N \qquad (14)$$

$$F_2(N_2) / N = \bar{s}_2 \text{ constant} \qquad (15)$$

This problem yields the necessary conditions

$$s_1 + \lambda s_2 = F_1' = \lambda F_2' \qquad (16)$$

where λ is a Lagrange multiplier associated with the constraint (15). The equations (14), (15), (16) and

$$s_1 = F_1(N_1) / N \qquad (17)$$

solve for $s_1, N_1, N_2, N, \lambda$ as functions of s_2. Thus along the curve $s_1 = \phi(s_2)$ population variables are endogenous. It is not necessary to establish the slope of ϕ for the argument that follows. All that is needed is the reasonable assumption that $\phi(0)$ (that is the efficient output of good 1 when good 2 is not produced) and $\phi^{-1}(0)$ (or the efficient output of good 2 when good 1 is not produced) are both positive. These curves are illustrated in figures 3 and 4. Figure 3 is drawn for the case in which island A can produce higher per capita output of good 2 for all values of per capita output of good 1, than island B. Now (12) involves two equations defining the overall per capita consumptions and outputs when both islands are combined and their per capita consumptions are equalized. It will be seen that a point in the (σ_1, σ_2) space is a linear combination of points on the production possibility curves of the two islands. The straight line joining points A and B in Figure 3 represents points in the attainable per capita consumption set when the two islands may both produce. The outer boundary of the feasible set of consumption vectors (σ_1, σ_2) is the efficient per capita consumption set. In Figure 3 it coincides with island A's per capita production possibility curve.

Indifference maps can also be drawn on Figure 3, and it is clear that because of the assumption of identical tastes the maps for $u(\sigma_1, \sigma_2)$, $u(s_1, s_2)$ and $u(s_1^*, s_2^*)$ (where these functions represent both A and B populated, A only, and B only populated, respectively) will be identical. It follows that, for the case shown in

[8] Criteria for optimum population with several goods and with trade for a small open economy are discussed in Pitchford (1974), chapter 5.

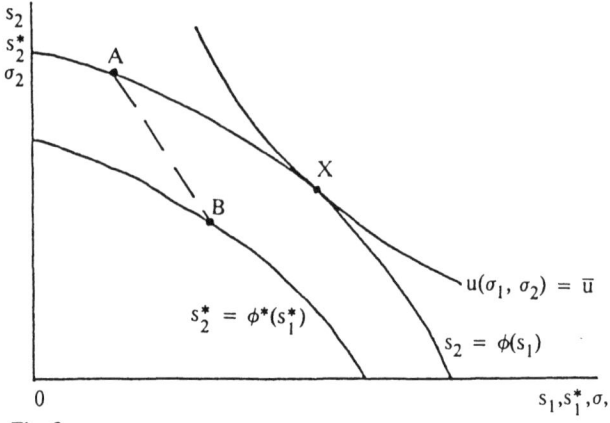

Fig. 3

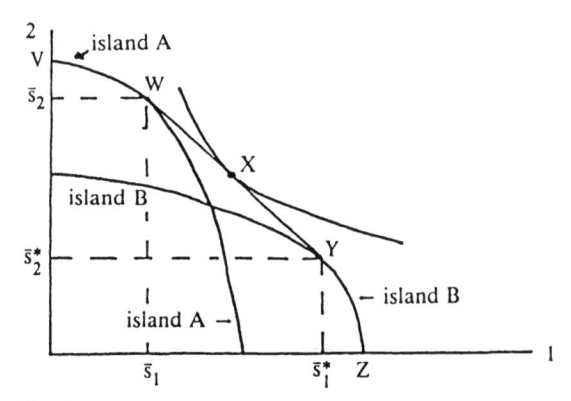

Fig. 4

Figure 3, the optimum will be at point X, which being on the production possibility curve of island A will mean island A alone is populated. Thus where the productivity of island A is such that its per capita production possibility curve lies entirely above that of island B, island B will not be populated on the basis of the individualistic criterion. Where this is not so the possibility exists that trade might make both islands sufficiently better off that island B is also populated, despite island A having to equalize its per capita consumptions with islands B. Figure 4 shows production possibility curves for the two islands that intersect.

Such a configuration could arise from there being different natural resource compositions and volumes on the two islands. The efficient boundary of the attainable set (σ_1, σ_2) is now given by VWXYZ where the linear segment WXY is tangential to both production possibility curves. This boundary is the *convex hull* of the set of individual island production possibility curves. That WXY is on this boundary follows from the fact that it has the equation

$$\begin{bmatrix} \sigma_1 \\ \sigma_2 \end{bmatrix} = \alpha \begin{bmatrix} \bar{s}_1 \\ \bar{s}_2 \end{bmatrix} + (1 - \alpha) \begin{bmatrix} \bar{s}_1^* \\ \bar{s}_2^* \end{bmatrix}, \ \alpha \in [0,1] \tag{12'}$$

An optimum is illustrated at X in which *both* islands are populated. Patterns of tastes could also be found such that only island A or island B is populated.

In short if island A's per capita productivity dominates that of island B in the sense shown in Figure 3 Meade's point still stands so that even with this form of dependence island B will not be settled under the individualistic criterion. If natural resource types and proportions produce the situation shown in Figure 4 where production possibility curves intersect, the gains from trade may make it worthwhile to populate island B. A government ruling many islands will extend its population under the individualistic criterion until it has exhausted all Figure 4 type gains.

The other form of dependence besides trade is the existence of public goods such as defence, a common language and education system, and other institutions whose cost can be shared between the islands. For any given level of supply of public goods the populating of island B will reduce their per capita cost of supply in island A, but the extra taxes which will have to be paid to equalize consumption with island B will be an offset to this benefit. To see what determines the outcome call the supply of public goods P, and using the one good case, consider the maximization of

$$u \left(\frac{F + F^* - P}{L}, P \right) \tag{20}$$

where $L = N + N^*$. The services of public goods are assumed to be provided from the output of the private good. Rewrite (20) to get

$$u \left\{ (y - \frac{P}{N}) \frac{N}{L} + y^* \frac{N^*}{L}, P \right\} \tag{20'}$$

$$u \left\{ y \frac{N}{L} + (y^* - \frac{P}{N^*}) \frac{N^*}{L}, P \right\} \tag{20''}$$

In (20') the level of per capita output of the private good is expressed as a linear combination of per capita output in island A net of the per capita cost of island A meeting the entire cost of the public good, and the per capita output of island B. In (20'') the cost of the public good is allocated entirely to island B. Now it is sufficient for island A alone to be populated at an optimum if

$$\hat{y} - (P/\hat{N}) > \hat{y}^*. \tag{21}$$

In this case island A's optimum *net* per capita output of the private good is greater than island B's optimum gross per capita output. Island A would be worse off if it had to equalize consumption per head with island B. On the other hand it is sufficient for the population of both islands if

$$\hat{y} - (P/\hat{N}) < \hat{y}^*, \text{ and} \tag{22}$$

$$\hat{y}^* - (P/\hat{N}^*) < \hat{y} \tag{22'}$$

With (22) and (22') holding neither island can provide at an optimum a given level of public goods from its own resources, and achieve a net output per head of the private good greater than that of the other. It pays each to share the cost of provision of the public good.

2.

Some would regard the preceding arguments to be somewhat damaging to the individual utility criterion. It would appear possible that world government devoted to maximizing such an objective with consumption equalization could result in an elitist community (island A) with much of the world's resources unexploited.[9] Such an outcome is not inevitable. As has been seen it all depends upon production conditions. However, supposing the worst so that some fertile areas of the world would be unpopulated on a *strict* interpretation of the per capita criterion, this is not in the author's view a reason to abandon the concepts the criterion embodies. Leaving island B unpopulated is unlikely to be in anyone's interests, even those privileged to live on island A, as will be shown. But perhaps it is not the utility criterion which has brought this about so much as the conditions with which it has been surrounded, namely one world government and consumption equalization. I turn to some arguments which give some support to the individualistic criterion and help save island B.

   1. If there is the possibility of more than one government, the residents of island A would prefer to see island B populated. As long as they don't have to equalize consumption with island B, trade with that island (and the sharing costs of some public goods), will normally improve welfare on island A. To confirm this consider the question of what population island A would prefer island B to have in order to maximize island A's welfare. Specifically, suppose island B's utility is given at some arbitrary level and ask what population level and distribution across sectors would maximize utility in A. It is required to

$$\text{Max}_{N_i, N_i^*, s_i, s_i^*} \quad u(s_1, s_2) \qquad i = 1,2 \tag{23}$$

subject to

$$s_1 N + s_1^* N = F_1 + F_1^* \tag{24}$$

$$s_2 N + s_2^* N = F_2 + F_2^* \tag{25}$$

$$s_1 N + p s_2 N = F_1 + p F_2 \tag{26}$$

$$u(s_1^*, s_2^*) = u^*(\cdot, \cdot) = \bar{u}^* \tag{27}$$

$$N = N_1 + N_2, \quad N^* = N_1^* + N_2^* \tag{28}$$

where s_i, s_i^* are per capita consumptions of good i on each island and p is endogenous.[10]

---

[9] A referee has pointed out similarities in the view expressed in this section and Rawls' (1972) thoughts on the sphere of applicability of his maximum criterion.

[10] The balanced trade condition (24) needs to be introduced when there is not a single government for the two islands.

Necessary conditions for an optimum population on island A are (24) to (28) and

$$u_1 s_1 + u_2 s_2 = u_1 F_1' = u_2 F_2' \tag{29}$$

$$u_1^* s_1^* + u_2^* s_2^* = u_1^* F_1^{*'} = u_2^* F_2^{*'} \tag{30}$$

$$p = u_2/u_1 = u_2^*/u_1^* = F_2'/F_1' = F_2^{*'}/F_1^{*'} \tag{31}$$

Condition (30) is the one of interest. It implies that if island A had its way it would prefer to trade with an island B populated according to the individualistic criterion, and, of course, this solution is preferable to the one in which island B is left unpopulated. However, if island A were forced to share a common per capita consumption level with island B we would be back to the situation in which they may prefer to see island B unpopulated. This view of the world suggests that rather than there being a sparsely populated world, with the possibility of many governments the individual geographic units involved could each be populated according to the individualistic criterion. Further the adoption of such a criterion by other countries could be seen to be of benefit to the home country. Where countries are federally governed without income equalization, the consequence of adopting an individualistic criterion could well be a series of regions each maximizing this criterion to their mutual benefit.

2. It has been assumed throughout that tastes are identical across islands. If they are not, the sorts of comparisons necessary to resolve these issues cannot be made. This again leaves scope for population of further regions, but not in terms of groups whose tastes largely coincide. The historical path to optimum population will be likely to ensure homogenous cultures and possibly tastes, within but not across regions. Differences in tastes give rise to further possibilities of gains from trade, so giving further grounds believing that the more productive regions would still like to see the less productive regions populated. Of course, if tastes are likely to differ markedly within regions there is again no point to the question of what an optimal population should be in terms of those criteria which assume identical tastes, and the applicability of the total utility concept must be seriously questioned.

3. There are some positive advantages of the individualistic over the total utility criterion. The total utility criterion is unlikely to be one which each individual in the society will endorse. This follows almost by definition as the total criterion takes the separate utility of individuals and adds them. The resultant objective is therefore likely to be one which will require intervention by the authorities in the implementation of an optimum plan. Moreover, as social and private utilities differ in a way which involves something more than the foresight of the authorities, the optimum will seem undesirable to the individual.[11] Of course incentives may be used to support the total utility optimum, but nevertheless, it will not normally accord with what individuals would choose if left to their own devices. If, however, individuals *choose* a total utility concept as the basis for their own individual welfare, then the total and individualistic criteria coincide. In the absence of this outcome the individual criterion has the merit that, externalities aside, individual and social

---

[11] A type of externality analogous to the congestion externality which can occur with the individualistic criterion is discussed in Pitchford (1985).

criteria for optimum population are the same. Therefore intervention to ensure an optimum will be confined to that needed to correct for various possible externalities.

3.

This paper has attempted to elucidate the nature of an individualistic utility based optimum population by showing how economic interdependencies such as trade and public goods determine how far population would be spread across regions of differing productivity. When all opportunities for beneficial trade and the sharing of the costs of public goods are exhausted it will not be optimal to extend population into further regions.

All this follows if there is one government and if that government insists on the equalization of consumption per capita in the populated world. Without one or both of these conditions it is in the interests of the more productive regions that those less productive should be populated, as long as they can trade. Further, if tastes differ across but not within regions the individualistic criterion would have a place in the determination of each region's optimum population. Nevertheless, this view of the world with each region populated according to the per capita criterion, does not tie down optimum population completely. What factors determine the division of the world into regions with separate governments? To explain them as due to historical accident may seem a practical solution, but the fact remains that optimal criteria do not determine them. Another aspect of this question is the fate of the poorest region. If it is in the interest of the wealthier regions to establish populations in poorer regions, how far will this subdivision of productive land go? One answer would be that it could extend until subsistence consumption is reached in the poorest region. The hardly seems a happy consequence of an optimal population criterion.[12] Presumably it would be up to sovereign governments to impose some minimum acceptable consumption levels by limiting the extent to which they will subdivide their territories into partially or fully self governing regions. It is likely that there would be political pressure to ensure this. Thus provided one accepts some historical process as determining self governing regions of the world, the individualistic criterion would still seem to have a place in relation to optimum population.

References

Dasgupta, P. S. (1969) On the Concept of Optimum Population. Review of Economic Studies
Meade, J. M. The Theory of Economic Policy. Volume II, Trade and Welfare, Oxford University Press, London, Chapter 4, and Mathematical Supplement, Chapter 1
Pitchford, J. D. (1974) Population in Economic Growth, North Holland, Amsterdam, Chapter 5
Pitchford, J. D. (1985) External Effects of Population Growth, Oxford Economic Papers
Rawls, J. (1972) A Theory of Justice, Oxford University Press, London

---

[12] The imposition of a Rawlsian criterion maximizing the minimum individual utility attained when population is a choice variable across islands would concentrate population in the individual utility maximizing consumption sharing group described in section II. Otherwise minimum per capita utility could be raised by depopulating an island, or by sharing consumption between islands.

An Analysis of International Migration: The Unilateral Case[1]

Murray C. Kemp and Hitoshi Kondo

1. Introduction

Any fully satisfactory analysis of population change, whether of the descriptive variety or of the welfare-theoretical variety, must contain within it a satisfactory analysis of the international migration of labour. However in the analysis of migration pitfalls abound; as a result, the subject remains in a quite primitive state, for the most part simply aping the theory of long-term international capital flows. In particular, the analysis of migration lacks a firm basis in the decision-making of individual households. Exempted from these comments is the recent paper by Galor (1986). That paper will be discussed at the end of Section 2.

Suppose that a family is contemplating the possibility of migrating to another country. It must decide whether to migrate at all; and, if the desirability of migration is accepted, it must decide whether the entire family or only some portion of it is to move and whether the move is to be permanent or temporary. To capture all dimensions of the family's problem one must employ an overlapping-generations model in which individuals live for three periods: childhood, adulthood and retirement. During childhood individuals make no decisions and play a purely passive role. During adulthood individuals work, save and raise families; moreover at the end of childhood individuals decide whether to migrate, permanently or temporarily, with their families or without them. These adult decisions concerning saving, family size and migration all depend on the opportunities available both at home and abroad; and what those opportunities are and how they are appraised depend on the family's preferences, on technological conditions at home and abroad, and on the several countries' endowments of factors (including labour). Evidently migration can arise from international disparities in any or all of preferences, technology and endowments. However, to avoid muddling the causal links, it would be advantageous to concentrate on one thing at a time. Here we develop a general-equilibrium theory of migration based on an international disparity of preferences. For the most part it will be assumed that the preferences of an individual are determined once and for all by his country of birth; if he migrates, he carries his preferences with him. However in a brief final section we consider some of the implications of relaxing that assumption. To further simplify the analysis we concentrate on steady states and assume both that all migration is permanent and that, during any given period, all migration is in the same direction.

---

[1] We acknowledge with gratitude the helpful comments of Oded Galor, Kar-yiu Wong, Klaus F. Zimmermann and the referee.

Microeconomic Studies
K. F. Zimmermann (Ed.)
Economic Theory of Optimal Population
© Springer-Verlag Berlin Heidelberg 1989

It will be shown that if an individual's preferences depend only on his country of birth then all steady-state migration is from the country with the relatively high rate of time preference to the country with the relatively low rate of time preference, but that if preferences can change after migration then steady-state migration might be in the opposite direction.

2. Preference-Based Migration

Two countries A and B produce a single commodity, which is the same in each country. This commodity can be consumed or accumulated for one period. The inputs are labour and capital (accumulated output). The same constant-returns production function prevails in each country. Thus

$$Y(t) = F[K(t), L(t)] = L(t) F[K(t)/L(t), 1] \equiv L(t)f[k(t)] \qquad (1)$$
$$F[K(t), 0] = 0$$

where $K(t)$ is the stock of capital and $L(t)$ the labour force during period t. All markets are competitive; hence

$$w(t) = \partial F[K(t), L(t)]/\partial L(t) = f[k(t)] - k(t)f'[k(t)] \qquad (2)$$
$$r(t) = \partial F[K(t), L(t)]/\partial K(t) = f'[k(t)]$$

where $w(t)$ is the wage rate and $r(t) - 1$ the rental of capital during period t.

Individuals live for three periods. During their childhood they make no decisions. During their adulthood they work, raise a family and save; possibly they migrate, at the beginning of the period and therefore without capital. During their retirement they live on their savings.

Each individual's preferences are represented by a utility function. The function takes the strictly separable form

$$u(t) = u_1[c_1(t)] + v[n(t)] + \alpha u_2[c_2(t+1)] \qquad (\alpha < 1) \qquad (3)$$

where $c_1(t)$ is the consumption of a typical adult during period t, $c_2(t+1)$ is the consumption of the same individual during retirement, $n(t)$ is the number of children raised by a typical adult during period t and $1/\alpha$ is a measure of the individual's time preference. Each of the functions u_1, u_2, v is increasing and strictly concave. (Later, the utility function and all variables will be given superscripts to indicate the country in which the individual was reared.) Individuals may or may not marry at the beginning of adulthood. Since (3) excludes any motive for making bequests, it also excludes the externality which marriage and bequests combine to generate. (See Kemp and Long (1982).) Whether or not individuals marry, $n(t)$ is defined as the number of children per adult. To enable us to later place a sign on certain expressions, the following restriction is placed on u_2.

(A1) The marginal utility of retirement consumption is not elastic; that is, $|c_2 u_2'' / u_2'| \leqq 1$.

There might be an international disparity in the form of any subset of the functions u_1, u_2, v and/or in the value assigned to α. For clarity of thought, however, it is essential that we concentrate on a single-parameter disparity. Here we assume that an individual's time preference is determined by the country of his childhood but that all individuals, wherever they are brought up, share the same functions u_1, u_2, v. Specifically, it is assumed that individuals reared in country A have a higher rate of time preference than individuals born in country B: $\alpha^A < \alpha^B$. Each individual, whatever his time preference, inelastically supplies one unit of labour.

Each individual has perfect myopic (one-period) foresight.

Autarkic economies The typical individual seeks to maximize (3) subject to the budget constraint

$$c_1(t) + \phi [n(t)] + c_2(t+1) / r(t+1) \leqq w(t) \tag{4}$$

where $\phi[n]$ is the cost in terms of output of raising n children ($\phi[0] = 0, \phi' > 0, \phi'' < 0$) and where $w(t)$ and $r(t+1)$ are taken as given. To ensure that the problem has a solution and that the solution is unique we add a further assumption.

(A2)   The elasticity of the marginal utility derived from children is not less than the elasticity of the marginal cost of raising children; that is, $|nv''/v'| \geqq |n\phi''/\phi'|$.

The first-order conditions for an interior solution are

$$u_1' [c_1(t)] = \lambda(t) \tag{5a}$$

$$v'[n(t)] = \lambda(t)\phi'[n(t)] \tag{5b}$$

$$\alpha u_2' [c_2(t+1)] = \lambda(t)/r(t+1) \tag{5c}$$

$$c_1(t) + \phi[n(t)] + c_2(t+1)/r(t+1) = w(t) \tag{5d}$$

Equation (5) yields unique values of the control variables $c_1(t)$, $c_2(t+1)$ and $n(t)$ in terms of $w(t)$ and $r(t+1)$. Those values, with (3), yield the indirect utility function $U[w(t), r(t+1)]$. Differentiating (5), and calling on (A1) and (A2), we obtain the partial-equilibrium comparative-statical results:

$$\partial c_1(t)/\partial w(t) = - \alpha u_2'' (v'' - \lambda\phi'')/D \geqq 0 \tag{6a}$$

$$\partial n(t)/\partial w(t) = - \alpha\phi' u_1'' u_2''/D > 0 \tag{6b}$$

$$\partial c_2(t+1)/\partial w(t) = - u_1'' (v'' - \lambda\phi'')/r(t+1) D \geqq 0 \tag{6c}$$

$$\partial c_1(t)/\partial r(t+1) = - \alpha(u_2' + c_2 u_2'') (v'' - \lambda\phi'')/r(t+1)^2 D \leqq 0 \tag{6d}$$

$$\partial n(t)/\partial r(t+1) = - \alpha\phi' u_1'' (u_2' + c_2 u_2'')/r(t+1)^2 D \leqq 0 \tag{6e}$$

$$\partial c_2(t+1)/\partial r(t+1) = \{-c_2 u_1'' (v'' - \lambda\phi'') + \lambda(v'' - \lambda\phi'' + \tag{6f}$$
$$(\phi')^2 u_1'')r(t+1)\}/(t+1)^3 D > 0$$

$$\partial c_1(t)/\partial \alpha = - u_2' (v'' - \lambda\phi'')/r(t+1) D \leqq 0 \tag{6g}$$

$$\partial n(t)/\partial \alpha = - \phi' u_2' u_1''/r(t+1) D < 0 \tag{6h}$$

$$\partial c_2(t+1)/\partial \alpha = u_2' (v'' - \lambda\phi'' + (\phi')^2 u_1'')/D > 0 \tag{6i}$$

where $D \equiv - \{ u_1'' (v'' - \lambda\phi'') / r(t+1)^2 + \alpha u_2'' (v'' - \lambda\phi'' + (\phi')^2 u_1'') \} < 0$ is the determinant of the bordered Hessian matrix associated with the problem.

Equations (2) and (5) make up a dynamic general-equilibrium autarkic system. Condensing it slightly, we obtain

$$\frac{u_1'\,[c_1(t)]}{\alpha u_2'\,[c_2(t+1)]} = f'\,[k(t+1)] \tag{7a}$$

$$\frac{v'\,[n(t)]}{u_1'\,[c_1(t)]} = \phi'\,[n(t)] \tag{7b}$$

$$c_1(t) + \phi[n(t)] + c_2(t+1)/f'\,[k(t+1)] = f[k(t)] - k(t)f'\,[k(t)] \tag{7c}$$

$$c_2(t+1) = n(t)k(t+1)f'\,[k(t+1)] \tag{7d}$$

where (7d) emerges from the relations $k\,(t+1) = s\,(t)L(t)/L(t+1)$, $L\,(t+1) = n(t)L(t)$ and $s(t) \equiv c_2(t+1)/r(t+1)$. Let $k(t+1) = H[k(t)]$ be the dynamic equation of $k(t)$, satisfying (7). It will be assumed that the autarkic system (7) has a unique and stable steady state $(\hat{c}_1, \hat{c}_2, \hat{n}, \hat{k},)$ with $\hat{k} = H[\hat{k}]$.[2]

We proceed to prove a series of preliminary propositions.

Lemma 1: Suppose that $k(t) = k(t+1) = k$. Then an increase in k gives rise to an increase in the number of children.

Proof: We have

$$\frac{dn(t)}{dk}\bigg|_{k(t)\,=\,k(t+1)\,=\,k} = \{-k\frac{\partial n(t)}{\partial w(t)} + \frac{\partial n(t)}{\partial r(t+1)}\} f'' > 0$$

where the inequality is an implication of (6b) and (6e). $\qquad$ Q.E.D.

Lemma 2: If $\alpha^A < \alpha^B$ then, for any common $\{w(t), r(t+1)\}$, $n^A(t) > n^B(t)$ and $s^A(t) < s^B(t)$.

Proof: From (6h), $\partial n(t)/\partial \alpha < 0$; and, from (6i), $\partial s(t)/\partial \alpha = (1/r(t+1))$ $(\partial c_2(t+1)/\partial \alpha) > 0$. $\qquad$ Q.E.D.

Lemma 3: If $\alpha^A < \alpha^B$ then, for any common $\{w(t), r(t+1)\}$,

$$\left| \frac{dr(t+1)}{dw(t)} \right|_{U^A\ const} > \left| \frac{dr(t+1)}{dw(t)} \right|_{U^B\ const}$$

Proof: We have

$$\frac{dr(t+1)}{dw(t)}\bigg|_{U^i\ const} = -\frac{\partial U^i[w(t),\,r(t+1)]/\partial w(t)}{\partial U^i[w(t),\,r(t+1)]/\partial r(t+1)}$$

$$= -r(t+1)/s^i(t)$$

where in writing the second equality use has been made of Roy's identity.[3] The proposition then follows from Lemma 2. $\qquad$ Q.E.D.

---

2) If $H' < 0$ then the uniqueness of the steady state is guaranteed.
3) For Roy's identity see, for example, Malinvaud (1985).

Lemma 4: If $\alpha^A < \alpha^B$ then, given that $k^A(t) = k^B(t) = k(t)$, $k^A(t+1) < k^B(t+1)$ and $n^A(t) > n^B(t)$ along the autarkic equilibrium paths.

Proof: Differentiating equilibrium equations (2) and

$$w(t) = c_1 [w(t),r(t+1), \alpha] + \phi[n[w(t),r(t+1),\alpha]] + n[w(t),r(t+1),\alpha] k(t+1)$$

with respect to α, we obtain

$$\frac{dk(t+1)}{d\alpha} = \frac{-\{(\partial c_1/\partial\alpha) + (\phi' + k(t+1)) (\partial n/\partial\alpha)\}}{\{(\partial c_1/\partial r) + (\phi' + k(t+1)) (\partial n/\partial r)\} f''[k(t+1)] + n} > 0$$

$$\frac{dn(t)}{d\alpha} = (\partial n/\partial r) (dr/dk) (dk/d\alpha) + (\partial n/\partial\alpha)$$

$$= \frac{n(\partial n/\partial\alpha)}{\{(\partial c_1/\partial r) + (\phi' + k(t+1)) (\partial n/\partial r)\} f''[k(t+1)] + n} < 0 \qquad \text{Q.E.D.}$$

Lemma 5: If $\alpha^A < \alpha^B$ and if the autarkic steady states are unique and stable then $\hat{k}^A < \hat{k}^B$.

Proof: From Lemma 4, for $k^B(t) = \hat{k}^A$, $k^B(t+1) > \hat{k}^A = H^A[\hat{k}^A]$.
It then follows immediately from the stability of the autarkic steady state $\hat{k}^B$ that $\hat{k}^A < \hat{k}^B$. \qquad Q.E.D.

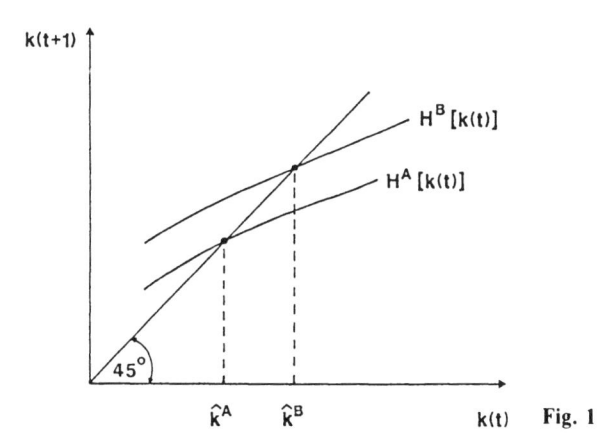

Fig. 1

Figure 1 illustrates the lemma for the case in which $dk(t+1) / dk(t) > 0$.

Open Economies   Consider now a world in which there are no barriers to migration.

Let $L^i(t)$ be interpreted now as the number of individuals who were reared in country i during period $t - 1$ and who therefore reach adulthood at the beginning of period t. Let $L^{ij}(t)$ be the number of migrants from i to j during period t, let $s^{ij}(t)$ be the saving of a typical migrant, and let $n^{ij}(t)$ be the number of children raised by the typical migrant. We shall say that $(p^i(t), p^j(t))$, where $p^i(t) \equiv (w^i(t), r^i(t+1))$ $(i = A, B)$, is an equilibrium price vector with unilateral migration if

$$0 < L^{ij}(t) < L^i(t) \text{ and } L^{ji}(t) = 0$$

$$U^i[p^i(t)] = U^i[p^j(t)] \text{ and } U^j[p^i(t)] \leqq U^j[p^j(t)]$$

If $(p^i(t), p^j(t))$ is an equilibrium price vector with unilateral migration and if $p^i(t) = p^i$, a constant $(i = A, B)$, then we shall say that $(p^i(t), p^j(t))$ is a stationary equilibrium price vector with unilateral migration. Let a *tilde* denote steady-state values; thus, in a steady state, $k^i(t) = \tilde{k}^i$, $n^i(t) = \tilde{n}^i$, $s^i(t) = \tilde{s}^i$. Henceforth it will be assumed that there is a unique stationary equilibrium with unilateral migration.

Lemma 6: In a stationary equilibrium with unilateral migration, the direction of migration is always the same.

Proof: Suppose that the direction of migration changes from some period to the next. Then, from the definition of an equilibrium price vector with unilateral migration, $U^A[\tilde{p}^A] = U^A[\tilde{p}^B]$ and $U^B[\tilde{p}^A] = U^B[\tilde{p}^B]$. Hence, from Lemma 3, $\tilde{p}^A = \tilde{p}^B$ $= \tilde{p}$. It follows that $\tilde{k}^A = \tilde{k}^B = \tilde{k}$ and, therefore, that $\tilde{s}^i = \tilde{s}^{ij}$, $\tilde{n}^i = \tilde{n}^{ij}$ for $i,j =$ A, B and $i \neq j$.

Suppose that migration is from country i to country j during periods t and $t+1$ and from j to i during period $t+2$. Then

$$k^i(t+1) = \frac{L^i(t) - L^{ij}(t)}{L^i(t+1) - L^{ij}(t+1)} \, s^i(t)$$

$$k^i(t+2) = \frac{L^i(t+1) - L^{ij}(t+1)}{L^i(t+2) + L^{ji}(t+2)} \, s^i(t+1)$$

Making use of the fact that $L^i(\tau) = n^i(\tau-1) (L^i(\tau-1) - L^{ij}(\tau-1))$ for $\tau = t+1$, $t+2$, and confining attention to the steady state,

$$\tilde{k}^i = \tilde{s}^i / (\tilde{n}^i(1 - \frac{L^{ij}(t+1)}{L^i(t+1)})) > \tilde{s}^i / \tilde{n}^i$$

$$\tilde{k}^i = \tilde{s}^i / (\tilde{n}^i(1 + \frac{L^{ji}(t+2)}{L^i(t+2)})) < \tilde{s}^i / \tilde{n}^i$$

which is a contradiction. If follows that if the direction of migration ever changes then it must change after every period.

Suppose therefore that migration is from i to j during periods t and $t+2$ and from j to i during $t+1$. Then

$$k^i(t+1) = \frac{L^i(t) - L^{ij}(t)}{L^i(t+1) + L^{ji}(t+1)} \, s^i(t) \tag{8a}$$

$$k^i(t+2) = \frac{L^i(t+1)}{L^i(t+2) - L^{ij}(t+2)} \, s^i(t+1) + \frac{L^{ji}(t+1)}{L^i(t+2) - L^{ij}(t+2)} \, s^{ji}(t+1) \tag{8b}$$

and

$$k^j(t+2) = \frac{L^j(t+1) - L^{ji}(t+1)}{L^j(t+2) + L^{ij}(t+2)} \, s^j(t+1) \tag{8c}$$

From (8a),

$$\bar{k}^i = \bar{s}^i / (\bar{n}^i (1 + \frac{L^{ji}(t+1)}{L^i(t+1)})) < \bar{s}^i / \bar{n}^i; \tag{8a'}$$

from (8c),

$$\bar{k}^j = \bar{s}^j / (\bar{n}^j (1 + \frac{L^{ij}(t+2)}{L^j(t+2)})) < \bar{s}^j / \bar{n}^j; \tag{8c'}$$

and, from (8b) and the fact that $\bar{n}^{ji} = \bar{n}^j$ and $\bar{s}^{ji} = \bar{s}^j$,

$$\bar{k}^j = \frac{\bar{n}^i L^i(t+1)}{L^i(t+2) - L^{ij}(t+2)} \frac{\bar{s}^i}{\bar{n}^i} + \frac{\bar{n}^j L^{ji}(t+1)}{L^i(t+2) - L^{ij}(t+2)} \frac{\bar{s}^j}{\bar{n}^j} \tag{8b'}$$

On the other hand, $L^i(t+2) = \bar{n}^i L^i(t+1) + \bar{n}^j L^{ji}(t+1)$. Hence the sum of the coefficients in (8b') is greater than one, which is contrary to (8a') and (8c').

If follows that if there exists a unique steady state with unilateral migration then the direction of migration is the same in every period. Q.E.D.

Lemma 7: In a steady state with unilateral migration from country i to country j and $k^i(t)$, $n^i(t)$ and $s^i(t)$ constant, the rate of emigration, $L^{ij}(t)/L^i(t)$, the rate of immigration, $L^{ij}(t)/(L^j(t) + L^{ij}(t))$, the rates of growth of the two work forces, $(L^i(t+1) - L^{ij}(t+1))/(L^i(t) - L^{ij}(t))$ and $(L^j(t+1) + L^{ij}(t+1))/(L^j(t) + L^{ij}(t))$, and the average birth rate in the host country are all constant.

Proof: We have, for country i,

$$k^i(t+1) = \frac{s^i(t) (L^i(t) - L^{ij}(t))}{L^i(t+1) - L^{ij}(t+1)}$$

$$= \frac{s^i(t) (L^i(t) - L^{ij}(t))}{n^i(t) (L^i(t) - L^{ij}(t)) - L^{ij}(t+1)}$$

$$= \frac{s^i(t)}{n^i(t) \{1 - L^{ij}(t+1)/L^i(t+1)\}}$$

implying that, in the steady state,

$$\bar{k}^i = \bar{s}^i / (\bar{n}^i \{ 1 - L^{ij}(t+1) / L^i(t+1) \}) \tag{9}$$

It follows that, in the steady state, the rate of emigration is $L^{ij}(t)/L^i(t) = \beta$, a constant.

The rate of growth of the labour force is then given by

$$\frac{L^i(t+1) - L^{ij}(t+1)}{L^i(t) - L^{ij}(t)} = \frac{L^i(t+1)}{L^i(t) - L^{ij}(t)} \left(1 - \frac{L^{ij}(t+1)}{L^i(t+1)}\right)$$

$$= \tilde{n}^i(1 - \beta)$$

and the rate of growth of emigration by

$$\frac{L^{ij}(t+1)}{L^{ij}(t)} = \frac{L^i(t) - L^{ij}(t)}{L^{ij}(t)} \frac{L^i(t+1) - L^{ij}(t+1)}{L^i(t) - L^{ij}(t)} \frac{L^{ij}(t+1)}{L^i(t+1) - L^{ij}(t+1)}$$

$$= \tilde{n}^i(1 - \beta)$$

Turning to country j, we have

$$k^j(t+1) = \frac{s^j(t)L^j(t) + s^{ij}(t)L^{ij}(t)}{n^j(t)L^j(t) + n^{ij}(t)L^{ij}(t) + L^{ij}(t+1)}$$

$$= \frac{s^j(t)\left\{ 1 + \dfrac{s^{ij}(t)}{s^j(t)} \dfrac{L^{ij}(t)}{L^j(t)} \right\}}{n^j(t)\left\{ 1 + \dfrac{n^{ij}(t)}{n^j(t)} \dfrac{L^{ij}(t)}{L^j(t)} + \dfrac{1}{n^j(t)} \dfrac{L^{ij}(t+1)}{L^j(t)} \right\}}$$

so that, in the steady state,

$$\bar{k}^j = \frac{\tilde{s}^j \left\{ 1 + \dfrac{\tilde{s}^{ij}}{\tilde{s}^j} \dfrac{L^{ij}(t)}{L^j(t)} \right\}}{\tilde{n}^j \left\{ 1 + \dfrac{\tilde{n}^{ij}}{\tilde{n}^j} \dfrac{L^{ij}(t)}{L^j(t)} + (1-\beta) \dfrac{\tilde{n}^i}{\tilde{n}^j} \dfrac{L^{ij}(t)}{L^j(t)} \right\}} \qquad (10)$$

It follows that the rate of immigration $L^{ij}(t)/(L^j(t) + L^{ij}(t)) = \gamma / (1+\gamma)$ where $\gamma = L^{ij}(t)/L^j(t)$ is a constant. It can then be shown that $L^j(t+1)/L^j(t) = \tilde{n}^j + \gamma\tilde{n}^{ij}$, so that the average birth rate is

$$\frac{L^j(t+1)}{L^j(t) + L^{ij}(t)} = \frac{L^j(t+1)/L^j(t)}{1 + (L^{ij}(t)/L^j(t))} = \frac{\tilde{n}^j + \gamma\tilde{n}^{ij}}{1+\gamma}$$

Finally, the rate of growth of the work-force is

$$\frac{L^j(t+1) + L^{ij}(t+1)}{L^j(t) + L^{ij}(t)} = \frac{L^j(t+1)}{L^j(t)} \frac{1 + (L^{ij}(t+1)/L^j(t+1))}{1 + (L^{ij}(t)/L^j(t))} = \tilde{n}^j + \gamma\tilde{n}^{ij}$$

$$\text{Q.E.D.}$$

It follows from Lemma 7, with (9) and (10), that

$$\bar{k}^i = \tilde{s}^i / (\tilde{n}^i (1 - \beta)) \qquad (11a)$$

$$\bar{k}^j = \frac{\tilde{s}^j}{\tilde{n}^j} \frac{1 + \gamma\tilde{s}^{ij} / \tilde{s}^j}{1 + (\gamma\tilde{n}^{ij} / \tilde{n}^j) + (\gamma(1 - \beta) \tilde{n}^i / \tilde{n}^j)} \qquad (11b)$$

Lemma 8: Suppose that $\alpha^A < \alpha^B$ and that there is a stationary equilibrium with unilateral migration.

(a) If the migration is from country A to country B then

$$\tilde{k}^A > \tilde{s}^A / \tilde{n}^A \text{ and } \tilde{k}^B < \tilde{s}^B / \tilde{n}^B$$

(b) If the migration is from country B to country A then

$$\tilde{k}^A < \tilde{s}^{BA} / \tilde{n}^{BA} \text{ and } \tilde{k}^B > \tilde{s}^B / \tilde{n}^B$$

Proof: (a) From Lemma 2, if the migration is from A to B,

$$\tilde{n}^{AB} / \tilde{n}^B > 1 \text{ and } \tilde{s}^{AB} / \tilde{s}^B < 1 \tag{12}$$

Then, from (11) and (12),

$$\tilde{k}^A = \tilde{s}^A / (\tilde{n}^A (1 - \beta)) > \tilde{s}^A / \tilde{n}^A$$

$$\tilde{k}^B = \frac{\tilde{s}^B}{\tilde{n}^B} \frac{1 + \gamma \tilde{s}^{AB} / \tilde{s}^B}{1 + (\gamma \tilde{n}^{AB} / \tilde{n}^B) + (\gamma (1-\beta)\tilde{n}^A / \tilde{n}^B)} < \tilde{s}^B / \tilde{n}^B$$

(b) If the migration is from B to A,

$$\tilde{n}^A / \tilde{n}^{BA} > 1 \text{ and } \tilde{s}^A / \tilde{s}^{BA} < 1 \tag{13}$$

From (11a),

$$\tilde{k}^B = \tilde{s}^B / (\tilde{n}^B (1 - \beta)) > \tilde{s}^B / \tilde{n}^B$$

and, from (11b) and (13),

$$\tilde{k}^A = \frac{\tilde{s}^{BA}}{\tilde{n}^{BA}} \frac{1 + \tilde{s}^A / (\gamma \tilde{s}^{BA})}{(1 + \tilde{n}^A \gamma n^{BA}) + (1-\beta)\tilde{n}^B / \tilde{n}^{BA}} < \tilde{s}^{BA} / \tilde{n}^{BA} \qquad \text{Q.E.D.}$$

Lemma 9: If $\alpha^A < \alpha^B$ and there is a unique steady state with unilateral migration from country i to country j then $\tilde{k}^j < \hat{k}^B$.

Proof: Consider Figure 2, in which QQ is the locus of feasible autarkic steady-state pairs (w, r) in each country and $H^B H^B$ is the locus of equilibrium autarkic pairs (w(t), r(t+1)) in country B. Since by assumption there is a unique autarkic steady state, the two loci intersect in the manner depicted.

Suppose that $\tilde{k}^j \geq \hat{k}^B$, so that $\tilde{w}^j \geq \hat{w}^B$ and $\tilde{r}^j \leq \hat{r}^B$. Suppose further that $w^B(t) = \tilde{w}^j$, so that $r^B(t+1) \geq \tilde{r}^j$.

Then, from (6d) and (6e),

$$s^B(\tilde{w}^j, \tilde{r}^j) \leq s^B(\tilde{w}^j, r^B(t+1))$$

$$n^B(\tilde{w}^j, \tilde{r}^j) \geq n^B(\tilde{w}^j, r^B(t+1))$$

and, therefore,

$$\frac{s^B(\tilde{w}^j, \tilde{r}^j)}{n^B(\tilde{w}^j, \tilde{r}^j)} \leq \frac{s^B(\tilde{w}^j, r^B(t+1))}{n^B(\tilde{w}^j, r^B(t+1))}$$

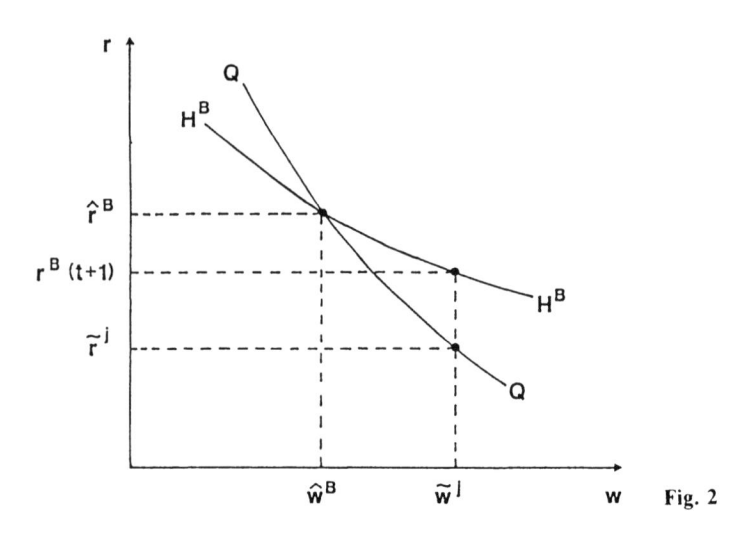

Fig. 2

Moreover, since

$$s^B(\tilde{w}^j, \tilde{r}^j) = \begin{cases} \tilde{s}^B & \text{if } j = B \\ \tilde{s}^{BA} & \text{if } j = A \end{cases}$$

$$n^B(\tilde{w}^j, \tilde{r}^j) = \begin{cases} \tilde{n}^B & \text{if } j = B \\ \tilde{n}^{BA} & \text{if } j = A \end{cases}$$

and, from Lemma 8,

$$\tilde{k}^j < \begin{cases} \tilde{s}^B / \tilde{n}^B & \text{if } j = B \\ \tilde{s}^{BA} / \tilde{n}^{BA} & \text{if } j = A \end{cases}$$

we have

$$\tilde{k}^i < \frac{s^B(\tilde{w}^j, \tilde{r}^j)}{n^B(\tilde{w}^j, \tilde{r}^j)} \leqq \frac{s^B(\tilde{w}^j, r^B(t+1))}{n^B(\tilde{w}^j, r^B(t+1))}$$

Since $f'[x]$ is monotonically decreasing in x it then follows that

$$\tilde{r}^j = f'[\tilde{k}^j] > r^B(t+1)$$

contrary to our assumption. Hence $\tilde{k}^j < \hat{k}^B$.   Q.E.D.

Lemma 10: If $\alpha^A < \alpha^B$ and there is a unique steady state with unilateral migration from country i to country j then $\tilde{k}^i > \hat{k}^i$.

Proof: Suppose that $\tilde{k}^i \leqq \hat{k}^i$. From the proof of Lemma 9,

$$\frac{s^i(\tilde{w}^i, \tilde{r}^i)}{n^i(\tilde{w}^i, \tilde{r}^i)} \geqq \frac{s^i(\tilde{w}^i, r^i(t+1))}{n^i(\tilde{w}^i, r^i(t+1))}$$

Moreover, from Lemma 8, $\tilde{k}^i > \tilde{s}^i / \tilde{n}^i$. Therefore $\tilde{r}^i = f'[\tilde{k}^i] < r^i(t+1)$, a contradiction. Hence $\tilde{k}^i > \hat{k}^i$.   Q.E.D.

Lemma 11: If $\alpha^A < \alpha^B$ and there is a unique steady state with unilateral migration then $\bar{k}^A \geqq \bar{k}^B$.

Proof: Suppose that $\bar{k}^A < \bar{k}^B$. Then $\bar{w}^A < \bar{w}^B$ and $\bar{r}^A > \bar{r}^B$; that is, $\bar{p}^B \equiv (\bar{w}^B, \bar{r}^B)$ lies to the right of $\bar{p}^A \equiv (\bar{w}^A, \bar{r}^A)$ on the locus QQ of Figure 2. Suppose further that in the steady state migration is from A to B. Therefore

$$U^A[\bar{p}^A] = U^A[\bar{p}^B], \quad U^B[\bar{p}^A] \leqq U^B[\bar{p}^B]$$

On the other hand, we know from Lemma 3 that the contours of U^A and U^B are negatively sloped with those of U^A steeper than those of U^B, so that each pair intersects only once; moreover $\bar{p}^B$ lies to the right of $\bar{p}^A$ and $U^A[\bar{p}^A] = U^A[\bar{p}^B]$. It follows that $\bar{p}^B$ lies below the curve $U^B[\bar{p}^A]$. Hence $U^B[\bar{p}^A] > U^B[\bar{p}^B]$, a contradiction. Thus $\bar{k}^A \geqq \bar{k}^B$.

By similar reasoning the same inequality is obtained when migration is from B to A.   Q.E.D.

That completes the preliminary calculations.

Theorem 1: Suppose that $\alpha^A < \alpha^B$ and that there exists a steady state with unilateral migration. Then the steady-state migration is from country A to country B, and

$$\hat{k}^A < \bar{k}^A, \hat{k}^B > \bar{k}^B, \hat{k}^A \geqq \hat{k}^B$$

$$\hat{n}^A < \bar{n}^A, \hat{n}^B > \bar{n}^B, \hat{n}^A \geqq \hat{n}^{AB}$$

Proof: Suppose that the migration is from B to A. Then, from Lemmas 9 and 11, $\hat{k}^B > \hat{k}^A \geqq \bar{k}^B$; and, from Lemma 10, $\hat{k}^B < \bar{k}^B$. This is a contradiction. The inequalities follow from Lemmas 1, 2, 9, 10 and 11.   Q.E.D.

Thus the steady-state migration is from the country with a high rate of time preference to the country with a low rate. Moreover the capital-labour ratio and the birth rate of residents (non-migrants) is higher in the former and lower in the latter than in the absence of migration.

Now we turn to the welfare implications of international labour migration. We cannot generally pin down the relationship between the locus of feasible steady-state pairs QQ and an isoquant U which is the locus of pairs giving the same utility, and this makes a welfare analysis ambiguous. However not all is lost.

Theorem 2: Suppose that $\alpha^A < \alpha^B$, that there exists a steady state with unilateral migration, and that QQ and U^i intersect at most once. If $\hat{r}^A < (>)\hat{n}^A$ then $U^A[\hat{p}^A] > (<)U^A[\tilde{p}]$ and if $\hat{r}^B < (>)\hat{n}^B$ then $U^B[\hat{p}^B] < (>)U^B[\tilde{p}]$, where $\tilde{p} = \tilde{p}^A = \tilde{p}^B$.

Proof: Since QQ and U^i intersect at most once, $\hat{k}^A < \bar{k}^A = \bar{k}^B < \hat{k}^B$, implying that $\tilde{p} = \tilde{p}^A = \tilde{p}^B$. The inequality $\hat{k}^A < \bar{k}^A$ implies that $\tilde{p}$ lies to the right of $\hat{p}^A$ on QQ. Evaluating $dr(t+1)/dw(t) \mid_{QQ} = 1/k(t)$ and $dr(t+1)/dw(t) \mid_{u\,const} = -r(t+1)/s(t)$ at $\hat{p}^A$ and recalling that $\hat{s}^A = \hat{n}^A\hat{k}^A$, we see that $U^A[\hat{p}^A]$ intersects QQ from below (above) if $\hat{r}^A =$ is less than (greater than) $\hat{n}^A$. Hence $U^A[\hat{p}^A] > (<)U^A[\tilde{p}]$ as $\hat{r}^A < (>)\hat{n}^A$.

The second half of the proposition can be proved in a similar way, beginning with the observation that $\hat{k}^B > \bar{k}^B$ implies that $\tilde{p}$ lies to the left of $\hat{p}^B$ on QQ.   Q.E.D.

Thus if the autarkic steady state of each country is characterized by under-investment (over-investment) relative to the Golden Rule then the utility of an individual reared in the source country will increase (fall) as the result of international labour mobility and the utility of an individual reared in the host country will decrease (rise). Moreover if the country with a high rate of time preference suffers from over-investment (under-investment) and if the country with a low rate of time preference suffers from under-investment (over-investment) relative to the Golden Rule, then international migration will lower (raise) the utility of all individuals in both countries.

We now comment briefly on the related work of Oded Galor (1986). Like us, Galor explored the pattern and welfare implications of international labour migration between two countries with different rates of time preference. In its general conception Galor's paper is highly original. However he made the implausible assumption that in each period and in each country the endowment of labour is exogenous and constant, independent of levels of migration; in particular, he assumed that, even if the entire workforce emigrates in one period, next period's workforce will be unchanged. Moreover he defines the cum-migration steady state in two different ways and this renders part of his analysis ambiguous. In our analysis, on the other hand, population growth is endogenous, costly and related to earlier and current rates of migration.

3. Migration and the Utility Function

It has been assumed in Section 2 that individuals carry their utility function with them when they migrate, and it has been shown that migration in the steady state is from the country with high time preference to the country with low time preference. However, as mentioned in Section 1, the individual's utility function might be influenced by his migration. We now consider a simple case in which the utility function $u(t)$ shifts monotonically and show that it is possible that the migration is from the country with low time preference to the country with high time preference.

Suppose that the utility function of a typical migrant from country i to country j is represented as $u^{ij}(t) = \psi_i[u^i(t)]$ where $\psi_i' > 0$. And suppose for the time being that the level of utility decreases as the result of migration, that is, that $u^{ij}(t) < u^i(t)$ for any common $p^i(t)$. Noting that the shape of the utility function, and also of the indirect utility function, does not change, $U^{ij}[p^i(t)] = \psi_i[U^i[p^i(t)]]$ and $U^{ij}[p^i(t)] < U^i[p^i(t)]$. Moreover $(p^i(t), p^j(t))$ is an equilibrium price vector with unilateral migration if $0 < L^{ij}(t) < L^i(t)$, $L^{ji}(t) = 0$, $U^i[p^i(t)] = U^{ij}[p^j(t)]$ and $\psi_j[U^i[p^i(t)]] \leqq U^i[p^i(t)]$. Therefore, in a stationary equilibrium, $U^{ij}[\bar{p}^i] < U^i[\bar{p}^i] = U^{ij}[\bar{p}^j]$ and $\psi_j[U^j[\bar{p}^j]] \leqq U^j[\bar{p}^j]$. In this case, Lemma 11 is not generally true and it is possible that $\bar{k}^A < \bar{k}^B$. This is not inconsistent with the necessary conditions of Lemmas 9 and 10 for migration from country B to country A. For example, if U^B intersects QQ twice, from below and then from above, $\bar{k}^A < \bar{k}^B$ and it is possible for migration to be from B to A.

On the other hand, if the level of utility increases by migration, $u^{ij}(t) > u^i(t)$. Then, in a stationary equilibrium, $U^{ij}[\bar{p}^i] > U^i[\bar{p}^i] = U^{ij}[\bar{p}^j]$ and $\psi_j[U^j[\bar{p}^i]] \leqq$

$U^j[\bar{p}^j]$. Since $\bar{p}^i$ lies above $U^{ij}[\bar{p}^j]$ and on QQ, then, in particular, Lemma 11 remains valid, with the strict inequality $\bar{k}^A > \bar{k}^B$. Thus, in this case, migration is from A to B, as asserted in Theorem 1.

It is emphasized that in this section we have been concerned only to point out the possible sensitivity of our findings to changes of assumption. It is not claimed that the simple case of a monotonically shifting utility function is especially realistic or theoretically crucial.

4. Summary

In this paper it has been shown how a theory of international migration might be erected on the basis of the life-cycle decision-making of individual households. A detailed analysis is provided of the particular case in which individuals are everywhere alike in all respects but their rates of time preference, which may differ from country to country. It is shown that if each individual's preferences depend only on his country of birth and if there are just two countries or groups of countries then all steady-state migration is from the country with the relatively high rate of time preference to the country with the relatively low but that if preferences can change after migration then steady-state migration might be in the opposite direction.

References

Galor, O. (1986) Time Preference and International Labour Migration. Journal of Economic Theory 38:1-20

Kemp, M. C. and Long, N. V. (1982) The Efficiency of Competitive Markets in a Context of Exhaustible Resources. In: W. Eichhorn et al. (Eds.) Economic Theory of Natural Resources, Physica-Verlag, Würzburg, 205-211. Reprinted in M. C. Kemp and N. V. Long (Eds.) Essays in the Economics of Exhaustible Resources, North-Holland, Amsterdam, 1984, 217-225

Malinvaud, E. (1985) Lectures on Microeconomic Theory, rev. (Ed.) North-Holland, Amsterdam

Population, International Trade and Indebtedness: A More General Analysis

1. Introduction

Our purpose in the present paper is to develop an open-economy, overlapping-generations model in which population, international trade and international indebtedness all appear as endogenous variables and in which intergenerational caring and bequests play a role. In particular, we examine the effects of international trade and investment on the steady-state values of capital ownership per worker, the capital-labour ratio, the level of income per family and the rate of population growth.

As predecessors we have Vicary (1983) and Kondo (1985). Both confined their attention to the small-country case. Moreover, Vicary's formulation neglects intergenerational caring (bequests) and, therefore, the relationship between the quantity and quality of children. This seems to be inadequate in its specification of the cost of raising children as he assumed that cost is an increasing and convex function of the rate of increase of the number of children. Basing himself as a model which accomodates bequests of both human and physical capital, Kondo reached several striking conclusions: some of them at variance with the earlier findings of Vicary. In particular, he showed that if the optimal family expenditure function is unrelated to the possibility of international trade and is decreasing in per-worker capital ownership and if the optimal demand for children is a decreasing function of per-worker capital ownership then, whatever the given international rate of interest, the opportunity to trade and invest internationally depresses the level of steady-state capital ownership per worker, raises the rate of population growth and increases the level of family income. However he assumed that parents' utilities depend not on the prospective utilities of their children but on the bequests made to their children. Evidently bequests are imperfect proxies for children's utilities.

On the other hand, Kemp and Kondo (1986) examined the properties of an optimal path for a closed economy with endogenous population and intergenerational caring. Making use of a general model in which parents' utilities depend on family consumption, on the number of children and on the prospective utility of a typical child, they showed that if the elasticity of the marginal utility of children is less than a certain number greater than one then per-worker capital ownership oscillates. Further, that there exists a non-trivial unique steady state and that the efficient path

---

[1] I am very grateful to Professor Murray C. Kemp and a referee for valuable suggestions and comments.

necessarily tends to the steady state or to a stable limit cycle. Finally, they showed that if, in addition to the above assumption, the marginal utility of children is at least as elastic as the marginal cost of raising children, then the rate of population growth also oscillates, but out of phase with the per-worker capital stock.

In the present paper we reconsider the analysis of Kemp and Kondo (1986) in the light of the opportunity of a country to trade and invest internationally. In Section 2 it is shown that in the small-country case, with the international rate of interest given, all of the Kemp-Kondo results concerning the optimal path remain valid. Moreover, shown it is that if the given international rate of interest is less (greater) than the steady-state autarkic rate then, comparing steady states, the international mobility of capital (i) reduces (increases) the rate of population growth, (ii) depresses (stimulates) per-worker capital ownership, (iii) reduces (increases) per-family income and (iv) leaves the small country with a deficit (surplus) on current account.

In Section 3 we abandon the small-country assumption and consider the implications of the opportunity to trade on the steady states of two countries each large enough to influence the world rate of interest. Those implications depend on the manner in which the two countries differ one from the other. Suppose that they differ only in the severity with which they discount the prospective utility of children. Confining attention to steady states, it is shown that (i) under autarky both per-worker capital ownership and per-family income are lower in the country with the lower discount factor, that (ii) in the world trading equilibrium the country with the higher discount factor is a net creditor, that (iii) in the country with the higher (lower) discount factor the rate of population growth is higher (lower) with trade than without, and that (iv) the opportunity to trade enlarges the inter-country disparity of per-worker capital ownership. Suppose, alternatively, that the two countries differ only in their technologies (production functions). It is shown that (i) autarkic per-worker capital ownership is greater and the rate of population growth lower in the country with the lower average labour productivity, that (ii) in the world trading equilibrium the country with the higher average productivity is a net debtor, that (iii) after trade the country with the lower average productivity enjoys a higher rate of population growth and a higher per-family income (in particular, the international disparity of population growth rates vanishes) and that (iv) the opportunity to trade depresses per-worker capital ownership in the country with the higher average productivity and enlarges the inter-country disparity of ownership.

2. A Small Country

2.1 The Model

Following Kemp and Kondo (1986),[2] we consider an economy capable of producing a single homogeneous commodity which can be consumed, invested or bequeathed. Individuals live for two periods of time, childhood and adulthood. During their childhood individuals make no decisions; during their adulthood they work, raise a family and make bequests. In each family there is a single parent, implying that bequests are received from just one parent. The inefficiency resulting from uncoordinated bequests from two sets of parents has been noted and studied by Kemp and Long (1982) and by Kemp and Kondo (1986). As suggested by the analysis of Kemp and Kondo, the single-parent assumption is, in the present context, quite harmless.

All individuals, of whatever generation, are identical in their preferences and innate abilities.

The utility u_t of a typical parent of period t depends on family consumption $c(t)$, on the number of children in the family $n(t)$ and on the prospective utility of a typical child u_{t+1}; that is,

$$u_t = \bar{u}\,[c(t),\, n(t),\, u_{t+1}] \tag{1}$$

If the utility function is additive in u_{t+1} and in some function u of the other variables, $c(t)$ and $n(t)$, the utility function (1) reduces to

$$u_t = \sum_{\tau=t}^{\infty} \delta^{\tau-t}\,[c(\tau),\, n(\tau)] \tag{2}$$

where δ $(0 < \delta < 1)$ is the constant discount factor and where $u_z \equiv \partial u/\partial z > 0$, $u_{zz} \equiv \partial^2 u/\partial z^2 < 0$ and $u_{zz'} \equiv \partial^2 u/\partial z\partial z' \geqq 0$ for $z,\, z' = c(t),\, n(t)$ and $z \neq z'$.

The family's budget constraint, on the other hand, is

$$c(t) + \phi[n(t)] + n(t)b(t+1) \leqq I(t) \tag{3}$$

where $I(t)$ is the family's income, $b(t+1)$ the bequest made to each child born during period t and $\phi[n(t)]$ the cost of raising n children, with $\phi' \equiv d\phi/dn(t) > 0$ and $\phi'' \equiv d^2\phi/dn(t)^2 < 0$.[3]

It remains to specify the family income function. Let the aggregate constant-returns production function be written

$$\begin{aligned} Y(t) &= F[K(t),\, L(t)] \\ &= L(t)\, F[K(t)/L(t),\, 1] \\ &\equiv L(t)\, f[k(t)] \end{aligned} \qquad (f' > 0,\ f'' < 0)$$

---

[2] A similar formulation was proposed by Razin and Ben-Zion (1975).

[3] Kemp and Kondo (1986) worked with the net production function (and net family income), so the cost of raising children did not appear explicitly in their paper.

where K(t) is the stock of capital, which lasts for just one period, L(t) is the workforce,[4] and k(t) is the per-worker capital stock or the capital-labour ratio in period t. With all markets perfectly competitive, the interest and wage rates satisfy

$$1 + r(t) = f'[k(t)] \tag{4}$$

and

$$w(t) = f[k(t)] - k(t)f'[k(t)] \tag{5}$$

respectively. Since per-worker capital ownership is equal to b(t),

$$I(t) = w(t) + [1 + r(t)]b(t) \tag{6}$$

or, substituting from (4) and (5),

$$I[b(t), k(t)] = f[k(t)] + [b(t) - k(t)]f'[k(t)] \tag{7}$$

Of course, with capital mobile between countries, b(t) may be greater or less than k(t).

From the point of view of the small country, the international rate of interest r is a given number which we take to be independent of time; thus $r(t) = \bar{r}$. From (4), then, the capital-labour ratio k is a constant also; thus $k(t) = \bar{k}$.

Finally, we formulate the optimizing problem of the typical family during period t. Defining

$$v[b(t)] \equiv \max \sum_{\tau=t}^{\infty} \delta^{\tau-t} u[c(\tau), n(\tau)]$$

for any t and any b(t), we have

$$v[b(t)] = \max_{c(t),\, n(t)} \{u[c(t), n(t)] + \delta v[b(t+1)]\} \tag{8}$$

where b(t + 1) satisfies

$$c(t) + \phi[n(t)] + n(t)b(t+1) = f[\bar{k}] + (b(t) - \bar{k})f'[\bar{k}] \tag{9}$$

(Notice that the function v depends on $\bar{k}$.) It will be assumed that the family's problem has a unique interior solution for any non-negative b(t).

2.2 Properties of the Optimal Path

An interior solution satisfies the first- and second-order conditions

$$u_c[c(t), n(t)] = \delta v'[b(t+1)]/n(t) \tag{10 a}$$

$$u_n[c(t), n(t)] = u_c[c(t), n(t)]\{\phi'[n(t)] + b(t+1)\} \tag{10 b}$$

and

---

[4] Since all individuals are indentical, they supply the same amount of labour, say one unit.

$$D \equiv \begin{vmatrix} u_{cc} + \dfrac{\delta v''}{n^2} & u_{cn} + \dfrac{u_c}{n} + \dfrac{u_n v''}{nv'} \\[4mm] u_{cn} + \dfrac{u_c}{n} + \dfrac{u_n v''}{nv'} & u_{nn} - u_c\phi'' + \dfrac{2u_n}{n} + \dfrac{u_n^2 v''}{\delta(v')^2} \end{vmatrix} > 0 \qquad (11)$$

Differentiating (10) totally, and solving,

$$\frac{dc(t)}{db(t)} = \frac{f'[\bar{k}]}{D} \frac{u_c}{n} \left[(u_{nn} - u_c\phi'' - \frac{u_n u_{cn}}{u_c}) \frac{v''}{v'} - (u_{cn} + \frac{u_c}{n}) \right] \qquad (12\,a)$$

$$\frac{dn(t)}{db(t)} = \frac{f'[\bar{k}]}{D} \frac{u_c}{n} \left[(\frac{u_n u_{cc}}{u_c} - u_{cn}) \frac{v''}{v'} + u_{cc} \right] \qquad (12\,b)$$

And, differentiating (8) and (9) with respect to b(t), then drawing on (10) and (12),

$$V'[b(t)] = u_c[c(t), n(t)]f'[\bar{k}] > 0 \qquad (13)$$

$$\frac{db(t+1)}{db(t)} = \frac{f'[\bar{k}]}{D} \frac{1}{n} \left[\frac{u_n u_{cc}}{n}(1-\epsilon) - u_c u_{cc}\phi'' - u_{cn}^2 - \frac{u_c u_{cn}}{n} \right] \qquad (14)$$

where $\epsilon \equiv -nu_{nn}/u_n$ is the elasticity of the marginal utility of children. From (4), therefore, $db(t+1)/db(t) < 0$ if and only if

$$\epsilon < 1 - \frac{n}{u_n u_{cc}} (u_c u_{cc}\phi'' + u_{cn}^2 + \frac{u_c u_{cn}}{n}) \qquad (15)$$

where the right-hand side of (15) is greater than one. Hence Proposition 1 of Kemp and Kondo (1986) remains valid for a small open economy.

Proposition 1: If the marginal utility derived from children satisfies condition (15) then, along an optimal path, per-worker capital ownership oscillates, each oscillation lasting for two periods (the lifetime of one generation).

The following additional proposition, the counterpart of Proposition 2 of Kemp and Kondo (1986), can be verified with the aid of (12).

Proposition 2: If the marginal utility derived from children satisfies condition (15) and is at least as elastic as the marginal cost of raising children then both the number of children and the rate of population growth $(n-1)$ oscillate, but out of phase with the per-worker capital stock.

Throughout our further discussion we will maintain the assumptions of Proposition 2.

From (10) and (13), c(t) and n(t) can be represented as functions of $b(t+1)$ and $\bar{k}$. Hence (9) can be re-written as the dynamic equation $b(t+1) = H[b(t), \bar{k}]$, with $\partial H[b(t), \bar{k}]/\partial b(t) < 0$. Moreover we have assumed that, for any non-negative b(t), the family's problem has a unique interior solution; and this implies that, for any $b(t), 0 < H[b(t), \bar{k}] < \infty$. It follows that, for given $\bar{k}$, there exists a unique and non-trivial steady state (c^*, n^*, b^*) such that

$$n^* = \delta f'[\bar{k}] \tag{16 a}$$

$$u_n[c^*, n^*] = u_c[c^*, n^*]\{\phi'[n^*] + b^*\} \tag{16 b}$$

$$c^* + \phi[n^*] + n^*b^* = f[\bar{k}] + (b^* - \bar{k})f'[\bar{k}] \tag{16 c}$$

(16a) may be interpreted as the modified Golden Rule, as noted by Razin and Ben-Zion (1975).

The steady state is locally stable if $|[\partial H/\partial b(t)]_{b(t)\ =\ b^*}| < 1$. However even if the steady state is locally unstable there is at least one stable limit cycle; and, if there are several limit cycles, the limit cycle farthest from the steady state b^* is necessarily stable. This can be demonstrated by superimposing the graphs of $b(t+1) = H[b(t), \bar{k}]$ and $b(t+1) = H^{-1}[b(t), \bar{k}]$, in the manner of Kemp and Kondo (1986). Hence Proposition 3 of Kemp and Kondo remains valid for a small open economy.

Proposition 3: If condition (15) is satisfied then for each given k there exists a unique and non-trivial steady state satisfying (16). The steady state may be locally stable or unstable. Globally, however, the solution $(c(t), n(t), b(t+1))$ tends either to a stable limit cycle or to the steady state, depending on initial conditions and on the stability characteristics of the steady state; it never goes to zero or infinity.

2.3 The Current Account Balance

The balance of trade is the excess of domestic product over domestic absorption. Since all individuals are identical, the balance of trade per worker is

$$m(t) = f[\bar{k}] - c(t) - \phi[n(t)] - n(t)\bar{k} \tag{17}$$

(Notice that, since capital lasts for only one period, domestic capital formation is equal to the stock of capital.)

The current account balance is here defined as the balance of trade plus the gross return of capital from abroad. Thus, making use of (9) and (17), the current account balance per worker is

$$h(t) \equiv m(t) + (1+\bar{r})(b(t) - \bar{k})$$

$$= f[\bar{k}] - c(t) - \phi[n(t)] - n(t)\bar{k} + f'[\bar{k}](b(t) - \bar{k})$$

$$= n(t)\{b(t+1) - \bar{k}\} \tag{18}$$

Hence, along an optimal path the country runs a current account surplus (or deficit) during period t if and only if the bequest to each child in period t (that is, per-worker capital ownership in period $t+1$) is greater than (or less than) the capital-labour ratio during period t. In a steady state,

$$h(t) = h^* = n^*(b^* - \bar{k}) \tag{19}$$

2.4 Comparative Steady States

We can now compare the autarkic and free-trade steady states. Let the superscript a indicate autarkic quantities. The autarkic steady state (c^{a*}, n^{a*}, b^{a*}) then satisfies (16) for $\bar{k} = b^{a*}$.

We begin by calculating the effect on $b(t+1)$ of a change in $\bar{k}$. Noting that any change in $\bar{k}$ shifts $v[b(t+1)]$, and making use of (13), we differentiate (10) with respect to $\bar{k}$ and solve, obtaining

$$\frac{\partial c(t)}{\partial \bar{k}} = \frac{f''[\bar{k}]}{f'[\bar{k}]} \frac{dc(t)}{db(t)} (b(t)-\bar{k}) + \frac{f''[\bar{k}]u_c\hat{u}_c}{Dv'} \left[u_{nn} - u_c\phi'' + \frac{u_n}{n} - \frac{u_n u_{cn}}{u_c} \right] \quad (20\ a)$$

$$\frac{\partial n(t)}{\partial \bar{k}} = \frac{f''[\bar{k}]}{f'[\bar{k}]} \frac{dn(t)}{db(t)} (b(t)-\bar{k}) + \frac{f''[\bar{k}]u_c\hat{u}_c}{Dv'} \left[\frac{u_n u_{cc}}{u_c} - u_{cn} - \frac{u_c}{n} \right] \quad (20\ b)$$

where $\hat{u}_c \equiv u_c[c(t+1), n(t+1)]$. Then, from (9), using (10) and (20),

$$\frac{\partial b(t+1)}{\partial \bar{k}} = \frac{1}{n} \left[(b(t)-\bar{k})f''[\bar{k}] - \frac{\partial c(t)}{\partial \bar{k}} - \frac{u_n}{u_c} \frac{\partial n(t)}{\partial \bar{k}} \right]$$

$$= \frac{f''[\bar{k}]}{f'[\bar{k}]} \frac{\partial H[b(t), \bar{k}]}{\partial b(t)} (b(t) - \bar{k})$$

$$- \frac{f''[\bar{k}]}{D} \frac{\delta \hat{u}_c}{n^2} \left[u_{nn} - u_c\phi'' - \frac{2u_n u_{cn}}{u_c} + \frac{u_n^2 u_{cc}}{u_c^2} \right] \quad (21)$$

Bearing in mind the assumption of Proposition 2 and the fact that $\partial H/\partial b(t) < 0$ we see that if $b(t) \leqq \bar{k}$ then $\partial b(t+1)/\partial \bar{k} = \partial H[b(t), \bar{k}]/\partial \bar{k} < 0$. From the uniqueness of the solution, $\bar{k}$ and b^* are in a one-to-one correspondence. Hence $H[b^{a*}, b^{a*}] \gtreqqless H[b^{a*}, \bar{k}]$ if $b^{a*} \lesseqqgtr \bar{k}$.

Case 1: Now suppose that the world rate of interest $\bar{r}$ is less than the steady-state autarkic rate of interest r^{a*}, so that the capital-labour ratio $\bar{k}$ satisfying (4) for $\bar{r}$ is greater than b^{a*}. Then both the steady-state wage rate and the steady-state wage-rental ratio are greater in an open economy than under autarky. Moreover, from (16a), the number of children per family and the rate of population growth in the steady state are smaller than under autarky.

On the other hand, since $\bar{k} > b^{a*}$, $H[b(t), \bar{k}] < H[b(t), b^{a*}]$ for $b(t) \leqq \bar{k}$. Hence $b^* = H[b^*, \bar{k}] < H[b^{a*}, b^{a*}] = b^{a*}$, that is, the opportunity to trade depresses per-worker capital ownership in the steady state. In view of (19), the country runs a deficit on current account, for $b^* < b^{a*} < \bar{k}$.

Finally, we consider the response of per-family income to the opportunity to trade. Let $G[b, k]$ be the optimal expenditure function satisfying (16a) and (16b). Then

$$\frac{\partial G[b, k]}{\partial b} = \frac{u_c}{u_{cn} - u_n u_{cc}/u_c} + n > 0 \tag{22}$$

$$\frac{\partial G[b, k]}{\partial k} = \delta f''[k] \left[\frac{u_n u_{cn}/u_c - u_{nn} + u_c \phi''}{u_{cn} - u_n u_{cc}/u_c} + \frac{u_n}{u_c} \right] < 0 \tag{23}$$

and, since $b^* < b^{a*} < \bar{k}$,

$$I[b^*, \bar{k}] = G[b^*, \bar{k}] < G[b^*, b^{a*}] < G[b^{a*}, b^{a*}] = I[b^{a*}, b^{a*}]$$

That is, steady-state per-family income is smaller in an open economy than in a closed economy, implying that the decline in interest income outweighs the rise in wage income. The drop in per-family income in turn brings about a decline not only in the rate of population growth (the number of children per family) but also in per-worker capital ownership (the bequest per child).

Case 2: Suppose alternatively that the international rate of interest $\bar{r}$ is greater than the steady-state autarkic rate r^{a*}. Then $\bar{k} < b^{a*}$, $\bar{w} < w^{a*}$ and $\bar{w}/(1+\bar{r}) < w^{a*}/(1+r^{a*})$, where $\bar{w} \equiv f[\bar{k}] - \bar{k}f'[\bar{k}]$. Moreover, from (16 a), $n^* > n^{a*}$; that is, the steady-state rate of population growth increases in response to the opportunity to trade.

For $b(t) \leqq \bar{k}$ ($< b^{a*}$), $H[b(t), \bar{k}] > H[b(t), b^{a*}] > b^{a*}$; hence b^* such that $b^* = H[b^*, \bar{k}]$ must exceed $\bar{k}$ and, from (19), the small country exports capital and is in current account surplus. Since $\bar{k} < b^{a*}$, $H[b^{a*}, \bar{k}] > H[b^{a*}, b^{a*}]$; hence b^* satisfying $b^* = H[b^*, \bar{k}]$ is greater than b^{a*}. Since $\bar{k} < b^{a*} < b^*$, we can then infer from (22) and (23) that

$$I[b^*, \bar{k}] = G[b^*, \bar{k}] > G[b^*, b^{a*}] > G[b^{a*}, b^{a*}] = I[b^{a*}, b^{a*}]$$

Thus the opportunity to trade raises both per-worker capital ownership and per-family income.

Proposition 4: Under the assumptions of Proposition 2, and comparing steady states, if the international rate of interest is smaller (greater) than the autarkic rate then the opportunity to trade (i) reduces (increases) the rate of population growth, (ii) depresses (raises) the level of per-worker capital ownership, (iii) reduces (increases) per-family income and (iv) leaves the small country with a deficit (surplus) on current account.

3. Two Large Countries

Our objectives in this section are an international comparison of autarkic steady states and an analysis of the effects of trade on the steady states of the two countries.

3.1 Two Countries With Different Discount Factors

Consider two large countries A and B which differ only in the rates of discount applied to the utility of children. Without loss of generality it is assumed that $\delta_A <$ δ_B, implying that parents care less for their children in country A than in country B.

3.2 Comparison of Autarkic Steady States

We begin by comparing the autarkic steady states of the two countries. Differentiating (10) with respect to δ,

$$\frac{\partial c(t)}{\partial \delta} = \frac{1}{D} \frac{u_c}{\delta n} \left[u_{nn} - u_c \phi'' + \frac{u_n}{n} - \frac{u_n u_{cn}}{u_c} \right]$$

$$\frac{\partial n(t)}{\partial \delta} = \frac{1}{D} \frac{u_c}{\delta n} \left[\frac{u_n u_{cc}}{u_c} - u_{cn} - \frac{u_c}{n} \right]$$

so that

$$\frac{\partial b(t+1)}{\partial \delta} = -\frac{1}{n} \left[\frac{\partial c(t)}{\partial \delta} + \frac{u_n}{u_c} \frac{\partial n(t)}{\partial \delta} \right]$$

$$= -\frac{1}{D} \frac{u_c}{\delta n} \left[u_{nn} - u_c \phi'' - \frac{2 u_n u_{cn}}{u_c} + \frac{u_n^2 u_{cc}}{u_c^2} \right] \tag{24}$$

Under the assumptions of Proposition 2, $\partial b(t+1)/\partial \delta > 0$; that is,

$$H_A[b(t), k] < H_B[b(t), k] \qquad\qquad \text{for any } b(t) \text{ and } k \tag{25}$$

It follows that $b_A^{a*} = H_A[b_A^{a*}, b_A^{a*}] < H_B[b_B^{a*}, b_B^{a*}] = b_B^{a*}$; for if $b_A^{a*} \geqq b_B^{a*}$ then $H_A[b_A^{a*}, b_A^{a*}] \geqq H_B[b_B^{a*}, b_B^{a*}] \geqq H_B[b_B^{a*}, b_A^{a*}] \geqq H_B[b_A^{a*}, b_A^{a*}]$, contrary to (25). Moreover, $I[b_A^{a*}, b_A^{a*}] = f[b_A^{a*}] < f[b_B^{a*}] = I[b_B^{a*}, b_B^{a*}]$. Thus autarkic steady-state per-worker capital ownership and autarkic steady-state per-family income are lower in country A than in country B. It then follows from (4) and (5) that the rate of interest is higher and the factor-price ratio lower in country A than in country B. However it is not clear what relationship the two autarkic rates of population growth bear to each other.

Proposition 5: Under the assumption of Proposition 2, and confining attention to autarkic steady states, both per-worker capital ownership and per-family income are lower in the country with the lower discount rate than in the country with the higher discount rate. Moreover the rate of interest is higher in the country with the lower discount rate.

3.3 Implications of Trade

Let us now introduce the opportunity to trade. Since the same production function prevails in each country, both the rate of interest and the capital-labour ratio will be equated across countries, with $r_A^{a*} > r^* > r_B^{a*}$ and $b_A^{a*} < k^* < b_B^{a*}$.

From the small-country analysis of Section 2, capital flows country B to country A in the international steady state. Hence per-worker capital ownership falls in country A, rises in country B, and the international disparity in per-worker capital ownership grows ($b_A^* < b_A^{a*} < k^* < b_B^{a*} < b_B^*$). This implies that the rate of population growth falls in country A, rises in country B and is smaller in the former than in the latter ($n_A^{a*} = \delta_A f'[b_A^{a*}] > \delta_A f'[k^*] = n_A^* < n_B^* = \delta_B f'[k^*] > \delta_B f'[b_B^{a*}] = n_B^{a*}$). Moreover, since

$$I\,[b_A^{a*}, k^*] < I[b_A^{a*}, b_A^{a*}] = f[b_A^{a*}] < f[b_B^{a*}] = I\,[b_B^{a*}, b_B^{a*}] < I\,[b_B^*, k^*]$$

per-family income falls in country A, rises in country B, and the international disparity in family income grows.

Proposition 6: Under the assumptions of Proposition 2, and confining attention to steady states, the opportunity to trade (i) reduces (increases) per-worker capital ownership and per-family income in the country with the lower (higher) discount rate, (ii) enlarges the international disparities in per-worker capital ownership and per-family income, (iii) reduces (increases) the rate of population growth in the country with the lower (higher) discount rate and (iv) leaves in current-account deficit (surplus) the country with the lower (higher) discount rate. Under trade, the rate of population growth is lower in the country with the lower discount rate.

3.4 Two Countries With Different Production Functions

Suppose alternatively that countries A and B differ only in their technologies. We proceed to compare the autarkic steady states of two countries and to examine the implications of trade for each country. For the purpose of the excercise it is assumed that the two countries differ only in the average productivity of labour, which is uniformly higher in country A; that is, it is assumed that $f_A[k] > f_B[k]$ and $f_A'[k] = f_B'[k]$ for all $k > 0$.

3.5 Comparison of Autarkic Steady States

We begin by showing that the level of autarkic steady-state per-worker capital ownership is lower in A than in B. Differentiating (10) with respect to f,

$$\frac{\partial c(t)}{\partial f} = \frac{1}{D}\,\frac{u_c}{n}\left[(u_{nn} - u_c\phi'' - \frac{u_n u_{cn}}{u_c})\frac{v''}{v'} - (u_{cn} + \frac{u_c}{n})\right]$$

$$\frac{\partial n(t)}{\partial f} = \frac{1}{D}\,\frac{u_c}{n}\left[(\frac{u_n u_{cc}}{u_c} - u_{cn})\frac{v''}{v'} + u_{cc}\right]$$

so that

$$\frac{\partial b(t+1)}{\partial f} = \frac{1}{Dn} \left[\frac{u_n u_{cc}}{n} (1 - \epsilon) - u_c u_{cc} \phi'' - u_{cn}^2 - \frac{u_c u_{cn}}{n} \right] \tag{26}$$

Hence, recalling (15),

$$H_A[b(t), k] < H_B[b(t), k] \qquad\qquad \text{for any } b(t) \text{ and } k \tag{27}$$

Suppose that $b_A^{a*} \gtreqqless b_B^{a*}$. Then, since H_i is decreasing in $b(t)$ and $H_i[b_i^{a*}, b_i^{a*}] \gtreqqless H_i[b_i^{a*}, k]$ if $b_i^{a*} \lesseqqgtr k$,

$$H_A[b_A^{a*}, b_A^{a*}] = b_A^{a*} \geqq b_B^{a*} = H_B[b_B^{a*}, b_B^{a*}] \geqq H_B[b_A^{a*}, b_B^{a*}] \geqq H_B[b_A^{a*}, b_A^{a*}]$$

which is contrary to (27). Hence $b_A^{a*} < b_B^{a*}$.

Therefore $1 + r_A^{a*} = f_A'[b_A^{a*}] > f_B'[b_B^{a*}] = 1 + r_B^{a*}$ and, by (16 a), $n_A^{a*} > n_B^{a*}$. However it is not generally possible to determine the international ranking of wage rates and per-family income.

Proposition 7: Under the assumptions of Proposition 2, and confining attention to steady states, autarkic per-worker capital ownership is lower, and the interest rate and the rate of population growth higher, in the country with higher average productivity.

3.6 Implications of Trade

We turn to the implications of trade for the steady states of the two countries. The opportunity to trade equates the rates of interest across countries, with $r_A^{a*} > r^* > r_B^{a*}$. Then the capital-labour ratio k^* is determined by the equilibrium condition $f_i'[k^*] = 1 + r^*$; evidently $b_A^{a*} < k^* < b_B^{a*}$.

From the small-country analysis of Section 2, capital flows from country B to country A in the international steady state. Moreover, $b_A^* < b_A^{a*} < k^* < b_B^{a*} < b_B^*$ and $n_A^{a*} > n_A^* = n_B^* > n_B^{a*}$. The rates of population growth in both countries are equal in the international steady state. On the other hand,

$$I_A[b_A^{a*}, b_A^{a*}] > I_A[b_A^*, k^*] < I_B[b_B^*, k^*] > I_B[b_B^{a*}, b_B^{a*}]$$

implying that per-family income falls in country A and rises in country B and it is less in the former than in the latter.

Proposition 8: Under the assumptions of Proposition 2, and confining attention to steady states, the opportunity to trade and invest internationally (i) reduces (increases) per-worker capital ownership in country with higher (lower) average labour productivity and enlarges the disparity between the two countries, (ii) reduces (increases) the rate of population growth and per-family income in the country with higher (lower) average productivity and (iii) leaves with a current-account deficit (surplus) the country with higher (lower) average productivity. It then follows that the rates of population growth in these two countries are equal in the international steady state.

4. Concluding Remarks

We have investigated the effects of the opportunity to trade and invest internationally on the steady-state values of capital ownership per worker and the rate of population growth in two large countries with different discount factors or different production technologies.

Endogenous population growth with modified Golden Rule equation (16a) plays an important role. If the rate of population growth is given exogenously then the modified Golden Rule implies the undesirable result that international trade between two countries leads to a constant flow of capital into the country with the higher autarkic rate of interest: so that, in the steady state, one country will have all the wealth. However, by allowing for endogenous population growth, we have managed to rule out this undesirable case.

Furthermore, the modified Golden Rule implies that only an international disparity in the rate of discount or in marginal productivity causes an international difference in the rate of population growth under trade. In other words, if preferences or technology differ between countries in any respects other than those just mentioned then, as a result of international trade, those differences are absorbed by the disparities in family consumption and per-worker capital ownership, and the rate of population growth is the same in each country.

We have developed, in this paper, a theoretical analysis of the relationship between international trade and the steady-state values of population growth, perworker capital and current account balance. In a further paper we hope to study the behaviour of the world economy away from the steady state and to consider the empirical relevance of our results.

References

Kemp, M. C. and Kondo H. (1986) Overlapping Generations Competitive Efficiency and Optimal Population. Journal of Public Economics 30: 237-247
Kemp, M. C. and Long, N. V. (1982) The Efficiency of Competitive Markets in a Context of Exhaustible Resources. In: W. Eichhorn et. al. (Eds.) Economic Theory of National Resources, Physica-Verlag, Würzburg, 205-211
Kondo, H. (1985) Population, International Trade and Indebtedness, University of New South Wales, Sydney
Razin, A. and Ben-Zion, U. (1975) An Intergenerational Model of Population Growth. American Economic Review 65: 923-933
Vicary, S. (1983) Endogenous Population Growth in an Overlapping-Generations Model with International Lending and Borrowing, Bulletin of Economic Research 35: 1-24

Author Index

Subject Index

Studies in Contemporary Economics

Editors: **D. Bös, G. Bombach, B. Gahlen, K. W. Rothschild**

G. Steinmann, Universität Paderborn; **K. F. Zimmermann,** Universität Mannheim; **G. Heilig,** Universität Bamberg (Hrsg.)

Probleme und Chancen demographischer Entwicklung in der Dritten Welt

Processings der 22. Arbeitstagung der Deutschen Gesellschaft für Bevölkerungswissenschaft zum Thema „Probleme und Chancen demographischer Entwicklung in der Dritten Welt". Universität-GH Paderborn, 1.–4. März 1988

1988. 20 Abbildungen. XII, 315 Seiten. ISBN 3-540-50321-8

Inhaltsübersicht: Perspektiven des Bevölkerungswachstums – Langfristige Trends und ökonomische Konsequenzen. – Die Ernährungsfrage. – Bevölkerung und wirtschaftliche Entwicklung. – Soziokulturelle Probleme in der Dritten Welt. Konsequenzen des Weltbevölkerungswachstums für die Industriestaaten. – Familienplanung in der Dritten Welt.

H. G. Zimmermann, Universität Bonn

Privates Sparen versus Sozialversicherung

1988. IV, 114 Seiten. ISBN 3-540-18863-0

Inhaltsübersicht: Einführung. – Intertemporale und interpersonelle Umverteilung: Privates Sparen versus Sozialversicherung. Lebensversicherung versus Sozialversicherung. – Die soziale Sicherheit als eigenständiger Wert: Privates Sparen versus Sozialversicherung, Lebensversicherung versus Sozialversicherung. Eine diskrete Version des Modells 2.1. Der Einfluß wechselnder Geburtenraten. – Zusammenfassung der Ergebnisse. – Literaturverzeichnis.

S. Homburg, Universität Köln

Theorie der Alterssicherung

1988. VI, 153 Seiten. ISBN 3-540-18835-5

Inhaltsübersicht: Einleitung. – Eine Typologie der Alterssicherungsverfahren. – Die einfache Mathematik der Alterssicherung. – Altersvorsorge und individuelle Ersparnis. – Positive Theorie der Alterssicherung. – Normative Theorie der Alterssicherung. – Zwei Variationen des Themas. – Politische Theorie der Alterssicherung. – Schluß. – Literaturverzeichnis. – Namenverzeichnis. – Sachverzeichnis.

M. Bösch, München

Umverteilung, Effizienz und demographische Abhängigkeit von Rentenversicherungssystemen

1987. VI, 209 Seiten. ISBN 3-540-17858-9

Inhaltsübersicht: Grundstruktur. – Umverteilungswirkungen des Umlagesystems. – Analyse kapitalgedeckter Systeme im Rahmen geschlossener Volkswirtschaften. – Effizienz von Rentenversicherungssystemen. – Rentenversicherungssysteme unter Berücksichtigung des Vererbungsmotivs. – Anhang. – Literaturverzeichnis.

Springer-Verlag Berlin Heidelberg New York London Paris Tokyo Hong Kong

Journal of
Population Economics

ISSN 0933-1433   Title No. 148

Editors: A. Cigno, Hull, England; P. Pestieau, Liège, Belgium; B. M. S. van Praag, Rotterdam, The Netherlands; R. Willis, Chicago, IL; K. F. Zimmermann (Managing Editor), Mannheim, FRG

Associate Editors: E. Boserup, F. Bourguignon, P. S. Dasgupta, F. T. Denton, R. R. Easterlin, J. Ermisch, G. Feichtinger, B. Felderer, R. A. Horvath, D. Kessler, W. Krämer, R. D. Lee, R. A. Moffitt, J. D. Pitchford, J. M. M. Ritzen, G. Schmitt-Rink, G. Steinmann, T. Tachibanaki, B.-A. Wickström, K. I. Wolpin

The **Journal of Population Economics** is an international quarterly in which high-quality articles dealing with broadly defined relationships between economic and demographic problems are published. Equal emphasis is given to theoretical and applied research. All articles must be relevant, well-written contributions based on a wide knowledge of the scholarly literature.

Some of the topics covered are: at the micro level, household formation, fertility choices, education, labor supply, and migration; at the macro level, economic growth with exogenous or endogenous population evolution, population policy, savings and pensions, social security, housing, and health care. Papers dealing with policy issues or development problems are also welcome.

The **Journal of Population Economics** is designed to be a forum for the study and discussion of these problems for ecconomists, demographers, sociologists, and researchers from other disciplines. It also provides an outlet for research involving many areas of specialization as well as reports of innovative findings. Another aim of the journal is to publish survey articles and evaluations of the work of others to make recent developments in the field of population economics more readily accessible to the widest possible audience.

Springer-Verlag Berlin
Heidelberg New York London
Paris Tokyo Hong Kong

The **Journal of Population Economics** is the official organ of the European Society of Population Economics.